Calgary Goes Skiing

A History of the Calgary Ski Club

Calgary Goes Skiing

A History of the Calgary Ski Club

David Mittelstadt

Copyright © 2005 David Mittlestadt

All rights reserved. No part of this publication may be reproduced, stored in a retrieval system, or transmitted in any form or by any means—electronic, mechanical, audio recording, or otherwise—without the written permission of the publisher or a photocopying licence from Access Copyright, Toronto, Canada.

Rocky Mountain Books
#108 – 17665 66A Avenue
Surrey, BC V3S 2A7
www.rmbooks.com

Library and Archives Canada Cataloguing in Publication

Mittelstadt, David, 1966-
  Calgary goes skiing : the story of the Calgary Ski Club / David Mittelstadt.

Includes index.
ISBN 1-894765-65-6

  1. Calgary Ski Club--History. I. Title.

GV854.8.C3M585 2005   796.93'06'0712338   C2005-903911-6

Edited by Alister Thomas
Book design by John Luckhurst
Cover design by John Luckhurst
Front cover photo: Cross-jump at Mt. Norquay, 1939.
  (Whyte Museum of the Canadian Rockies, V108-1095, Lloyd Harmon.)

Printed in Canada

Rocky Mountain Books acknowledges the financial support for its publishing program from the Government of Canada through the
Book Publishing Industry Development Program (BPIDP).

This book is printed on 100% recycled paper, processed chlorine free and printed with vegetable-based inks.

Contents

CHAPTER ONE
Calgary Goes Skiing 1

CHAPTER TWO
A Very Brief History of Skiing 5

CHAPTER THREE
Skiing Comes to Calgary 27

CHAPTER FOUR
The Glory Years 64

CHAPTER FIVE
Movers and Shakers 113

CHAPTER SIX
Swinging Singles 155

CHAPTER SEVEN
Hard Times 198

CONCLUSION
Back to the Future 219

ACKNOWLEDGEMENTS 222

ENDNOTES 223

INDEX 232

Lake Louise Detail

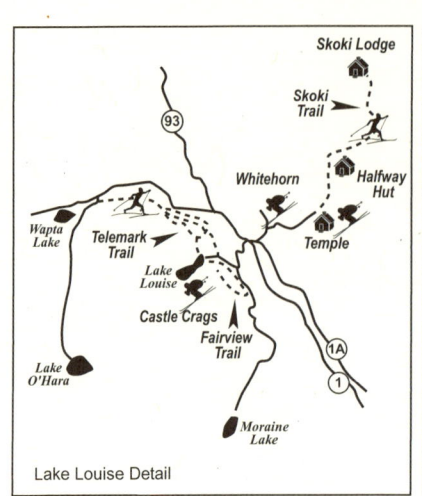

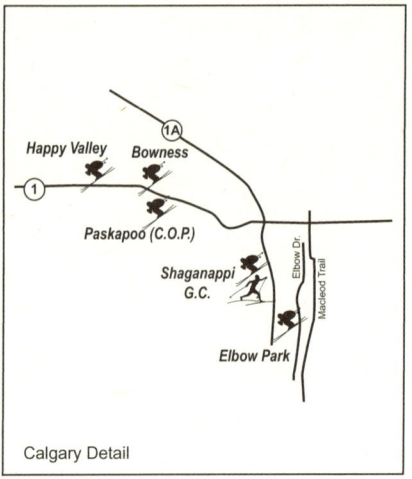

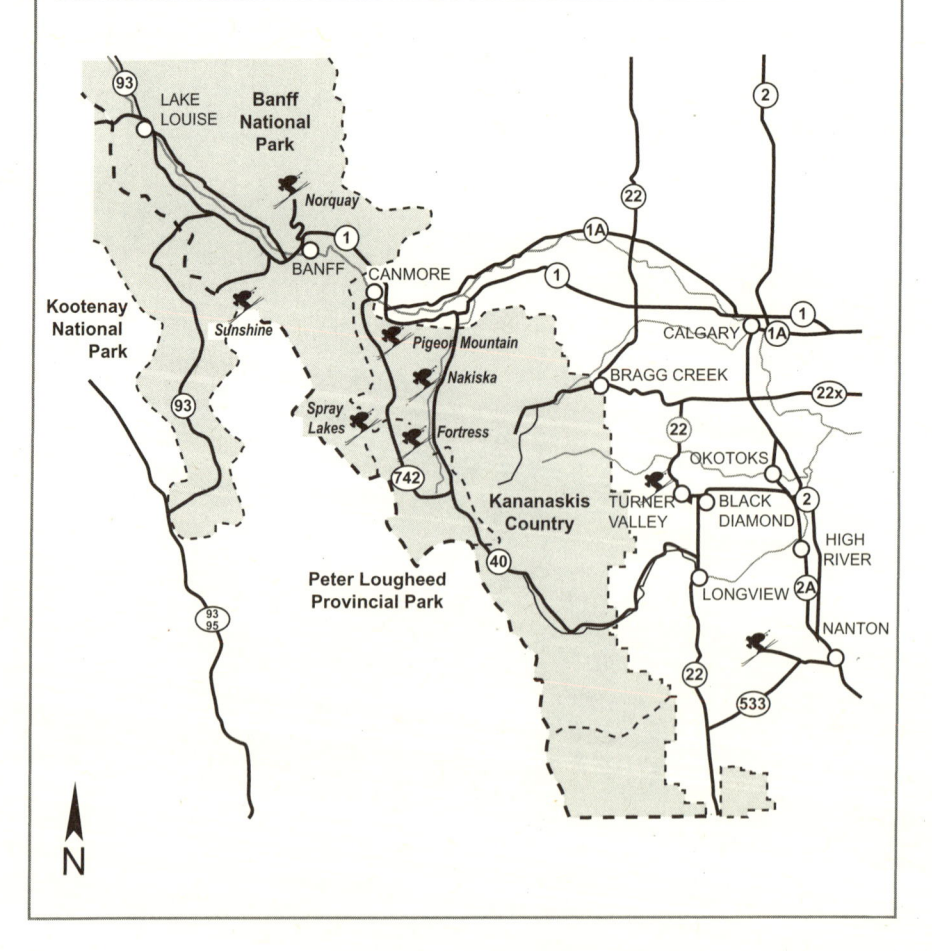

Calgary Detail

CHAPTER ONE

Calgary Goes Skiing

WHY WE SKI—THE CALGARY
SKI CLUB—THE GROWTH OF A SPORT—
CLUBS MATTERED—SUMMED UP—
RAISON D'ETRE

Skiing is a way of life. The truly addicted forgo career, family and security all for the chance to play on the snow. The ski bum lives only to ski. It's a cliché, almost as old as the sport. Whether it is the thrill of speed, the kinaesthetic pleasure, the idealistic simplicity or the easy-going lifestyle associated with skiing, people get hooked like few other sports. And a lucky few live the life. Of course, most of us can only dream of skiing like that. We fit our obsession around jobs and family. But whether a skier goes out 10 days or 100 each year, the love is the same. And it was just as true for the sport's pioneers.

In 1935, skiing arrived to stay in a small prairie city on the edge of the Rocky Mountains. A small group of enthusiasts, who had met and discovered their shared passion a couple of years before, incorporated the Calgary Ski Club. Despite the city's unreliable snow cover—as true in the thirties as today—these young adventurers established a glamorous new sport in the city. Skiing was just then sweeping North America as the thing to do. Before the club appeared, in the winter Calgarians curled, they skated and they played hockey, but they didn't ski. The Calgary Ski Club was responsible for turning Calgary into a skier's city.

This book tells the story of the Calgary Ski Club. It traces the club's beginnings from a few Scandinavian ski jumpers. It looks at the contributions the club made in its early years towards establishing the sport in Calgary, the club's involvement in alpine ski racing, its attempts to start a ski hill in the city. It shows how over time, the growth of skiing as a business changed the club, and how the growth and development of Calgary also affected the CSC. It remembers some of the people who were the heart and soul of the club, their accomplishments and their contributions to the sport.

When ski resorts were a new invention and ski instructor a new job description, skiers gathered in the fellowship of clubs to pursue their passion. Skiing is an ancient form of locomotion on snow, but it was not until the late 19th century that it developed into a recreational pastime and a competitive sport. Ski clubs played a fundamental role. The transformation of skiing coincided with the beginnings of mass tourism, which brought people to mountain regions like the Alps for leisure. Even more important was the Victorian culture of sport and recreational clubs. Nearly all pastimes had their clubs—rugby clubs, horticultural clubs, music clubs, debating clubs, curling clubs. Clubs were how people explored their interests and met the like-minded, and often the only place to do so. In a ski club, one learned how to ski, met others with whom to ski, went to places to ski and even developed skiing venues.

The Calgary Ski Club belonged to this tradition. Looking out over the Sunshine Village Ski Resort in Banff National Park from the top of Brewster Peak, it is hard to believe that a scant 70 years ago there was only one lonely cabin, which stood shut in for the winter. The sport was in its infancy in Banff, where a few enthusiasts skied on the sides of Mt. Norquay above the town. In Calgary, a handful of skiers had found each other practising on scattered hillsides in the city. They came together to promote the sport. The new club recruited members, convinced local retailers to carry ski equipment, gave lessons for beginners and provided transportation with chartered buses and trains to the Banff area. In cooperation with skiers and ski clubs in Banff, the CSC also helped develop the Norquay ski area.

After the war, the CSC grew quickly. Through the 1950s, it worked to further promote skiing in the Calgary area and attempted to establish its own ski hill in the city limits. Members of the club raced, went ski touring in the high mountains around Banff and flocked in increasing numbers to growing ski areas at Norquay, Sunshine and Lake Louise. In the 1960s, responding to demographic changes, the club focused much more on families and children. The club was centred on high-performance junior competition and ran programs to encourage kids to take up skiing. It was heavily involved in advocating better skiing facilities in the mountain parks and supporting Olympic bids for the Calgary-Banff area.

In the following decade, the club underwent a major transformation. By 1970, the CSC's constituency of young adults had deserted it for the Petroleum Ski Club, formed in 1968 and dedicated to recreational skiing. When interest in junior racing declined and moved to specialized clubs, the CSC went into a precipitous decline. A new group of skiers, primarily newcomers the booming economy attracted, rescued the club. They radically shifted the CSC's focus to recreational skiing and expanded into summer pursuits like hiking and canoeing to become a year-round recreational club. Some members were concerned that the CSC was drifting away from skiing, but the club jumped into the cross-country boom of the seventies with enthusiasm.

Since its 50th anniversary in 1985, the Calgary Ski Club has contended with some challenges. The poor economic conditions in the city through the eighties and early nineties drove membership down and created financial difficulties for the club. The baby boomers aged and started families and many dropped out of skiing. The club retrenched, focusing on its core outdoor recreation like hiking and skiing and developing an innovative cross-country program. Despite a resurgence in the downhill ski industry, however, the club's membership has not bounced back. The Calgary Ski Club is typical of many outdoor clubs in the city, which have generally shown a steady decline in membership even as outdoor recreation has boomed. This fact poses the question of what the future holds for the Calgary Ski Club.

A brief outline of the club's history makes it clear that the CSC has played an important role in establishing the ski industry in the Rocky Mountains. When skiing was new, the clubs—the CSC in Calgary, the Edmonton Ski Club in Edmonton and the Ski Runners of the Canadian Rockies in Banff—helped develop venues for skiing and provided the patrons. The CSC and other clubs also pioneered ski lessons, transportation to the mountains, a ski patrol to keep a crowded ski hill safe, and overnight bus trips to exciting new ski destinations. The CSC lobbied hard for the expansion and improvement of ski areas in Banff National Park. Once the potential of skiing became clear, businesses took over many of the services the clubs offered and established the sport as a major recreational industry. Ironically, this has moved ski clubs to the periphery.

The CSC has reflected the changes in the way people ski. In the early days, without mechanical lifts, people skied uphill, downhill and cross-country, usually on the same pair of big wooden skis. Technological changes split skiing into different disciplines with specialized equipment: the alpine skier with heavy boots, skis and fixed heels, dependent on the lift; the self-propelled cross-country skier with narrow skinny skis; and the ski mountaineer. Skiers increasingly focused on one discipline or another. The CSC often led the way. It started a program for backcountry skiing and ski mountaineering in the 1960s, at a time when this style of skiing had fallen into disfavour in North America. In the 1970s, the club embraced cross-country skiing. The increasing fragmentation of the ski scene, however, has also challenged clubs like the CSC, which in its early years served all skiers and styles of skiing. Specialized clubs, dedicated to racing, cross-country skiing or recreational downhill skiing, have usurped the role of the generalist ski club.

The story of the Calgary Ski Club also has larger historical significance. Historians have largely ignored the world of sport until relatively recently, and skiing in particular. One aspect of ski history that almost no one has studied is the contribution of ski clubs to the growth of the sport. So, while this book is first and foremost a history of the CSC, it also shows the dynamic connection between the club and its larger context, not just with skiing but also with Calgary, Banff and the Rocky Mountains. Even less has been written about recreational sports clubs and their culture than about skiing. There are not many club histories, other than simple commemorative works, to be found in the realm of any sport so this book is a pioneering work. The history of the CSC is also a step forward in better understanding our sporting culture.

Lest this all sound too serious, the main reason people joined the Calgary Ski Club, whether in 1935 or 1985, was to have some fun. This essentially is what skiing was and is about. This book shows how the CSC got its start and how it developed and how it fit into the general evolution of skiing. It also captures some of the spirit of adventure and excitement that skiers of each new generation felt. The gentle hiss of skis running through powder snow, the thrill of carving a turn on a high-speed downhill, the elegance of striding effortlessly along a wooded trail—these things have not changed much over the years and are our link today to the skiers of yesteryear.

CHAPTER TWO

A Very Brief History of Skiing

THE DISTANT PAST—SKIING DIASPORA—ALPINE TRANSFORMATION—LIFT LINES—BANFF

Scandinavians discovered something a long time before everyone else: sliding about on snow is a lot of fun. It was apparently a well-kept secret. Of course, in the days when fur and wool were the only choice for outerwear, central heating was a fireplace and winter generally meant borderline starvation, most people didn't think about recreation when the snow flew. Even when they did, the rest of the winter world made do with skating, curling, or heavens forbid, the slog of snowshoeing. When skiing emerged from Norway in the nineteenth century, the only other people getting some thrills on snow were a few crazy Englishmen in the process of inventing bobsledding in the Alps. The world was ready for something exciting to do in the winter.

Once skiing escaped from Scandinavia, it spread to every part of the world with snow. The Calgary Ski Club received its charter in the 1930s, when skiing was experiencing a new surge of popularity as a winter pastime. The club, and skiing in the region around Calgary, was part of a much larger pattern of development. It was a pattern that saw skiing evolve in less than a hundred years from a Scandinavian tradition into a popular form of recreation and a major industry in Europe and North America. A brief look at the history of skiing, especially the development of the downhill variety, will set the stage for the story of the club's first years.

THE DISTANT PAST

Skiing is either very old or relatively new, depending on how it is defined. As a means of locomotion over winter snows, skiing is ancient, dating back thousands of years. Archaeologists have found wooden skis in Scandinavia and Russia reliably dated as early as 4500 BC, and ancient rock wall carvings show unmistakable images of skiers.[1] The Norse sagas mention skiing and some Norse deities are described as skiers. The most famous early account dates from the Norwegian civil war in the thirteenth century, when King Sverre sent his infant son Haakon to safety over the mountains with two scouts, the "Birchlegs." The feat is still commemorated with the Birkebeinerrennet cross-country race.[2] There are medieval accounts of hunters in Scandinavia, who astounded visitors with their ability to get across deep snow on their wooden boards. Norway's first record of postal delivery on skis dates from 1530,[3] and doctors, midwives and priests were all known to use skis. There were military applications as well. In 1718, Norwegians troops on using skis defeated a Swedish army on foot.[4]

Early skis were simple. In many regions, they were originally of uneven length, with a short "pushing" ski and a long gliding ski, although by the late nineteenth century equal length skis were the norm. They were made of wood and might measure anywhere from eight to 12 feet long.[5] A simple leather strap across the foot held it onto the ski; soldiers in the eighteenth century added a heel strap to help keep the ski on while sliding downhill.[6] At some early date, someone discovered that animal skin—sealskin worked particularly well—could be fixed on the bottom of a ski to keep it from sliding backwards. The hairs lay flat to allow glide in one direction, but would stand up when the ski moved back. One long pole helped provide propulsion and balance, and the skier dragged it behind on a downhill and used it like a rudder and a brake. Generally, with loose bindings and soft leather boots, skis were difficult to control at any kind of speed.

The sport of skiing is a much more modern invention. The line between utility and pleasure was no doubt blurred, and people for centuries have known that sliding about on snow is fun.[7] As a leisure activity, pursued solely for pleasure, however, skiing is not 150 years old. Its most popular variant, lift-served downhill skiing has not quite turned 75. It was not until the middle of the nineteenth century that competitions were established in Scandinavia.[8] These included long distance jumping; the langlauf, a long cross-country race; and the villom, a kind of downhill race, involving a high-speed descent down a slope with obstacles. Cross-country racing and jumping would become the signature competitions of the Norwegians and the Swedes. They were curiously uninterested in downhill racing, the direction skiing would go as both sport and recreation once it was introduced to the Alps.

Some innovations helped establish skiing as a competitive endeavour. Sondre Norheim, from the Telemark region of Norway, is sometimes called the father of modern skiing. Dissatisfied with the performance of his skis, in the 1860s Norheim made some crucial changes.[9] Using twisted birch root, he made bindings that kept the foot more firmly attached to the ski. He also manufactured a ski that was narrower in the middle than at the tip and tail—the creation of side-cut, which as every modern skier knows, determines how well a ski turns. The improved skis allowed Norheim and his skiing companions to invent two methods of manoeuvring, the "telemark" turn and the "christiania" turn. The telemark used a lunge position, knees bent with the tip of rear ski coming up to the front foot. The christiania, or "christie," was the familiar parallel turn. Norheim and his friends amazed crowds at a jumping competition in Oslo in 1868 and his new style spread through Norway and beyond.[10]

SKIING TO THE WORLD

The Scandinavians were already exporting skiing to the world. As a fundamental part of Nordic culture, especially in Norway, skis went wherever Scandinavians went. Beginning in the mid-nineteenth century, along with the Swedes and the Finns, the Norwegians began a "skiing diaspora" which would establish the sport the world over.

One of the first places skis appeared were the mining camps in the American West. In the Sierra Nevada Mountains of California and then later in the Colorado Rockies, skis were introduced as a way to travel between mining camps in the winter. "Snowshoe" Thomson carried mail in the Nevadas starting in 1856 on skis (often called "Norwegian snowshoes," hence the nickname) while the Reverend John L. Dyer travelled by skis through the Colorado mountains in the 1860s to preach.[11] The miners also had their own wildly popular downhill races. Competitors would blast straight down a slope as fast as possible. The skier who went furthest won. Mining camp competed against mining camp amid ferocious betting and revelry. This scene was repeated elsewhere, such as in Kiandra, Australia, where Norwegian miners and prospectors formed the first known ski club in the world in 1861.[12] After the American mining boom ended, skiing disappeared for a generation or two in the west.[13]

Ironically, it was on the flat prairies that skiing made the greatest early inroads in the United States. Scandinavian immigrants also brought their sport to the Midwest. From 1880 to around 1910, ski clubs sprang up in Scandinavian communities throughout Minnesota and Wisconsin. The clubs focused on jumping, which had become a most prestigious and popular skiing event in Norway. It was, in the words of one writer, "... a clannish affair. Their ski clubs ... were formed not so much to propagate the sport as to provide the means of organising jumping meets and congenial, ethnic socialising."[14] The jumpers, who also promoted traditional cross-country races, founded the Norwegian-dominated National Ski Association in 1904.

The introduction of skiing in Canada mirrored the United States. Scandinavian immigrants introduced it to different parts of the country. One account claims Finns brought skis to Eastern Canada in the 1840s, another mentions people on skis around Ottawa in the 1850s. One of the first documented instances of skiing was in 1879, when the Canadian Illustrated News reported a Norwegian man had travelled between Montreal and Quebec City on skis.[15] Out west, immigrant railway workers were seen using skis in the 1880s. Early Canadian skiing centred on the mining and logging towns of the British Columbia interior, like Rossland and Revelstoke, where large numbers of Scandinavians had settled. As early as 1888, skiers were racing down the slopes of Red Mountain at Rossland in a fashion reminiscent of the miners of the American West.[16]

Enthusiasts in Revelstoke formed the first organized club in Canada in 1891.[17] The Revelstoke Ski Club promoted ski jumping and cross-country races, much like the clubs of Minnesota. In Rossland, a club formed in the 1890s for skiing and other winter sports. In 1898 the Rossland winter carnival began, which featured ski jumping and races down Red Mountain. While not limited to Norwegians and Swedes, the ski club of Revelstoke consisted of seasoned skiers, mostly of northern European extraction, who were looking for a venue to compete, not to promote skiing in general. Jumping was primarily a spectator sport, mostly restricted to those with skiing in their blood.

Although a bit later than the U.S., skiing also made an appearance out on the Canadian prairies. Ski jump towers rose above the skyline in places like Camrose, Alberta, where a large community of Swedes and Norwegians

The height of fashion: skiers circa 1910. (CSC Collection.)

formed the Fram Ski Club in 1911, the province's oldest ski club.[18] Residents of Edmonton soon followed suit, and for several years there were spirited jumping competitions between the two clubs, which skiers from Revelstoke and other B.C. clubs often attended.[19] Wherever more than three or four Scandinavians could be found, a ski club would soon appear along with a jumping tower. Skiing wouldn't become widely popular, however, until it evolved in the Alps.

Europe

Surprisingly, few Europeans outside of Scandinavia, even in the alpine countries, were familiar with skiing before the 1880s. Historians have traced a few Norwegians who took their skis to Europe. A small number of Austrian, Germans and Swiss had seen or heard about the sport and started experimenting.[20] The famous Norwegian explorer Fritjohf Nansen's 1888 trip across Greenland on skis created a great deal of interest, especially among European mountaineers. They immediately saw it as a way to access the high mountains in winter.[21] By the end of the nineteenth century, skiing was no longer an oddity, as ski clubs sprung up in Germany, Austria and

Switzerland. The British played an interesting role in getting the sport established in the Alps. They were great tourists in the nineteenth century, and several adventurous Englishmen learned to ski in Norway. They took their new skill to Switzerland, a favourite haunt of upper class British travellers. An English colonel by the name of Napier came to Davos, Switzerland with his Norwegian manservant and a pair of skis around 1889. English expatriates formed the Davos Ski Club in 1903.

Once skiing took hold in the Alps, it wasn't long before it began to evolve. One early Austrian enthusiast—some say fanatic—Mathias Zdarsky, taught himself to ski using snowplow or "stem" turns. He became convinced this was the only way to descend steep alpine terrain with control. With the fervour of a true believer, he criticized the Norwegian style of skiing, with its favoured telemark turn and emphasis on cross-country skiing, as ineffective in alpine conditions. He attracted many adherents. An Austrian military man, Colonel Bilgeri, introduced skiing to the Austrian army. He also came up with the innovation of using two short poles instead of one to help with propulsion on the flats and balance going downhill. The usefulness of skis for winter mountaineering was clear, and ski touring in the high country of the Alps emerged as a popular variant of the sport, more exciting and challenging than simple cross-country "running" below the tree line. Even more importantly, on the steep slopes of the Alps, people explored the thrills of skiing downhill.

Skiing as Sport and Recreation

As a recreation, skiing owes a great deal to the Victorians. During the later Victorian era, a new leisure culture was built upon three foundations: the creation of a large middle class with disposable income and time for recreation; the promotion of physical exercise as an antidote for the ills of urbanization and industrialization; and the transformation of games and pastimes into sport, which conveyed moral and spiritual benefits through competition.[22] The concept that sport was a way of building "character"—meaning sportsmanlike behaviour—was uniquely Victorian. Great believers in organization, the Victorians used the club as a way of gathering like-minded individuals together to better enjoy and promote all sorts of activities, but especially sports.[23] The club would be a vital instrument in the popularization of skiing. While ski enthusiasts were not necessarily middle or upper class, the growth of the sport was closely linked to the number of people with the time and money to pursue it. Skiing was not the only winter activity to benefit: curling, skating, tobogganing and others experienced booms in popularity.

Thanks to technological advances in transportation and communication, the Victorians also popularized tourism, and nowhere more than in the Alps of Europe. By the 1870s, activities like hiking and climbing in the mountains were all the rage in upper class and upper-middle class circles, especially in England. On a bet, a group of wealthy Englishmen stayed at St. Moritz for a month during the winter, and so enjoyed themselves that the idea of the winter resort was born.[24] The adoption of skiing as a winter pastime was not far behind. The Victorian era was also a time of nationalism, and sports and recreation often became arenas for exercising national pride. In Norway, skiing quickly transformed from being the way farmers and woodcutters travelled in winter into a fundamental part of national identity and character, the Idreat, personifying a vigorous northern people.[25] Non-Norwegians would also feel the appeal of skiing as a manly, character building sport that set one apart from the crowd.

Conditions were ideal for people to discover skiing as a thrilling winter sport. The British had a lot to do with this, especially Arnold Lunn. He was probably the world's first ski bum, as well as instrumental in pointing skiing in a new direction, downhill. The Scandinavians certainly knew how to ski down hills, but did not practice descending slopes as an end in itself. In the Alps, however, winter tourists and local sportsmen were skiing mostly as an amusing new pastime, and it wasn't long before enthusiasts were looking for ways to make it more exciting (jumping, though practised, was apparently a little too exciting for most people). The most obvious was to emphasize skiing down. Son of a wealthy tour operator, Lunn emerged as a leader of a group of Brits in Murren, Switzerland, who more and more focused on "downhill running," especially racing.[26] Instead of long ski tours into the high country, the British and their local imitators started repeatedly skiing the same slopes, climbing up again for the pleasure of another run down. The emphasis was on speed.

This had interesting consequences: for one, the slopes became packed and this encouraged downhill technique to evolve. The Murren skiers started the famous Kandahar downhill race in 1911. Lunn refined existing races around obstacles into the slalom, a timed competition down a course marked by flags, designed to test a skier's manoeuvring skill. It was wildly popular and quickly became a standard type of race. Lunn also led the fight to get downhill and slalom racing accepted for recognized competition. The Scandinavian dominated Federation International de Ski had been formed in 1924, after the first Winter Olympics were held. Only jumping and cross-country were recognized for the Olympics.[27] By 1930, this had changed, and downhill skiing and racing rapidly eclipsed the older forms of competition.

BACK ACROSS THE POND

The Alpine approach to skiing soon influenced development on the other side of the Atlantic, where a ski scene was thriving on the Eastern Seaboard, with clubs leading the way. While the jumping clubs that dominated North American skiing at the end of the nineteenth century didn't widely popularize the sport, some adventurous souls took it up. Many were college students and members of the leisured classes in the eastern U.S. and Canada. Skis, imported from Norway, were provided for winter guests at the exclusive Lake Placid Club in 1904.[28] The Montreal Ski Club was founded the same year, and inspired students at Dartmouth College in upper New York State to start the Dartmouth Outing Club in 1909, with an emphasis on skiing and snowshoeing. Other schools emulated the Dartmouth Club, and their graduates founded other clubs for skiing. The clubs that sprung up in the eastern U.S. introduced the curious to skiing, but also explored the potential of the forested mountains of New England, building club lodges and cutting trails in the woods for skiing.

Much the same thing happened in Eastern Canada. Thanks to a large population, skiing caught on early in Montreal and the Laurentian Mountains. A true winter city, Montreal had a strong tradition of winter sports like curling, skating, snowshoeing and tobogganing, organized into many clubs.[29] Montreal ski pioneers remembered people experimenting on the slopes of Mount Royal as early as 1881. A group of McGill professors took up the sport and in 1904 a small group of enthusiasts founded the Montreal Ski Club. While not the first ski club in Canada (that honour went to Revelstoke), Montreal's club was perhaps more influential. Scandinavian members provided instruction, but the club attracted enthusiasts from prominent Montreal families and promoted skiing beyond ethnic boundaries.[30] Another club was formed in Quebec City in 1908, and ski clubs proliferated swiftly. While jumping was still a big part of the sport, Montreal skiers also enjoyed cross-country rambles and downhill running on Mount Royal. Even before the First World War, the Montreal club began to organize outings to the Laurentian Mountains.[31]

Skiing soon spread to Ontario. The Ottawa Ski Club formed around 1910 with a sizable Norwegian contingent, and was joined by the Cliffside Club in 1919.[32] Skiers from the two clubs explored the nearby Gatineau Hills and found that old logging tracks made admirable ski trails. Skiing also appeared in other parts of Ontario, including the flat lands around Toronto. The sport was taken up enthusiastically by the middle class professionals of the city, and the Toronto Ski Club was started in 1908. Despite lacking natural ski terrain, the club grew quickly, and would prove energetic and innovative in developing venues for skiing, especially at the nearby Summit Golf Club. Canada's national volunteer ski patrol would grow out of the Toronto club.[33]

After the First World War, skiing experienced a surge of popularity. Older clubs rebounded and new clubs formed.[34] In 1920, the clubs in Quebec and Ontario formed the Canadian Amateur Ski Association. Interest in jumping declined, but interest in other aspects of skiing increased correspondingly. Membership increased into the hundreds and then thousands for the clubs in Ottawa and Toronto, and clubs undertook to provide instruction for members and establish proficiency tests. The clubs also created venues for skiing as well as clubhouses and lodges in ski country, or encouraged local entrepreneurs.[35] Trails were cut throughout the Gatineau and Laurentian Mountains for ski touring in the twenties. In 1927, the Montreal Ski Club convinced the Canadian Pacific to start running special ski trains on the weekends to the Laurentians, and many Americans from New York joined Canadian skiers, staying in the many quaint rural inns found throughout the area or renting old farmhouses.[36]

Clubs were introducing more and more people to skiing. But even more importantly, some of the people joining clubs in the U.S. and Canada could afford travel to Europe. They were exposed to new innovations in skiing technique and skiing gear, especially the popularity of "downhill running" over the older Nordic disciplines of jumping, cross-country racing and ski touring—and they brought their experiences back.

TRANSFORMATION

Downhill skiing and racing in Europe during the 1920s and 1930s drove many innovations in equipment. This is not the place to trace the evolution of skiing gear, but improvements to skis and bindings were important to the growth of the sport. Early recreational skiers used long wooden skis, narrow for cross-country travel, wide for ski jumping. Bindings were improvements on Norheim's innovation, but still primitive and did not allow for much control over the ski. The growing popularity of downhill running started a cycle of improvement and specialization for ski gear. While skis remained wood, homemade skis were replaced by mass-produced versions of much higher quality, and also shorter and more specialized. A young Austrian machinist, Rudolf Lettner, screwed metal edges onto his skis in 1928 to keep the wood from splintering, and discovered that they made turns much easier on hard snow. After a bit of controversy, metal edges became popular.

Bindings went through a rapid transformation. Various ways of clamping the front of boot to the ski were invented—a Norwegian named Huitfeldt invented the first, called toe irons.[37] This was later complemented by a cable around the back of the boot, tightened by a throw on front of the ski—the "Kandahar" was a popular brand. In the 1930s, a new feature was added to some bindings: the back of the cable was attached to the ski by a spring or a hook, clamping the foot to the ski and adding immeasurably to control going downhill.[38] The heel was kept loose for travelling uphill and cross-country, then fixed for downhill runs. Keen racers often used "beartraps," a binding

High tech: leather boots and cable throw bindings, circa 1930s.
(WHYTE MUSEUM OF THE CANADIAN ROCKIES, V108-1553, LLOYD HARMON.)

where a long thong was wrapped around the boot, threaded through eyelets on the binding and buckled tight. The new bindings made it difficult to adopt a telemark stance and contributed to the decline of this style of turning. Specialized ski boots complemented better bindings. While still leather, footwear became higher, stiffer and more supportive. These changes made skiing faster and easier, but also more dangerous. Commentators noticed a dramatic rise in injuries, especially broken legs and ankles.

Along with better equipment came better technique. An Austrian, Hannes Schneider, invented the "Arlberg" method (sometimes called the Arlberg swing or simply the Arlberg) which combined the British emphasis on downhill speed with the controlled skiing of Zdarsky. Schneider added a distinctive crouching stance to the "christy" turn, making precise, high-speed turns possible on the equipment of the day. More importantly, he organized a logical progressive system that took beginners from snowplows to parallel turns. Criticized as rigid and time consuming—each stage had to be mastered perfectly before the student was allowed to progress—the Arlberg set a standard for teaching and allowed many more people to master the sport. Visiting skiers took the Arlberg back to North America. European ski instructors followed, including Schneider himself, a refugee from the Nazis in the 1930s. By the mid-thirties, a burgeoning race scene introduced more technique and good skiers were using quite modern looking parallel turns.

Most of the changes in gear and technique were for downhill skiing. Specialized equipment also evolved for cross-country racing, with skis becoming narrower and lighter. Most skiers opted for heavier gear for better downhill control, and used it for ski touring or cross-country jaunts, which were still a big part the sport in the thirties and forties. The invention of the ski lift changed this.

Lift Lines

As "downhill running" became more and more popular, people also began to look for ways to increase the time spent going down rather than up. Back during the California mining boom, one mine carried people up in the ore buckets on Sundays for a run down.[39] Other early attempts at assisted uphill travel included towing toboggans. In Europe, existing cog railways and teleferiques, cable cars built for summer sightseers, were pressed into service with some success.[40] But the revolution started at the beginning of the 1930s when more or less simultaneously in Switzerland and Shawbridge,

A glamorous image: CPR poster, circa 1930s. (Glenbow Archives Poster 36.)

Quebec, the rope tow was invented. It utilized a rope strung up the hill and run through the drive train of an old car.[41] Soon mechanics were putting cars up on blocks throughout North America and rigging up tows. Skiers merely had to grab hold of the rope to get pulled up the hill for a run down. They were tricky to use, but had immediate appeal to many skiers, even if some old-timers turned up their noses at the contraptions. More importantly, people were willing to pay for the privilege of getting towed up hill. The commercial ski hill was born.

By the mid-twenties, the sport was growing fast in North America. Widespread prosperity gave more and more people the means to pursue activities like skiing, and in a growing consumer culture, the desire.[42] No longer a matter of building character and strong bodies, sport was now recreation. Skiing became increasingly associated with a desirable, glamorous lifestyle. Advertisers began to use skiing to sell everything from cars to cigarettes.[43] More importantly, ski gear became more available when companies manufactured it domestically. The 1932 Winter Olympics at Lake Placid, which the Lake Placid Club largely organized, further promoted skiing to the public. Most of the new enthusiasts were middle or upper class, able to afford the gear, the time and the travel.

Skiing reappeared in the western U.S. A new generation brought European-style ski touring and downhill skiing to places like Mt. Hood in Oregon and Denver. Local enthusiasts established skiing in more remote places like Jackson Hole, Wyoming or Alta in Utah. During the Depression, government make-work projects included creating ski facilities, whether clearing slopes and trails in the east or building the magnificent Timberline Lodge at Mt. Hood. And business was fast awakening to the potential of the sport. Aside from local entrepreneurs, moneyed enthusiasts like Fred Pabst of the brewing Pabsts built lodges and ski tows throughout the northeastern U.S. and even in Quebec.

The craze for downhill and slalom skiing reached Canada in the late twenties, and the focus of skiers switched from cross-country trails to finding or clearing good downhill slopes. Montreal skiers further developed the slopes at Shawbridge and Hill 70 near St. Saveur (home of the famous Red Birds Ski Club, devoted to racing). They also discovered Mt. Tremblant and cleared runs on the mountain. Alex Foster built one of the world's first rope tows in Shawbridge in 1932 and more followed. In 1937, an American real estate developer built a lodge at Tremblant, cut runs specifically for skiing

Snow fun: Calgary Herald *advertisement, 1935.* (GLENBOW ARCHIVES.)

and installed tows, creating what might be considered Canada's first purpose-built commercial ski resort.[44] Ottawa skiers had Camp Fortune in the Gatineaus.[45] The Toronto Ski Club, meanwhile, grew into one of the largest clubs in Canada, with an astonishing 3,000 members by 1936.[46] All the eastern clubs had big memberships: Ottawa was also about 2,000 members strong. Among them was John Southam, of the Southam newspaper family, who would move west in 1930 to manage the *Calgary Herald* and become a charter member of the Calgary Ski Club.

Sun Valley, Idaho, established in 1936, pointed the direction that skiing would go in the future. Averell Harriman, head of the Union Pacific Railway, wanted to increase winter passenger traffic on his railway. An avid skier and Austrian nobleman, Count Felix Schaffgotsch, found a beautiful valley near Ketchum, Idaho for Harriman, on a spur line of his railroad. Harriman built a high-end resort to rival anything in Europe, which would feature such innovations as the world's first chairlift, developed by Union Pacific engineers from a banana loader. A bunch of Hollywood celebrities attended Sun Valley's opening, reinforcing the glamorous image of skiing and giving the sport another boost in popularity. It also changed what people in North America thought a ski area should be.

By the end of the thirties, skiing had evolved into something like the sport familiar today. People could drive or take a train from a big city to a ski area, where they could get a pull up a hill and run down it many times. Many skiers still travelled under their own power, either taking to trails for cross-country jaunts or ski touring into the high mountains and backwoods in search of solitude and untouched snow, but this was changing. Among competitors, the emphasis on downhill and slalom racing had eclipsed ski jumping and cross-country racing outside of Scandinavia. The recreational skier thought increasingly in terms of going to a hill and repeatedly climbing it—or being pulled up—for the pleasure of going down.

SKIING IN BANFF AND THE ROCKY MOUNTAINS

The story of the Calgary Ski Club is part of the development of skiing around Banff. The sport came relatively late to the Canadian Rockies. Skis did make some early appearances. There were reports that Scandinavians employed on construction crews in the 1880s near Silver City, a short-lived town by Castle Mountain, travelled on skis in the winter.[47] A few years later, in 1893, an American visitor to the Banff Sanatorium saw local resident George

Paris on snowshoes. He told Paris about the skis Norwegian immigrants used back home in North Dakota and promised to send him a pair.[48] They came that winter and Paris immediately became the first ski casualty in Banff after crashing on a hill near the sanatorium. He gave up skiing, but a few other locals experimented with the sport, using his skis or their own handmade copies. The famed mountain guide, Conrad Kain, brought a pair of skis with him to Banff in 1910 and built a ski jump on Tunnel Mountain.[49] A few local boys enthusiastically took to the novel entertainment. Jack Stanley, a friend of Kain and owner of a local sawmill, built some skis.

Skiing didn't get well established around Banff, however, until near the end of the First World War. In 1916, local businessmen Norman Luxton and B.W. Collinson decided to promote the town as a winter destination and organized the first Banff Winter Carnival for February 1917.[50] Among the attractions were ski jumping, skijoring with horses and cross-country races. The top racers and jumpers in the west came to compete. Among the skiers from Revelstoke, Camrose and Edmonton was Gus Johnson of Camrose. Johnson, another ubiquitous Norwegian, stayed in the mountains and organized the Banff Ski Club, bringing along a whole generation of young

Original Mt. Norquay lodge, circa 1928.
(WHYTE MUSEUM OF THE CANADIAN ROCKIES, V189 PA 157-33, LLOYD HARMON.)

local skiers, including Cyril Paris, son of George Paris, and brothers Cliff White and Peter Whyte (Peter changed the spelling of his last name). Two other skiers, Chris Gottaas and Jack Moxness, came to the first festival from Calgary to compete.[51] They would return home to be the founders of the first Calgary Ski Club.

The Banff Winter Carnival went on to be a great success. Under Johnson's leadership, the Banff Ski Club also thrived. The young skiers, especially Cyril Paris and Cliff White, began exploring the high country around Banff and discovered forest fires and logging had formed ready-made ski slopes on Mount Norquay.[52] An American visitor, entomologist Owen Bryant of Boston, heard about these explorations and suggested building a ski cabin at Norquay, like those found throughout his native New England. He provided the financing to hire Gus Johnson to build the cabin and clear off the brush to create new runs. Paris, White and other enthusiasts got permission from the park authorities for the cabin. When the building was finally finished in 1928, it established the slopes of Norquay as a skiing venue and put Banff on the map as a ski destination. More importantly, Norquay would quickly become popular among skiers from Calgary. Depression work crews built a road up to the resort in 1935, making it possible to drive up to the base of the slopes.

Some skiing had also been going on near Lake Louise since the early twenties, thanks to the Swiss Guides.[53] The CPR employed the guides at the Chateau in the winter clearing snow from the hotel roof. Some of the guides had skis and gave lessons to interested locals. The CPR stationmaster, Stan Boyle, and his family became avid skiers and along with the guides formed the Lake Louise Ski Club.[54] The guides also explored the high country around Lake Louise, and told Cyril Paris about the fabulous skiing that they had found in Ptarmigan Valley to the north. Paris and Cliff White and other Banff skiers investigated the area in 1930, and were in turn amazed by the potential.

Paris and White soon hatched a plan to build a lodge in the Skoki Valley. They formed the Ski Club of the Canadian Rockies, took over the Norquay lease and got permission from the Dominion Parks Branch to build a cabin at Skoki. Selling shares in the ski club financed the new building. Skoki Lodge attracted a loyal American clientele but struggled, lacking the money for a needed expansion. Sir Norman Watson, a wealthy British industrialist, bought majority ownership in Skoki in 1935.[55] Watson had much bigger

Skoki Lodge, 1941. (CSC Collection, Ozzie LaRue.)

plans than simply expanding Skoki. He envisioned a series of European-style chalets in the area, run by Swiss peasants who would support themselves in the summer herding cattle in the alpine meadows. This eccentric notion never came to pass, but Watson did build Temple Lodge on the east side of Whitehorn Mountain, which was the start of the Lake Louise ski resort.

Norquay and Skoki were not the only important ski developments in the Banff area. In 1928, ski pioneers Erling Strom and the Marquis D'Albizzi, both instructors at Lake Placid, visited the Rockies and saw the apparently limitless terrain for skiing. In the face of much skepticism from local packers and guides, they established a ski camp at Assiniboine. Using a CPR cabin built for summer trail rides, they took clients in on skis for stays of several weeks. Strom ran the camp in the early spring for 14 years. Closer to Banff, tour operator Jim Brewster and some friends investigated the skiing possibilities around Sunshine Meadows, where the CPR had another cabin for trail riders. Jim and his brother Pat leased the cabin for ski trips, and bought it outright in 1936.[56] Visitors travelled partway by vehicle, partway by horse, then finished up the trip to the cabin on skis. In the late thirties, enthusiasts around Jasper formed a club and developed runs on Whistler Mountain.[57]

Skiing was not restricted to lodges and tourism. High-country ski touring and ski mountaineering were also popular around Banff, especially at

One horsepower snow machine: Mary Reid going to Sunshine, circa 1936.
(GLENBOW ARCHIVES, NA 4317-3.)

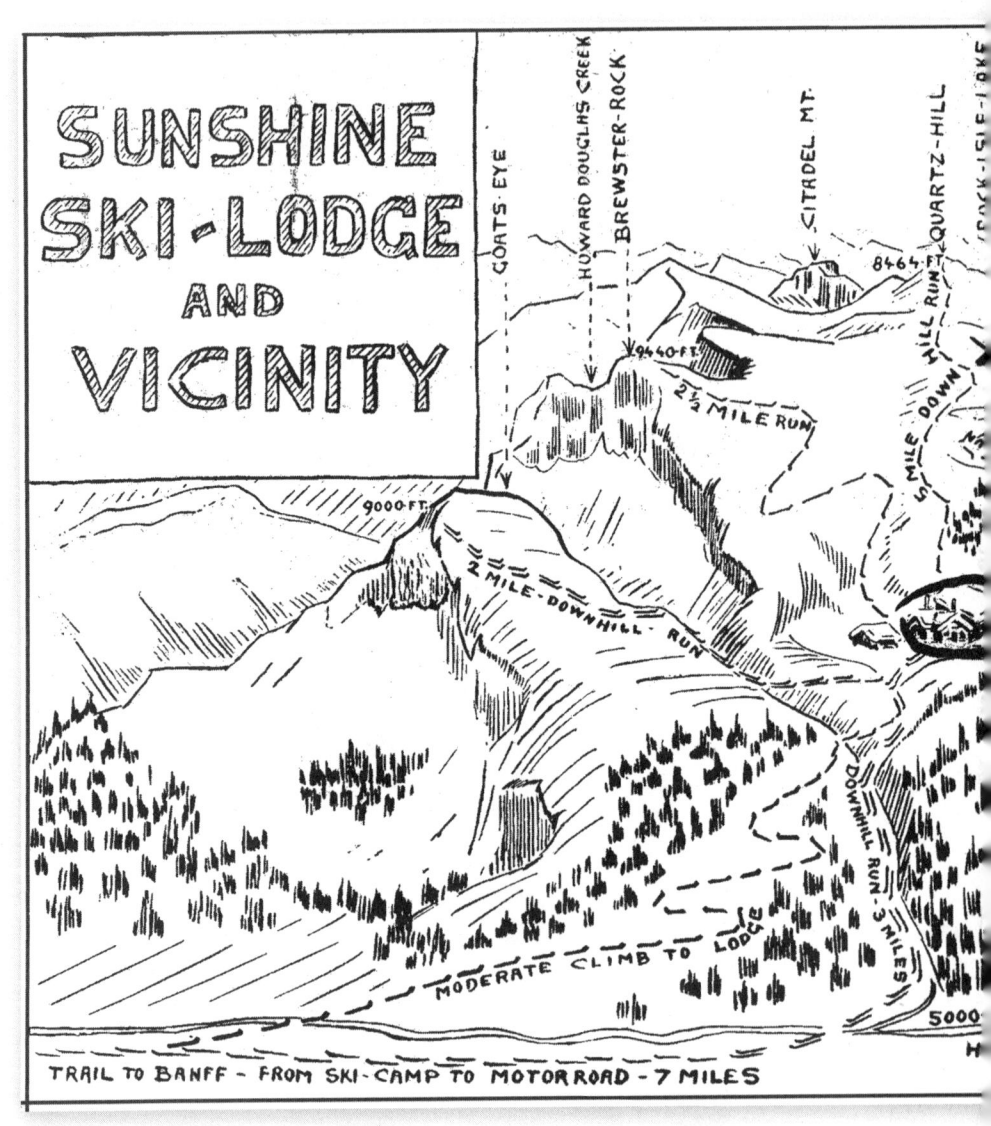

Ski touring paradise: early map of Sunshine. (GLENBOW ARCHIVES PA 2351-74.)

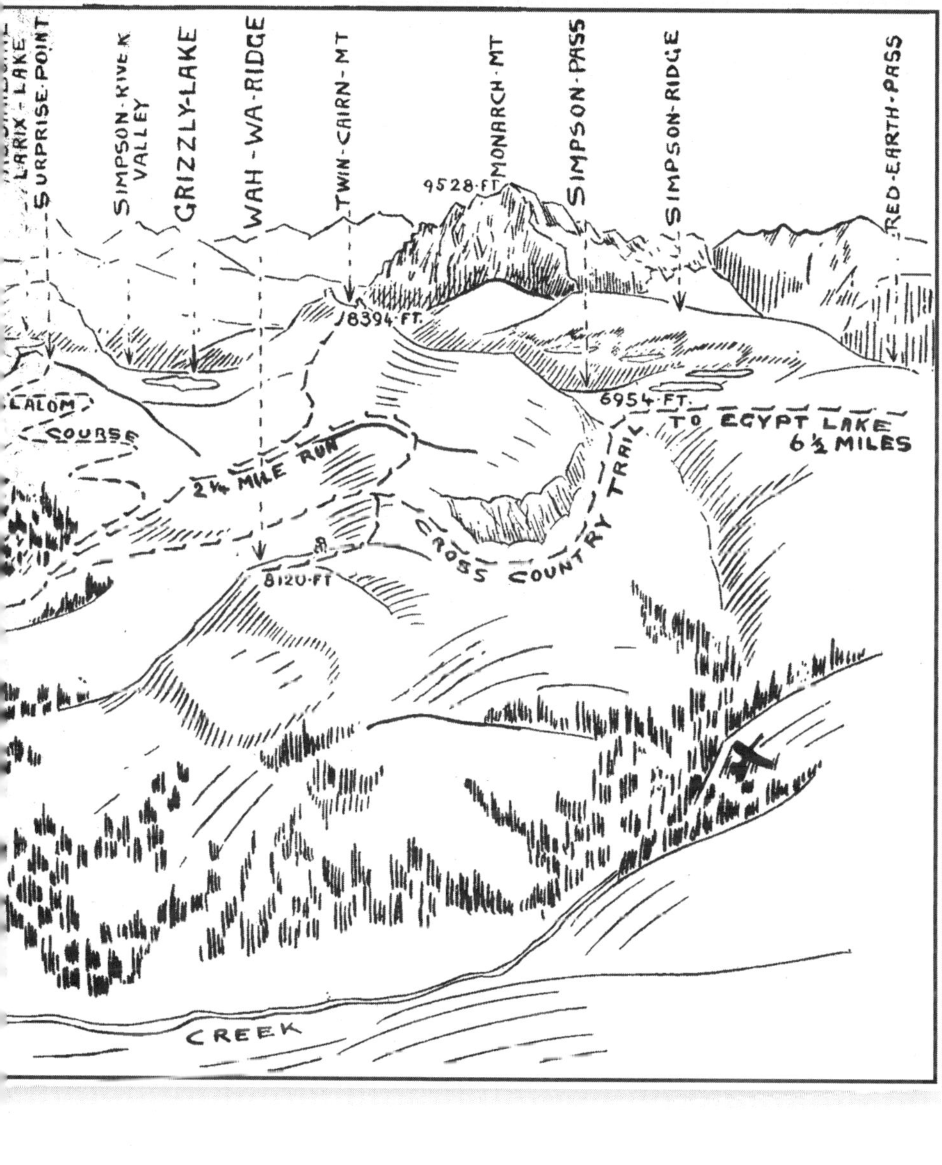

LARIX - LAKE
SURPRISE·POINT
SIMPSON·RIVER
VALLEY
GRIZZLY-LAKE
WAH-WA-RIDGE
TWIN-CAIRN-MT
9528·FT
MONARCH·MT
SIMPSON-PASS
SIMPSON-RIDGE
RED-EARTH-PASS
8394·FT.
6954·FT.
TO EGYPT LAKE
6½ MILES
LALOM
COURSE
2¼ MILE RUN
CROSS COUNTRY TRAIL
8120·FT
CREEK

Skoki. The Canadian Alpine Journal published its first articles on ski mountaineering in the Rockies and Coast Range in 1931, and the following year had a whole section devoted to the subject. In 1936, the Alpine Club of Canada held its inaugural ski camp at Lake O'Hara, and built the Stanley Mitchell Hut in the Little Yoho Valley specifically to encourage skiing. Calgary skiers would play their part in high-country explorations. In 1935, Calgary Ski Club members made the first ski ascent of Mt. Balfour on the Wapta Icefields.[58]

By the 1930s, local enthusiasts had established skiing around Banff, and a few more far-sighted residents and businessmen saw the potential for winter tourism and encouraged the sport. A new Banff club, the Ski Runners of Canadian Rockies, was formed in 1933 to promote skiing. Modelled on the Trail Riders of the Canadian Rockies, prospective members had to ski 25 miles of mountain trails to qualify. Visitors and immigrants to Banff introduced new styles of skiing, such as the Arlberg method and downhill and slalom racing. Norquay became a popular site for competitions, culminating in the 1937 Dominion Ski Championships. Ski Runners of the Canadian Rockies hosted this event along with the Calgary Ski Club, which eight keen individuals had chartered just two years before after a chance meeting on a golf course—on skis, of course.

CHAPTER THREE

Skiing Comes to Calgary

Jump—Pioneers—Rebirth—Growth—
Where to Ski—Tee Time—Bragg Creek—
Norquay—School's In—Racing—
Whupping Edmonton Championships—
High Country—Social Calendar

Calgary had never seen anything like it. On the edge of the escarpment overlooking the Elbow River on the south edge of town stood a 40-foot wooden tower. It had a snow-covered ramp on one side that stretched partway down the hillside and terminated abruptly in a jump. As a crowd of thousands held their breath, a daredevil on long skis started down the ramp. Gathering speed, he hurtled off the jump, flew gracefully through the air and landed, breaking hard to stop before reaching the end of snow and pitching headfirst into a muddy field. Ninety-five feet was a disappointment for Anders Haugen, the world record holder at 213 feet, but the conditions were not ideal. The assembled spectators, standing in the mud and slush of a February chinook, loved it. It was 1919 and skiing had made a spectacular debut in the city, under the auspices of the Calgary Ski Club.

The snow-capped Rocky Mountains may dominate the skyline, but Calgary is really a prairie city, and a relatively warm and dry one thanks to the famous chinook winds. There are some significant topographical features, nevertheless, the climate is not a natural one for skiing—snow cover was no more reliable 70 years ago than it is now. The sport of skiing thus got off to a relatively slow start in the city. The first Calgary Ski Club, a band of Scandinavian immigrants pursuing jumping, did not last. It was not until the 1930s, when the sport really took off in North America, that Calgarians started to catch ski fever Another band of enthusiasts realized that although the city was not the most desirable location for skiing, some of the best ski terrain in the world was not far away in Banff National Park.

The Calgary Ski Club was reborn, and taking a cue from the established ski clubs of the east, aggressively promoted the sport. The club recruited new members, convinced stores to carry equipment, arranged convenient and inexpensive transportation to the mountains, provided instruction for beginners and worked with Banff skiers to improve venues such as Mt. Norquay. Within a few short years, thanks to their efforts, skiing went from something seen in newsreels to the hottest new sport in Calgary.

The Pioneers

As far as winter sports went, Calgary, an Anglo-Scottish city, was mad for curling with hockey a close second. The city did not have a large population of Scandinavian immigrants, and this may account for the late appearance of skiing. Edmonton and Camrose both had active ski clubs before the First World War, thanks to the many Norwegians and Swedes in central Alberta. Interestingly, a 1913 article in the *Edmonton Bulletin* announced that "jumpers from the Camrose, Entwistle and Calgary ski clubs will compete in this weekend's tournament."[59] No Calgary competitors were at the event, however, so any club based in Calgary must have been short lived. It was a half-dozen years later, in 1919, that skiing made its first known debut in Calgary in spectacular fashion, thanks to—naturally—a group of Scandinavians.

Christian Gottaas would later move to Camrose, but in 1917 he lived in Calgary, and was one of a handful of skiers around the city. Gottaas, a labourer at the Calgary Foundry, went out to Banff for the first winter carnival with his friend, Jack Moxness. They competed in the cross-country race, and Gottaas came in second. Back in Calgary, Gottaas and Moxness met up with Rudy Verne, a recently arrived Swede, and some other ski-minded souls. In the fall of 1919, the little group, including J. Digeraas and A.N. Simpson, decided to form a ski club and find a place in the city to build a jumping hill. As the *Calgary Herald* reported:

> Upon the initiative of Rudolf Verne of this city, the Calgary Ski Club was constituted yesterday when a few Scandinavian ski enthusiasts gathered to discuss the possibility of facing up a first class hill for jumping.[60]

Verne was a born organizer: the following winter he also founded and was first president of the Calgary Art Skating Club. Although not a journalist by trade (he was a clerk for the Canadian Bank of Commerce) Verne wrote a couple of articles on skiing for the *Herald*, including one on the Banff Winter Carnival. The article noted with satisfaction the hiring of Gus Johnson of Camrose to run the skiing events.

The founders of the new club were much like their forebears in Revelstoke and Rossland. The Calgarians planned to focus on the traditional forms of ski competition, cross-country and jumping, but they were evangelical about the sport. "The aim of the Calgary Ski Club is to promote skiing in all its different branches by way of expert instruction to beginners as well as competitions for more advanced members."[61] The membership fee was a stiff five dollars for men and three for ladies, raised to ten and five respectively, a disincentive to the curious at a time when five dollars a day was a decent wage. The club needed money to pay for a ski jump.

The group had chosen the south escarpment of the Elbow River, overlooking Riverdale Avenue in the district of Elbow Park, as a site for a jump. Realtor Freddy Lowes, a well-known Calgary sportsman, owned the property and happily gave the club permission to use it. In return the club made him the honourary president. A tower was still necessary to create enough speed

The ski jump in Elbow Park, 1920. (Glenbow Archives, PA 2319-5.)

Grandstanding: some very brave ski jumpers demonstrate their sport, 1921.
(GLENBOW ARCHIVES, NB 16-504 WILLIAM J. OLIVER.)

for a decent jump, and within a few weeks, the club had hired a contractor to put up a 40-foot structure.[62] No time was lost organizing the first contest for February 16 and 17, 1920. The dates took advantage of the fact the Banff Winter Carnival was scheduled for the previous week. This ensured that top jumpers, some of international calibre, would be on hand to inaugurate the Elbow Park jump.

The event roused considerable interest among Calgarians, and the tournament drew crowds estimated at more than 3,000.[63] The club arranged special streetcars to deliver spectators to the area.[64] True to expectations, the Calgary club got some top talent to come to the city, including the reigning world champion, Anders Haugen of the U.S., and the Canadian champion, Nels Nelson of Revelstoke. Ominously, just before the big day, the weather warmed up, and the club members found themselves frantically carting snow over to the jump to create a long enough run-out for the landing. On the day of the competition, reduced to just one day, the crowd wallowed in slush and mud. Sticky conditions meant the longest jump of the day was only 95 feet and the short run-out meant competitors had to resort to frantic manoeuvres to stop, much to the interest of spectators.

The competition was still spectacular and attracted the attention of E.L. Richardson, general manager of the Calgary Exhibition and Stampede. Richardson, no doubt impressed by the success of the Banff Winter Carnival, wanted to organize one for Calgary. Ski jumping was clearly a crowd-pleaser. Verne joined the organizing committee as the representative for skiing and art skating.[65] However, the jump in Elbow Park was too far away from the exhibition grounds in Victoria Park. The solution was to build a new jump. The grounds lacked a suitable hill, so a steel-frame tower was built on top of the grandstand. The local papers claimed the jump tower would be nearly 80 feet high, on top of the 55-foot height of the stand.[66] Although jumping was one of the carnival highlights, there was also a cross-country race for men and women as well as skijoring.

The ski jumpers were promoted as the major attraction of the carnival (next to the bonspiel), and the first event in 1921 attracted North America's top competitors. They also went to the Banff carnival and then out to Revelstoke for another tournament. The organizers in the three cities made sure their dates did not conflict.[67] Like the Elbow Park competition, the jumps at the first carnival were disappointing. Snow was in short supply and the tower was poorly designed. Verne would recount in later years that the company supplying the steel had changed the design, resulting in a terrifyingly steep run down and a badly angled ramp that threw jumpers too high—many of the competitors blanched upon inspecting the jump. None dropped out, and numerous crashes added to the entertainment. The problem of ensuring sufficient snow, however, would return to plague the carnival again and again. The following year Richardson had to ship snow from Lake Louise by rail to the grounds. Even the usually optimistic *Calgary Herald* commented that perhaps Calgary was not the best place for a winter carnival.[68]

Ski jumping continued at the winter carnival for three years, but not under the auspices of the Calgary Ski Club. In 1921, Richardson hired Nel Nelson, the famous Revelstoke jumper, to redesign the ski jump and supervise the event for the following year. A couple of Calgary skiers continued to compete, but the city's ski club had disappeared. One reason for its demise was likely because Verne left Calgary shortly after founding it. By 1921, he was busy exploring the mountains north of Vancouver. By his own account, Verne and a Norwegian friend climbed a trail in West Vancouver until they "came out on a great Alpine plateau, a winter fairyland and skiers' paradise."[69] Grouse Mountain Ski Resort can be found there today. Verne had gone to

Vancouver to take a job as an instructor at the Connaught Skating Club.[70] He also started the Olympic Sport Shop and a ski factory, continued racing and jumping, and was a founder of the Hollyburn Pacific Ski Club, a group of mostly Swedish enthusiasts who established a ski lodge on Hollyburn Ridge. Verne would also serve as the Western vice-president of Canadian Amateur Ski Association.[71]

Vancouver's gain was Calgary's loss. Skiing did not catch on in the city for another decade. Part of the blame was probably jumping itself: although popular for spectators, it was the realm of daredevils and did not draw people to skiing. The city was not quite ready to embrace the new-fangled sport and the club faded into obscurity. Skiing was left to the odd individual or two messing about on their own, mostly kids occasionally seen on the hillsides in Elbow Park near Christ Church or above Riley Park in Hillhurst.[72] But the sport remained an oddity in Calgary.

The Club Reborn

John Southam was a scion of the Southam publishing family of Ottawa. In many ways, he represented the new wave of skiers who adopted the sport in the late twenties and early thirties: well educated, well connected, from a prominent establishment family. The grandson of William Southam, he went into the family newspaper business after finishing school and was sent to Calgary in 1932 to work as the assistant business manager for the *Herald*. An avid outdoorsman, Southam had discovered skiing in Ottawa. He was a member of one of the city's ski clubs, which were large, very well organized, and had lodges in the Gatineaus. Eastern Canadian skiers had also discovered the fun of downhill and slalom racing. Southam cut his teeth in this burgeoning ski scene. When he came to Calgary as a young man in his early twenties, not only was he a proficient skier but he knew what a club could do for promoting the sport.

And the sport needed promoting. Despite the proximity of Banff, Southam must have been surprised to find that there wasn't any kind of club in the city, and for that matter, apparently no skiers. Going out for a jaunt on the hills around Calgary, he must have wondered if he was in some sort of exile. Jack Farish, one of the charter members of the resurgent Calgary Ski Club, remembers Southam's story of how he finally found some like-minded souls. After a good snowfall, Southam headed out for a ski:

He packed a sandwich and drove his car out to the bottom of this hill [where Strathcona Heights and Coach Hill are now situated] one bright sunny morning towards the end of February. There had been quite a fall of fresh snow the night before. He noticed another track coming across his at an angle and then he saw two other skiers. He went over to where these other skiers were having lunch beside some big boulders. This is where he met Dudley Batchelor ... and Gordon Moodie. They didn't have any experience at skiing like he did and as they visited over lunch they got to talking about how helpful if would be if a club was organized to help teach people to ski and improve ski areas in an organized way, and in general, further the interests of skiing.[73]

Later stories would say that when Southam came across the two, they had a copy of Hannes Schneider's Wonder of Skiing in one hand and a flask of liquid courage in another.[74]

With this first meeting, the seed was planted. Batchelor and Moodie did not know of any other skiers in the city, but Southam soon found another couple of recruits, again through mere happenstance. As Alan Carscallen later recollected:

One day in the early thirties ... my friend Charlie Michener and I were skiing on the hills of the Calgary Golf and Country Club when a man appeared on the horizon and starting waving his ski pole and shouting at us. We thought we were being evicted from the grounds but as he came closer we saw it was John Southam. That's how we first met him. He had mistaken us for Dudley Batchelor and Gordon Moodie who he thought were the only other two people in Calgary who had skis.[75]

Carscallen was also enthusiastic about the idea of forming a club. Sometime in 1933 Southam took the initiative and put a notice in the *Herald* calling a meeting of interested skiers.[76] A small group had their first meeting at the *Herald* offices, and the Calgary Ski Club was reborn.

That first season the club was made up of just a handful of skiers: Alan Turney, Fred Ausenhaus and Dr. Gordon "Doc" Campbell joined the group, but it still numbered less than 10. Skiers were so rare in Calgary that anyone

Founders: Jack Farish and John Southam at Sunshine, ca. 1936.
(GLENBOW ARCHIVES, PA 2176-3.)

new stuck out from the crowd—Carscallen remembers seeing a fellow on 8th Avenue wearing a tuque and a skiing-style jacket. Sure enough, Monsieur Simard had recently arrived from Quebec to take a Rocky Mountain ski vacation, and Carscallen and Batchelor whisked him off for the weekend.[77] Paradoxically, such a small community—you knew just about everyone who skied—helped the club, as the city's skiers were happy to band together. When Ozzie LaRue, who had learned to ski in Saskatchewan of all places, moved to the city in 1937 he immediately joined the club, looking for people to get out with.

In 1935, the club took the step of formally incorporating under the provincial societies act. The aim was simple: "To encourage, promote and advance the sport of skiing in all its branches, and allied sports; to cooperate with other ski bodies for the advancement of skiing and to further develop the friendship and good fellowship of its members." Eight members were listed as founders: Gordon Moodie, draftsman, City Hall; Alan H. Carscallen, teacher, Calgary Commercial High School; John Southam, manager, *Calgary Herald*; Alan H. Turney, manager, bond department, James Richardson; Dudley E. Batchelor, bookkeeper, City Hall; Fred N. Ausenhaus, electrician; Gordon A. Campbell, physician; and John Farish, insurance. With the exception of Ausenhaus, the new founders were members of the educated middle class who could afford the not inconsiderable expense of skiing. And they were young: Southam was all of 24 years old. The group was the new face of skiing; the sort of people responsible for the sport's explosive growth in North America during the 1930s.

Calgarians keen to try skiing at the time faced some obstacles. There was no recognized venue. There were no instructors to teach proper technique. There were no stores in the city that sold ski equipment. The sport was tenuously established in Banff, but for a Calgarian access to the mountains in winter was not particularly easy—if you tried to drive—or convenient for skiing—if you took the train. In short, there was almost a complete vacuum as far as local skiers were concerned, outside of a handful of enthusiasts, and there was a lot of work to be done.

Rapid Growth

One of the first things the neophyte club addressed was equipment. A local source of quality ski gear was needed. Southam took the initiative, visiting the Bay and Eaton's in turn, only to be turned down. No market, declared both store managers. Next Southam tried the sporting goods stores, which mostly served hunters and fishermen. Andy Russell, of Russell's Sporting Goods, agreed to give ski gear a try. His only question was whether Southam thought there were enough skiers to warrant it. Southam confidently told him there soon would be! Russell's, at that time located next to the Wales Hotel downtown, quickly became a rendezvous for local skiers who could repair to the hotel bar to plan trips. Russell, though not a skier, was happy to help with organizing trips, thus beginning a long relationship between his shop and the CSC. The shop was the meeting place for the club's chartered bus trips, and Russell sold memberships to the club.

Once Russell's began to carry ski gear, the department stores followed, selling skis, boots, poles and bindings, usually called "harness." The Kandahar-style cable binding was popular, as was the beartrap, the long thong that held the foot to the ski. Most people bought relatively wide, general-purpose downhill skis and used them for cross-country jaunts and ski touring. Russell soon carried the metal edges coming into vogue and learned how to install them. Even Russell's, however, had almost nothing in the way of skiing-specific clothing. Almost all the early members of the club remember buying Grenfell cloth and having jackets made. The double mitts used by garbage

Ladies welcome: CSC skier at Norquay, circa 1930s. (CSC COLLECTION.)

collectors and outside labourers were popular, while plus-fours, canvas or tweed trousers completed the costume—natty but not very adequate when the wind and snow were blowing.

Having gear available made it much easier to introduce people to skiing. There was a lot of interest in the sport in the city, and the club grew quickly. By the end of 1934, the club claimed 55 members, and at the beginning of 1936, the number had almost tripled to 147.[78] For the 1938/39 season, the total was almost 400, consisting of 330 seniors and 64 juniors.[79] Almost all the new members were beginners—the founders, some of who had been barely able to ski themselves a couple of years before, now had to teach others. But the growth in Calgary wasn't just an accident; true to its charter, the club carried out membership drives that got more and more people out skiing. These new ski enthusiasts were not just young men—women joined the club in large numbers. Although the exact gender split isn't known, the 1936 governing council of the club had two women among the eight councillors, and several women, including Ruby Roberts, Jean Irving, Verna Cavanaugh and Mary Thompson, were all prominent in the early years of the club.

Among the many Calgarians the club introduced to skiing were several members of the city's mountaineering community. Jack Farish remembers recruiting several local members of the Alpine Club—Alexander Calhoun, Sidney Vallance, and Dick Rushworth—into the CSC. Vallance, head of the Calgary section for many years, became an enthusiastic promoter of skiing and ski mountaineering in the Alpine Club. Alan Carscallen, in turn, would join the Alpine Club and helped organize skiing trips for the mountaineering organization, like the summer ski camp on the Columbia Icefields in 1938. The ACC decided not to extend a special membership to the ski club upon a formal request from Jack Farish, but the two clubs would maintain informal links for many years based on common members.

The club had its own publicist in the form of Reginald Hayden. He was a sports writer for the *Calgary Herald*, an avid skier and a member of the CSC—he would serve on the club council. He and Southam likely schemed to get a regular ski column into the paper. Starting in 1936, Hayden wrote a weekly, then twice-weekly column, "Ski Notes and Queries," named after the yearbook of the Ski Club of Great Britain, dealing with ski news in Calgary and the Rockies. Needless to say, the club's activities were well reported.

Where to Ski?

From inception, the club was faced with a vexing question: where to ski? Vexing because the choice was the mountains, which required travel, or around the city, which required snow. Mt. Norquay was the easiest to reach and the most developed in Banff. Further afield there was Sunshine, Skoki and Assiniboine, but the first two required at least a weekend commitment and Assiniboine, a week. Not all skiers could easily afford travelling to Banff every weekend, so the club also explored alternatives closer to Calgary. The major obstacle for skiing around the city—a distinct lack of reliable snow cover—made Norquay the unofficial home of the club in the 1930s and the focus of much of its energy. The challenges of getting to the mountains helped the CSC coalesce. Founder Gordon Moodie later said that the club was really born "in the rest period between runs—erratic, wobbly runs on Norquay's nursery slopes ..."[80]

The founders of the new club quickly established that it was possible to visit Norquay on a weekend day trip. Carscallen remembered his first trip to Banff. He drove out with a couple of others on the old Coach Road. Although not well maintained in the winter, it was quite passable, a good sign. Once in Banff, the Calgarians found the town was a far cry from the buzzing tourist mecca of today—in winter it was very sleepy, most of the hotels were closed. The town itself lacked facilities for skiing and skiers—Norquay was where the action was. But the ski slopes weren't easy to get to—the road up to the lodge had just been started, so Carscallen and friends did what Banff residents had been doing for a decade—they took a horse-drawn sleigh partway to the camp, then got out and walked the rest of the way with shouldered skis. "It hadn't occurred to us that people could ski uphill."[81]

The slopes above the ski lodge were not as extensive as they would become, but still far better than anything in the vicinity of Calgary. The Norquay ski camp was also the stomping grounds for a small but talented bunch of Banff skiers, like Norm Knight, Rupe Edwards, the Paris brothers, the White family, and recent immigrants such as Austrian Vic Kutschera, credited with introducing the Arlberg method to Banff.[82] The Ski Runners of the Canadian Rockies, formed recently as a winter equivalent to the Trail Riders and the Skyline Hikers of the Canadian Rockies, regarded the hill as their home base, a place to practice before undertaking more rigorous ski touring in the high country. Members of the Ski Runners spent a great deal of time improving the slopes. With the exception of John Southam, the Banff skiers were much more advanced than the Calgarians but this just whetted their appetite. Carscallen, for one, came away firmly convinced that the club should aim to take Calgary skiers to Banff. After enjoying a day out, they returned to Calgary the same day, arriving late in the evening. Several more trips followed that winter.

Tee Time

Closer to home, the choices were limited. Southam and Carscallen had met at the Calgary Golf and Country Club, and the city's golf courses were the favoured local venues for club skiers. The tended fairways were the attraction; little snow was required to make them usable. Skiing on a golf course was cross-country skiing, but the terrain was a little more varied terrain than a playing field. There were also small hills for practice at the Calgary Golf and Country Club on the Elbow River, the Regal Golf Course in the northeast and the Bowness course on the western outskirts of the city.

The CSC got permission from the country club to ski on its grounds, conveniently located on the south edge of the city. Using the same heavy gear they took to the mountains, enthusiasts would slog around when there was enough snow—and sometimes when there wasn't. The snow cover was usually transitory, and skiing in marginal conditions had unfortunate consequences. At the end of November 1937, an early snowfall brought out throngs to the country club, estimated at 300, and as the *Herald*'s ski correspondent reported, the golf club started to turn away non-members, afraid that the greens would get damaged. Jack Farish remembered that "the Country Club was very good to us for a while ... but then some of our members got too pushy and skied too late into the spring and wrecked some of their greens, so we got kicked out of there."

Concern over damage to the courses was not restricted to the private golf and country club. The club approached the City of Calgary for permission to ski on the Municipal Golf Course, now known as Shaganappi. In 1938, Jack Insley, the club treasurer, requested permission from the city parks department to use the area for ski lessons for school kids.[83] Parks superintendent William Reader granted permission, but with the caveat that the club not cause any damage to shrubs, trees and grass.[84] The superintendent also expressed concern that club use might encourage non-club members from skiing on the course. Clearly, there were some major drawbacks to golf courses as ski areas.

Outside of the golf courses, enthusiasts just headed for the nearest hillside when there was enough snow. Southam had met up with Moodie and Batchelor on the slopes of what is now known as Signal Hill. Jack Farish remembered skiing near the Technical Institute grounds by 10th Avenue NW, and driving out to the Twin Bridges on the road to Bragg Creek and skiing around there. Skiers would go as far as the area around Priddis and Millarville in search of snow. There were some significant hazards to these impromptu slopes. As Reg Hayden pointed out to his readers:

> While enjoyable skiing is possible on these hills with a good fall of snow, skiers should be very careful to thoroughly inspect the slopes before using them, as there is not sufficient snow at present to properly cover up rocks and other dangerous obstacles ...[85]

That, sadly, was the usual situation around the city. Skiing in Calgary and area remained a sporadic affair. The problem was simply the extremely unreliable snow. The 1930s were a decade known for drought; 1937/38 was an exceptionally good season in the mountains, but not in the city, and for several years after there were only a handful of occasions when it was possible to break out the boards in Calgary.

BRAGG CREEK EXPERIMENTS

The other alternative the club investigated was the hills around the hamlet of Bragg Creek, just west of the city. During the season of 1937/38, Bragg Creek had snow while Calgary was bare. Skiers from the city headed for the hamlet and duly noted the possibilities of the area. A few locals had started skiing and early in 1938 formed a ski club.[86]

CSC councillors Albert Riley and Henry Samuelson carried out an official club reconnaissance in January 1938. They returned excited, reporting a myriad of old pony trails ripe for skiing and plenty of prospective slopes with a little clearing of brush.[87] The access was good: thanks to drilling activity in the area, the road to the hamlet was ploughed. One hill, near the dude ranch of Jake Fullerton, area pioneer and outfitter, looked particularly enticing. The club executive discovered Fullerton was one of the founders of the Bragg Creek club and very keen to further skiing in the area. He had his own plans to build a cabin and clear some runs. Nothing more was done that season, but the following fall the CSC organized a work party in September to help Fullerton with clearing, and the club looked forward eagerly to trying the area that winter.[88]

The real test came a couple of months later after some heavy early snowfalls. For Sunday, November 27, the club organized a special bus trip to Bragg Creek and the Fullerton Ranch. About a hundred skiers showed up.[89] The day was not really a success. No one had plowed the road, and it was barely passable, requiring a lot of pushing. The clearing work had not progressed sufficiently to create good runs, and the snow conditions left much to be desired—soft, heavy and melting. The cabin was not yet built. One steep slope, nicknamed Two-Pine in deference to Norquay's Lone Pine run, offered some good skiing for the experienced, but the beginners on the trip floundered. Still, the veterans of the club noted that there was great potential for the area, if more clearing was done, and there was a general feeling of optimism.

The Bragg Creek experiment, however, did not come to fruition. The CSC promised more volunteer labour. Fullerton continued to clear stumps and trees and built the needed cabin. But then the snow stayed away the rest of the 1938/39 season and the impetus faltered. Unreliable snow again was the problem, as anyone who visits the present cross country facility at Bragg Creek can attest. While Calgary skiers continued to visit the hills around the hamlet as an alternative to the mountains when conditions warranted, it would be another three decades before skiing came to Bragg Creek to stay.[90]

NORQUAY: THE CSC'S HOME AWAY FROM HOME

It was clear to the club that serious skiing meant skiing at Norquay, so dedicated skiers planned on making the jaunt to Banff on the weekend. The Norquay Ski Camp had the advantage of being close to Banff and the railway station. The road was completed in 1935, making it possible for a car or bus to drive to the base of the slopes. Norquay had a lodge, the small cabin the Banff Ski Club built, and it had good slopes along with natural open spaces. Banff skiers had been clearing new runs.

One of the crucial services the club offered Calgary skiers was arranging their transportation to Banff, cheaper than they could do it themselves. Alan Carscallen, club president in 1936, later said that it was probably the single most important motivator for forming the club.[91] Car-pooling was one option, and from the beginning, the club made arrangements for car pools. The winter drive to Banff was still a difficult and somewhat uncertain process, however, and many people didn't own a car. Something a little more reliable was needed. The club then chartered a bus on the weekend to get skiers out to the hill, charging a small round trip fare for club members—around $2. The bus usually departed from Russell's Sporting Goods downtown early on Sunday morning, returning in the evening, allowing skiers to get in a full afternoon at Norquay. The drawback was that the bus used the same bad roads as cars, and sometimes couldn't get through.

What the club really wanted was a ski train. By this time, the ski special concept, which had first taken off in the Laurentians, was well established all over North America. Following the lead of the Canadian Pacific, wherever there was skiing and large population centres in proximity, railroads had started offering lower rates for skiers and often scheduled special trains to take urban skiers to the snow. Half the fun of skiing in the Laurentians was taking the train, crowded with other cheerful enthusiasts, out for the day or weekend. Skiers sang, gossiped, told stories and flirted with the opposite sex.

In Calgary, the club executive approached G.D. Brophy of the CPR in 1935 about setting up a ski train.[92] Skeptical of the need for a scheduled ski special, the CPR was amenable to a lower excursion rate for the CSC on the regular train. The club made arrangements with Brewster's in Banff for a bus

Skiers disembarking in Banff, Alan Carscallen on far right, John Southam third from right. (WHYTE MUSEUM OF THE CANADIAN ROCKIES, V108 1144, LLOYD HARMON.)

to take skiers from the station to Norquay. For $5, a CSC member got a round trip ticket to the hill. The only drawback was the schedule: by train and then bus, skiers usually arrived at the camp slightly before noon. It was still the best way to get out to the mountains.

The special fare was quite a success, with an estimated 700 skiers using the train over nine weeks in 1936.[93] The following year, the CPR scheduled an earlier train for skiers and the local "ski special" was born.[94] The CPR usually began offering its excursion rates in January and discontinued the service in April. Run on Sundays (many people still had to work all or part of Saturday in the 1930s), the train soon attracted a sizable crowd. For the 1937/38 season, the club estimated ridership averaged 100 per week. Eventually, certain coaches were set aside for skiers.[95] Bruce Compton, an early club stalwart, recalled that up to seven or eight coaches might be filled with skiers, while Ross McPhalen, president in 1944, claimed that ski trains out to Banff sometimes numbered more than 20 cars![96] They had much the same fun atmosphere of the famous trains of the Laurentians, and the club even produced a songbook for sing-a-longs on the journey to and from Banff.

Skiing at Norquay was of course a far cry from what contemporary skiers experience. Facilities at the hill were very limited. The old lodge was a log cabin barely more than 30 by 20 feet, with a fireplace and a lunch counter inside. No one had to pay to use the hill and the lodge was also open to the public: the operators made a little money from the lunch counter. Early in the season, skiers might spend the first part of the day tramping down any new snow on the hill to build up the base and create a good surface for running slalom races. With no lift, not even a rope tow, skiers climbed up, usually just shouldering their skis and walking—not many had specialized climbing skins. On busy days, the combination of climbing up the same slopes used for coming down created chaos that was sometimes dangerous.

Most of the CSC skiers, who tended to be beginners, stuck to the practice slopes across from the lodge. The Lone Pine run, named for a landmark tree located above the practice slopes, was a favourite for more advanced skiers. They also visited the Bowl on the upper slopes. Another famous run was the Gully, the start of the narrow trail down to Banff, which was the scene of many nasty accidents. The trail crossed the road three times, and one skier famously collided with a bus. Even a keen skier was usually only able to do half a dozen runs in the course of a day. Rocks and other natural hazards abounded. Broken skis, and bones, were not uncommon.

Busy day: Mt. Norquay slopes, circa 1938. (GLENBOW ARCHIVES, NA 4317-7.)

Membership in the club gave Calgary skiers certain benefits at the lodge, including an area set aside for the exclusive use of the Ski Runners and the CSC. The club earned this privilege because it certainly contributed to the early development of Norquay. There are no statistics to quote, but on the weekends Calgarians often made up the majority of skiers in the early years. For the 1937/38 season, the club estimated Calgarians made 4,000 visits to Norquay.[97] Up to 300 skiers might come out from the city for the day. The residents of Banff, keen skiers that they were, couldn't match those kinds of numbers. While not everyone from Calgary belonged to the CSC, the club, through its car-pooling, buses and preferred rates on the train, certainly accounted for many of those on the hill, and established the ritual for Calgarians of travelling to Banff to ski. The sponsorship of racing, which the CSC shared with the Ski Runners, also helped popularize Banff as a ski destination, bringing it to the notice of eastern Canadian skiers.

Aside from patronage, the club also lent material aid to developing the hill. Along with the lodge operators and the Ski Runners, the club's executive peppered the parks superintendent and Dominion Parks Branch for changes to the hill, be it permission to clear more timber to increase the runs or requesting improvements to the road.⁹⁸ Both clubs lobbied the government to spend money on improving the hill, and were somewhat successful—the parks department built a costly new ski jump for the 1937 Dominion Championships. Some club members helped clear runs in the early years, although the distance from Calgary meant that the Banff skiers did far more of this work. During the snowless early season of 1938/39, the CSC and the Ski Runners decided to brush the slopes of Norquay to reduce the amount of snow needed to make them skiable. Realizing volunteer labour would not do the job quickly enough, the two clubs put up money to hire a crew of labourers—the Ski Runners raised the lion's share—and a great deal of work was done in December, 1938. ⁹⁹

That same month, the original Norquay lodge burnt down. Late the next fall, a new and much better lodge was built. The CSC found several Calgary investors and thus played a major role in the new building. Jim Cross had skied with the club on several occasions. A keen supporter of amateur sports, he donated a cup for the annual Calgary-Edmonton club ski meet. Lawyer and future multi-millionaire Eric Harvie was related by marriage to John Southam and was the club's legal advisor. He was known to get out on skis with his sons.¹⁰⁰ The CPR was involved, for obvious reasons. Along with several Banff businessmen, including Jim Morrison, who had been managing the old lodge, the Calgarians formed a new company, Canadian Rockies Winter Sports Inc., took over the lease for the cabin and rebuilt it in style. The club solicited members to buy shares in the new company to help further.¹⁰¹ For a small fee, the two ski clubs were given exclusive rights to part of the building to act as a clubhouse with Ross McPhalen, the 1944 president, negotiating the arrangement for the CSC.¹⁰²

The new company had bigger plans for Norquay than simply building the lodge. The site was to become a "winter sports centre." More than anything else, the CSC and the Ski Runners wanted a rope tow. By the late 1930s, tows were proliferating at ski areas and skiers wanted them. The Calgary club seriously considered building one, which demonstrates just how committed the CSC was to Norquay. The club went so far as to investigate types and make an official application to the Parks Branch in 1939 for permission to install it, conditional on being able to charge a fee for its use.¹⁰³ In the event Canadian Rockies Winter Sports stepped in. Using a McLaughlin Sedan, Jim Morrison built the first much-anticipated rope tow in January 1941.¹⁰⁴ Skiers still had to climb to get to the top of the Bowl or the Lone Pine, but with the tow

Interior of the new lodge, circa 1939.
(Whyte Museum of the Canadian Rockies, V189 PA 157-37 Alan Carscallen.)

Norquay could offer as good a skiing experience as almost any Eastern Canadian resort. The war ended more expansion plans; nonetheless lift-served skiing had arrived in the Rockies.[105]

Along with the Ski Runners, the CSC formed a big part of the ski fraternity at Norquay, with the club eagerly participating in the Banff Winter Carnival. The carnival was a popular occasion, and due to the skiing events, a major date on the CSC calendar. In 1935, Jean Irving, one of the early women members of the club, was elected as the Winter Carnival Queen. Verna Cavanaugh, whose father donated a cup to the club for racing, followed her the next year. They would not be the only CSC women to ascend the carnival throne. Banff and Norquay had become the club's spiritual home.

School's In

Many of the people signing up with the Calgary Ski Club were raw beginners. The club could get people out to Banff, but it wasn't much good if they couldn't ski. Remembering their own attempts to learn the sport, founding members, like Carscallen and Moodie, knew that skiing was not something easily mastered alone. Free instruction in the basics for members thus became one of the club's main offerings and one of its most important contributions to promoting the sport.

To find suitable teachers, the CSC had to look to the Banff ski community. In January 1936, Norm Knight and Rupe Edwards, two talented Banff skiers, were engaged as the official club instructors.[106] Knight had worked at Mount Rainier in the U.S. and would later be an instructor at Lake Placid. Edwards would also travel widely working as a ski instructor. They started the Sunshine Ski School, but also taught at Norquay. CSC members could have free instruction on Sundays at Mount Norquay with the two, paid for by the club. Austrian born Vic Kutschera, who had come to Banff in 1928, was another popular CSC instructor. He was the chief climbing and skiing guide at Skoki. Like other ski clubs of the era, the CSC instituted a badge system for members to gauge their progress but also to encourage them to improve their skiing. To earn the permanent badge of the club meant passing a proficiency test.[107]

Free instruction was both popular and successful and it was hard to keep up with demand. Over thirty people might show up for a lesson. To meet the need, the club decided to turn some of its members into assistant instructors. Some of the better or more experienced skiers, including Harry and Bill Armstrong, Alan Carscallen, Bill Ross and Ozzie LaRue, took lessons from Knight on how to instruct. It was not exactly Canadian Ski Instructors Alliance-standard, but good enough to take some pressure off the pro instructors. The volunteer instructors were especially useful for a program started in the late thirties to teach children how to ski. The club ran classes, weather and snow conditions permitting, at different locations around the city, such as the Municipal, Regal and Bowness golf courses and Christ Church hill in Elbow Park. The inaugural effort for the winter of 1938/39 drew 80 youngsters.

Another motivation for providing instruction was safety, which was quickly becoming a real concern for local skiers. Going straight down, or "schussing," was still a popular way of descending a slope, especially among the unskilled. With more and more people showing up at Norquay, schussing was becoming dangerous. The club mantra was "controlled skiing," meaning keeping speed in check by turning and being able to avoid obstacles—especially other skiers.

Something will have to be done about these 'schussers.' Sunday saw a lot taking it straight, many, mostly those from Banff, succeeding. But there was an even larger number who wound up in undignified postures after plowing great furrows in the snow. Results could easily have been more dangerous than they actually were. The 'schusser' sometimes forgets he is not the only person liable to be hurt. On a crowded slippery slope, others are placed in danger, and even though he may holler 'track!' the speed demon is responsible for many accidents. [108]

Reg Hayden's complaint ignited a minor controversy between the Banff and Calgary skiers over where the reckless skiers were coming. It was clear that safety was an issue. The CSC felt that one way it could be addressed was with teaching and training, and continued to offer instruction in various forms for several decades.

RACING

Skiing at Norquay meant that the Calgarians were soon bitten by the alpine racing bug. The club quickly produced some competent skiers; it wasn't long before they wanted to test their skills. In the early 1930s, skiers around the world were eagerly participating in the new disciplines of slalom and downhill racing, and Banff was no exception. Two Englishwomen on a skiing trip to the Rockies introduced the slalom in 1929.[109] Before long, weekend races were common among the Banff skiers, and the new Ski Runners club enthusiastically embraced competitions. A number of talented local athletes emerged, including Norm Knight, Rupe Edwards, Ted and Cyril Paris. As instructors and role models they would teach the Calgary Ski Club all about the new sport.

The club's embrace of competition was not surprising. Racing was seen as a way to create better skiers. "Competition is a means of developing good skiers. Competition develops good ski technique, which in turns requires a thorough knowledge of controlled skiing. It is one of the objectives of the Calgary Club to teach all its members to ski under control."[110] While not every skier necessarily wanted to race, for many, a sport required some competition. And racing was also a way of promoting skiing.

John Southam had doubtlessly done some racing out east, and, in fact, organized a trip of the better Ski Runners to a competition at Mt. Rainier,

Washington during the 1933/34 season.[111] He keenly advocated the club's involvement in racing. The CSC joined the Western Canada Amateur Ski Association, which oversaw competitions in the west, and supported the decision to merge the WCASA with the Canadian Amateur Ski Association in 1935. Southam joined the western advisory board for CASA and the following year was made the chair of CASA's new Rocky Mountain Zone. Alan Carscallen would serve in the same capacity.

It wasn't long before the club had its own competitions. What began as informal slalom races, usually after a morning of instruction, soon became a yearly club championship. Businesses and individuals sponsored trophies. By 1937, club skiers competed for the Cavanaugh Trophy for men's slalom, the Russell Cup for men's downhill and the coveted Hudson Bay Cup for best combined. The ladies had the *Herald* Cup for the women's slalom race—there was, as yet, no ladies downhill race. The CSC skiers could also match themselves against the Ski Runners in races their club organized. A provincial championship was established before the war. Women got into racing as well as men, and Verna Cavanaugh was one early CSC enthusiast for slalom racing. Bill Ross and the Armstrong brothers, Harry and Bill, were among the better club racers. Harry liked racing so much that he travelled as far as Washington State for more competitions.

One happy ski family: members of CSC and Ski Runners, circa 1930s.
(CSC COLLECTION.)

Even at this early date, the club realized that the racers of the future would come from the ranks of their young members. The CSC had a junior membership, and in 1938 held a slalom race for the younger members. Among the competitors was Bob Freeze, a major figure in the club in the late 1940s and early 1960s. A junior club championship was soon created. The juniors also helped promote the sport. Two junior members, Bill Bennett and Alan Carlyle, approached the Calgary School Board with a proposal for an interscholastic ski committee.[112] It would organize instruction, outings and competition for Calgary schools. A ski club had already been formed at Central High, with Carlyle as the vice-president. Western Canada High also formed a club, and the two schools met in battle for the first time in March 1939 for a slalom race on the Regal Golf Course.[113] Joe Maguire and Henry Samuelson, two adult members of the CSC, ran the event.

Racing swiftly became a big part of the Calgary Ski Club's identity, even if the majority of the members didn't race. The club was barely two years old when, along with the Ski Runners, it was chosen to host the Western Canadian Championships. Aside from the challenges of organizing a ski meet in what was still a relatively isolated location, it demonstrated the young group's interest in organized competition. It also cemented the club's commitment to Norquay as its home hill and the close relationship between the CSC and the Ski Runners, "one happy ski fraternity," as one Calgarian called it.

Sadly, two competitive disciplines club members mostly ignored were cross-country racing and ski jumping. The latter remained the domain of the Scandinavians—it was just too daunting for most people new to the sport. Fred Ausenhaus, the only founding member with Nordic roots, built a jump for the club but it was little used. The langlauf also didn't attract too many practitioners, even when Hayden in his column encouraged people to try it. Many club members were avid ski tourers—but like today's backcountry skiers, they spent most of their time looking for good downhill runs in pristine powder.

Beating the Edmonton Eskimos

Inevitably, the Calgary and Edmonton ski clubs had to have a race. In some ways skiing was more advanced in the capital. Edmonton had a very active ski club, dedicated to jumping, before World War One. When interest in skiing revived in the late 1920s, not just one but eventually five ski clubs were formed—the Edmonton Ski Club, the Voyageurs Ski Club and the

Ripping it up: Ted Paris shows good form, 1939.
(WHYTE MUSEUM OF THE CANADIAN ROCKIES, V108 1070, LLOYD HARMON)

Eskimos Ski Club were but three. The city had a "ski council" promoting cooperation between the different clubs at a time when Calgary skiers were still wandering alone on golf courses. Blessed with better snow conditions and cursed by more distant mountains, the Edmonton clubs were more successful developing their own skiing facilities. Edmonton skiers also helped develop skiing around Jasper, making the long trek in increasing numbers in the late 1930s.

The Calgarians, weaned on the slopes of Norquay, were the better skiers. This was made clear over the first few years of the annual meet. Edmonton enthusiasts experimented with trips to Banff not long after the CSC was established, and their Calgary brethren welcomed them with open arms. The first organized venture to Norquay in 1937 attracted 165 skiers on a specially chartered train. They were accompanied out to the mountains by over a hundred Calgarians, making for one of the busiest days at the hill to that date.[114] The Edmontonians' trip was celebrated with an inter-city slalom race with the CSC, and it became a yearly event that continued in the post-war years. The Calgarians easily romped to victory in the inaugural race. In the tradition of the day, prominent Calgary businessman and sometime skier J.B. Cross donated a cup for the race, raising the stakes considerably.

The standard of Edmonton skiing rose quickly and within a couple of years Calgary's supremacy was being challenged. Finally, in 1941, the northerners captured the cup after a hard-fought race, even though Calgary star Harry Armstrong was on hand to compete. Writing in the *Herald*, one-time CSC president Albert Riley gave two reasons for Edmonton's success. Ex-Banff resident and ski instructor Peter Vadja now lived in the capital; and Edmonton skiers had had snow since November, and could ski every night of the week thanks to floodlights at their club hills.[115] The competition was fierce for the Cross Cup, but the Edmonton skiers' visits to Banff were considered high points in the Calgary ski season. The weekend had a carnival air. Win or lose, the Calgarians enjoyed the visits from the capital's skiers—and they usually won.

THE DOMINION CHAMPIONSHIPS

Running the Western Canada Championships in 1936 was just a warm-up. The choice of Banff for the 1937 Dominion Ski Championships was a sign of how quickly skiing had progressed in the region. The decision also showed how quickly the two sponsoring clubs, the Calgary Ski Club and the Ski

Runners of the Canadian Rockies, had matured. The Canadian Amateur Ski Association, eager to develop skiing in the west, agreed to subsidise the two clubs for the Dominions and bring the best skiers in the nation to Banff.

The Dominion meet was not just a Canadian event; international competitors could enter. Along with every competitive skier of note in Canada, American Olympic stars Dick Durrance and Alf Lindley came as well as legendary jumper Alf Engen. Hjalmar Hvvam, the future inventor of one of the world's first releasable ski bindings, was there and two-time World Champion Walter Prager, formerly of Switzerland and now coaching at Dartmouth. The Swiss Universities Ski Team, on a competitive tour of North America, came straight out from the Dartmouth Winter Carnival. The great Norwegian ski champion of the time, Sverre Kolterud, accompanied by Erling Strom as guide and translator, also made an appearance. He struck fear into the hearts of all those gathered—there were predictions he might win every event.

The results were a little more even than that. Engen won the jumping competition and young Dartmouth cross-country racer Howard Chivers the langlauf. Kolterud took the Nordic combined title. In the alpine events, Pierre Francioli of the Swiss team won the slalom, downhill and the Alpine

Officialdom: Alan Carscallen, head of organising committee, on left, 1940.
(WHYTE MUSEUM OF THE CANADIAN ROCKIES, V108 1414, LLOYD HARMON)

combined titles. Against this formidable competition, the Canadians didn't do too badly. Tom Mobraaten of Vancouver was third in the jumping competition, while youngster Louis Cochand from Quebec was third in both the slalom and downhill. CSC and SRCR skiers did not make much impression in the standings—Norm Knight's very creditable eighth in slalom and 14th place in the downhill were the best results—but earned high marks for putting on a fine tournament.

Despite a chinook several days before the tournament and generally poor snow conditions, all the events went off without a hitch. The Ski Runners had set the courses and the downhill was compared favourably to the course at the 1936 Olympics. Both clubs provided the people power to marshal the courses, organise and do the other grunt work of preparation. The CSC undertook to publish a souvenir booklet for the event. The park administration built a new jump in support and helped clear the courses. The CPR pitched in with a special early train for spectators from Calgary to see the ski-jumping competition and supplied a charter train from eastern Canada. The competitors were responsible for their own transportation and accommodation, though the clubs arranged discounts. The competition scene was still a small one: aside from local skiers, there were probably no more than a hundred participants from out of town. The two clubs did put on a dance every night of the tournament and a banquet was given for all the competitors at the end of the championships.

Joined by two fledgling groups, the Lake Louise Ski Club and the Canmore Ski Club, the CSC and the Ski Runners did it again in 1940. Alan Carscallen, now Western vice-president of CASA, led the organization team. With the addition of junior championships, women's competitions and the Four-Way title for best all-round skier, the event was even bigger. The organizing committee of the Banff Winter Carnival lent a hand. Traffic control was a major issue, as many spectators drove up, attracted by the large car park installed with the new lodge.

Due to the war, the 1940 Dominions was a much more Canadian event, without the same constellation of international stars as the 1937 tournament. The four-way competition roused particular interest. The Canadian Amateur Ski Association had established the title the year before for the best skier overall in all four racing disciplines. It was an attempt, perhaps, to bolster cross-country and jumping. A young Quebec skier won it for 1940. Two Banff skiers, one of the Paris brothers in the senior race and Bud Gourlay in the junior race, pulled off an upset and became the Dominion downhill champions. CSC skiers did not make much of an impression racing, but once again, as traffic wardens, gate-keepers, course marshals, time-keepers and bank-rollers, the club contributed to a successful event. The second Dominion further established Banff as a skiing destination.

HIGH COUNTRY ADVENTURES

Racing was a big part of the club's identity, but for many members skiing at Norquay was merely preparation for touring the high country, enjoying the powder snow and long runs on alpine slopes. As one member wrote in the 1936 Canadian Ski Yearbook, "Instruction classes and Norquay slopes are only a means to an end, for later we offer ... the highly individual happiness of High Touring at Sunshine and Skoki."[116] CSC skiers pursued ski mountaineering and backcountry touring with a pioneering spirit. "The Calgary Ski Club," wrote Gordon Moodie, "has pushed this serious exploration eagerly—exploration headed by the best and shrewdest mountain guides. Experience has been hard won and well assimilated and always passed on—mindful of the Club's chief goal: The Advancement of Skiing."[117] Ski touring was very much a part of the club's early years.

The established high-country "camps," the lodges at Skoki and Sunshine drew most of the Calgary crowd. Club skiers utilized Assiniboine the least because the lodge generally required a trip of at least four or five days, usually a week, to be worthwhile. Despite some formidable logistical obstacles, Skoki and Sunshine could be reached quickly enough to be weekend destinations. The club negotiated reduced rates for members at both locations. Even so, it was quite an adventure, not to mention exhausting, to get into either lodge for a two-day weekend. Carscallen recalled making the trip out to Skoki:

> ... that involved driving to Lake Louise. The road was closed—the road was not officially open—beyond Banff in wintertime. There was no Trans-Canada but there was a summer road of course to Louise so you took your own chance and you drove to Louise probably late Friday evening, having driven from Calgary after work, stopped at the Dominion Café for food and a little bit of fortified coffee and so on. You would usually get to Louise just before midnight and leave your car near the station at Lake Louise and then start out to ski to Skoki.[118]

Arriving at Skoki first thing in the morning, the hardy Calgarians would have a nap before heading out for an afternoon of ski touring. After skiing most of Sunday, they would head back to their car, arriving after dark and making it to Calgary in the small hours. Surprisingly, not everyone who did the trip was a strong skier. Carscallen remembered one time when someone brought a bunch of young ladies who were beginners—one had never skied before. They gamely made the lodge, much to the amazement and disapproval of Vic Kutschera and Rupe Edwards, who were working as guides at Skoki that year.[119]

The snow conditions and seemingly limitless terrain for touring and downhill runs brought Calgary skiers into Skoki in increasing numbers, usually on long weekends or for a ski week. Ozzie LaRue recalls going to Skoki several times a year in the late 1930s. Most trips to the lodge by club members were informal affairs, but the CSC also planned a three-day sponsored club trip for the glorious days of early spring in 1936.[120] Calgarians also went to Skoki to race for the Rankin and the Sir Norman Watson Cups. These events usually overwhelmed the lodge's facilities—some of the racers slept in tents.

Skiers heading into Skoki noted the excellent skiing closer to the road, and it wasn't long before Sir Norman Watson decided to put a lodge closer to the highway. It was intended to be the first in a series of ski chalets in the area. Temple Lodge opened in 1939, only three miles from the highway and much easier to reach than Skoki. The lodge only slept 24 guests, but it was possible to go there for a day trip, especially after the Dominion Parks Branch built a summer road up to it. By 1940, a tractor could tow a sled full of skiers to the lodge. The slopes around Temple became increasingly popular destinations for day-tripping Calgarians, especially after the war.

An early experiment mixing skiing and aircraft took place at Skoki, thanks to Carscallen and Gordon Moodie. They were interested in photography, and in the depths of the Depression, making a little extra money. The idea was to sell photographs showing the fabulous skiing potential of the Rocky Mountains to the CPR publicity department, with an added twist of taking them from the air.[121] They decided to start with Skoki and get some aerial shots of the Rankin Cup race. Things did not go according to plan. Renting a movie camera and chartering two pilots and planes, they set out from Chestermere Lake. Carscallen actually made it to the vicinity of Skoki, but couldn't land due to the weather. Meanwhile, Moodie and his pilot had engine trouble and crash-landed on Ghost Lake.

Undaunted, they tried again a few weeks later, finding a bush pilot who was looking for work. This time they made it to Skoki, but had more trouble—at a higher altitude, the plane didn't have enough power to take off with both passengers. Moodie had to ski out from the lodge while Carscallen and the pilot continued on to Assiniboine for more photos. They never made it. Over the Bow River, the engine conked out and they landed on the river ice. The plane crashed again when the pilot tried to take off without Carscallen, and remained on the edge of the river. Carscallen and Moodie abandoned the photo project, with not much to show for their time and expense except a good story and a few sales to the CPR.

Within a few years, Sunshine began to emerge quickly as a worthwhile weekend destination for Calgarians. Alan Carscallen went to the new camp five years in a row around Christmas, starting with the lodge's first year of operation, 1934.[122] At first, skiers travelled part of the way from Banff on horseback then skied almost the entire length of Healy Creek. It was an exhausting day even for strong skiers. The Brewsters, owners of the lodge, realized that better access was going to be crucial. They ploughed the road out to Healy Creek and transported skiers to that point by truck or bus. The family also lobbied the government to improve and extend the summer road up the Healy Creek drainage.[123] When they acquired a tracked vehicle, "Sunshine Susie," in 1938, the ski was reduced to about three miles, about the same as it is now. CSC skiers, who previously booked the cabin for long weekends, now made the trip in for the weekend or even just a day. Reg Hayden, Hank Samuelson and Doug Smith accomplished this feat for the first time in December of 1938.[124] Although they were limited to one run off Brewster Mountain, the trip set an important precedent. Within a few years, an extension of the road meant that "Susie" could often make it right up to the lodge.

Skoki and Sunshine offered fabulous skiing and a comfortable cabin to rendezvous at every night. The club also looked for other good ski touring areas close to a road and suitable for day trips. One popular spot was the vicinity of Lake Louise. Meeting up with the Lake Louise Ski Club, the CSC sponsored an outing to the area in 1937, skiing at Castle Crags across the lake from the Chateau. About 30 Calgary skiers boarded the bus chartered for the event. Castle Crags quickly became a popular club trip and was repeated several times in the next couple of years. Club skiers poked around the Victoria Glacier further up the valley and also skied up around Mt. Fairview. In 1941, the club organized a trip to Castle Mountain, touring up Altrude Creek.[125]

It's all ours: guests at Sunshine, circa 1940. (CSC COLLECTION.)

A few members of the club were more adventurous and tried ski mountaineering. Jack Farish and Alan Carscallen were also hikers and climbers and members of the local chapter of the Alpine Club, along with Ken Betts and others. Gordon Moodie and "Dud" Batchelor were also keen on mountain adventures. In 1934, Carscallen, Moodie and Batchelor, along with Vic Kutschera and Gordon Campbell, enjoyed fine spring skiing in the Yoho Valley. The most hazardous part of the expedition was the drive on a gravel mountain road in an old roadster, festooned with skiing and camping gear. In 1935, Moodie and Batchelor decided to tackle the first ski ascent of Mt. Balfour, high up on the Wapta Icefield. They teamed up with Kutschera and Lloyd Harmon of Banff. Although it was June, the party skied most of the way to timberline via Sherbrooke Lake. Over a couple of otherwise uneventful days, they easily made it to the top of Balfour and enjoyed superlative spring skiing on the way down.

High-country skiing was a self-propelled affair. Skiers climbed with herringbones, wax or climbing skins to do runs off Brewster Rock and Twin Cairns at Sunshine or Fossil Mountain and Merlin Ridge near Skoki. It was hard work, but for any serious skier it was touted as the ultimate experience. As an anonymous member of the Calgary Ski Club wrote for the 1937 Canadian Ski Year Book:

> … there is only one real reason for joining a ski club, for spending so many happy hours and so many tedious hours on practice slopes; only one excuse for the red tape and elaborate official falderal of ski organization. That reason is high Alpine Skiing … And until you have skied above tree line you haven't skied. You haven't lived!

For most people in the Calgary Ski Club, the reality was somewhat different. Before World War II, most club skiers didn't venture far beyond the nursery slopes of Norquay. Many were newcomers to the sport, and unravelling the mysteries of snowplows, stem Christies and the Arlberg was more than enough to keep them occupied. The club would long retain a romantic regard for days in the high country, yet its future would be part of the explosive growth of lift-served skiing.

Self propelled: ski touring at Sunshine, circa 1936. (GLENBOW ARCHIVES, PA 2716-22.)

The Social Calendar

The club put a lot of effort into the promotion of skiing, but it was not all serious work. Nor was the club all skiing. There were also the dances and parties. The Calgary Ski Club and skiing in general attracted young, adventurous adults to its ranks. John Southam was only 24 in 1933, and that was probably close to the average. A bunch of athletic 20-year-olds are inevitably going to have parties. Clubs and societies were also important parts of socializing in that era. Most organizations had dances or parties, formal and informal. These were an important part of the social life of young adults in the age before nightclubs and other diversions were common. For one thing, clubs and societies could get liquor licenses. Social functions, aside from the natural desire to extend the fun and comradeship on the hill to the city, were also a good time to recruit new members to the club.

The executive decided that the club needed a permanent headquarters, in the form of clubrooms. Most clubs had some kind of meeting place. The ski club wanted a permanent location to set up a library and hold lectures and get-togethers of a less academic character. The perfect spot soon materialised. Carscallen's landlord, Sam Diamond, heard that he was looking for rooms and told him about Braemar Lodge, one of his properties. It was a

Good digs: clubroom in Braemar Lodge, 1936. (CSC Collection.)

hotel and rooming house of good character, run by two elderly Englishwomen. There was a large space perfect for a lounge plus two additional rooms for an office and meeting. Braemar was ideal, with plenty of atmosphere: "…there was one very nice room, beautiful big fireplace in it and dark beamed ceiling, somewhat on the English pub motif."[126]

Even better, Diamond offered Carscallen the rooms free of charge, and the club had a dance there almost immediately. The deal was almost too perfect, and the catch soon emerged. Diamond had also suggested that the club apply for a liquor license. Since the rooms were intended for social functions, Carscallen thought this was a good idea. Eric Harvie, the club's legal counsel, advised them not to rush into anything. It soon became apparent why Diamond had been so generous with the club: obtaining a liquor license in 1936 Calgary was no easy task, and clearly Diamond thought that the club might have a better chance of getting one for the premises than he did. According to Carscallen, when the club decided the following year not to get the license, Diamond was not amused and evicted them.

Eviction was very inconvenient because the social side of the club was growing as fast as the skiing side. One popular excuse for a get-together was to watch ski movies. People had started making ski films as early as the 1920s. The club's venerable tradition of showing ski films started soon after it got the Braemar Lodge room, with movies of the 1936 Western Canadian Championships at Banff. Hannes Schneider's films of European skiing were very popular. Movies from race meets, promotional films of different ski resorts and instructional movies filled many evenings. Showing a film or two or three became a regular feature of both official meetings and social get-togethers.

The club started having regular "ski-meetings" during the season, combining a little business, like planning trips, with a lot of socializing including music and a bit of dancing. After losing the Braemar location, the club rented Penley's Academy on 8th Avenue downtown for evenings:

> Fun! Wasn't it? Why our first ski meeting at Penley's, of course. Didn't you get a kick out of old Pete Pryke christying around the corners, and Gordy Hart tempo turning on his seat trying to follow Hannes Schneider on the screen. It was great![127]

For a good time off the slopes, nothing beat the dances. The season usually began and ended with a proper formal dance; 150 couples came to the ball that concluded the 1934/35 season. Less formal dances were held through the winter, often with a theme. One of the first dances at the Braemar was a "Hillbilly Hoedown." The Hard Times Ball, held with youthful defiance of the prevailing economic climate, became an annual event. Partygoers dressed in their "best rags" for the evening. The dances were not staid affairs, not even the formal ball that ended the season, which was almost always held at the Bowness Country Club. As one unnamed clubber remembered:

> Everyone brought their own liquor since the Golf Club was not licensed—however, you could buy mix from them. We had some really lively bands and the party used to go on into the wee hours of the morning. I remember driving some people home from the party about 3 o'clock one time and then going back to the party![128]

By 1938, the club had to restrict the end of season ball to club members because word had got out it was a good time and too many people were crashing it.[129]

The socializing, which included train trips to the mountains, helped build club spirit. Members could also proudly wear a CSC pin to show their allegiance to their sport and their club. Fred Taylor, architect, artist, avid skier and brother of brewery magnate E.P. Taylor, designed the first pins, which became available in 1936. The design consisted of a large letter C, with a skier in the letter performing that signature move of the 1930s, the gelandesprung.[130] The pin, the first in a series produced over the years, was greatly prized and a sure conversation starter. Bruce Compton remembered this about the pin designed under his auspices in the late 1940s. "They attracted a lot of attention and members were very proud of them. Everywhere you went people would stop you to ask what the pin meant—skiing was a very elite sport in those days."[131]

A Good Beginning

At the start of the war, the Calgary Ski Club could look back at its first few years with pride. Now almost 400 strong, it had come a long way from eight founding members, some of whom could barely ski. The Calgary Ski Club had done a great deal to bring skiing to Calgarians. In fact it had done almost too good a job. Interest in skiing was burgeoning, but not every new skier was automatically joining the club. "There was a big gang of Calgary skiers on the hill, but we still note with chagrin that there are a lot of them who are not members of the club," noted Connie Mackie, the club's secretary-treasurer, in the weekly newsletter early in 1941.[132] No one was suggesting that every Calgary skier had to be a club member, and really, it was a sign that the sport was now well established.

The Calgary Ski Club could take a lot of credit for this. In addition to providing instruction to make skiing safer and more fun for members, the club was also bringing the sport to school children, building skiers for the future. In partnership with the Ski Runners, the club had run two Dominion championships, hosting some of the best skiers in the world. The CSC itself had taken to racing and ran several of its own popular contests. It had organized cheap transportation to allow Calgary skiers to enjoy the pleasures of skiing in Banff, especially at Mt. Norquay. Through their patronage, the club had contributed to establishing Norquay, Sunshine and Skoki as viable concerns, setting the stage for future growth of the sport. There were a lot of good reasons to join the Calgary Ski Club. And CSC people were spreading the gospel outside of the city: ex-members would help found clubs in Canmore and Red Deer.[133]

Calgary was going skiing.

CHAPTER FOUR

The Glory Years

POST-WAR DEVELOPMENTS—THE WAR YEARS—
BOOM TIMES—A HOME HILL—RACING—
SKI PATROL—GUIDES—TRAINS & BUSES &
FUN—THE SKI ANNUAL

If only there was something like the ski trains today. It was the late 1940s. Early on a frosty Sunday morning, while the rest of Calgary slept, the city's train station teemed with life. From across the city they came, skis over shoulders, garbed in colourful sweaters and an odd mix of jackets and parkas. Just about every skier in the city was there, all eager to start the trip to Banff. As the train rolled out of Calgary, some snoozed or read a book, but most chattered about plans for the day. Guitars might appear and someone would strike up a tune. By the time the train swayed over Morley Flats and the mountains drew near, the whole train echoed with song. A few wineskins even came out. In Banff everybody rushed onto the buses to Norquay or Sunshine. On the way home that evening, the train was much quieter.

The ski trains were not the only party on wheels the Calgary Ski Club hosted. Imagine loading up on a bus on a Friday night in 1953. An intrepid band of skiers planned to make the drive all the way to Whitefish, Montana that night and arrive in the wee hours. Then it would be a full day of skiing, dinner, dancing, another day of skiing and the long drive back to Calgary. The bus bumped at times over snowy, icy, gravel roads—the highway was not paved all the way to the border. The skiers might or might not make it to the hill at Whitefish, but they might dance on restaurant tables in Shelby, Montana, as a blizzard shook the windows. It's no wonder that every CSC old-timer will tell you a lot of romances—and marriages—came out of the ski club.

The 1940s and 1950s were the Calgary Ski Club's golden era. The club's success mirrored that of the sport of skiing in general, and was also a reflection of the explosive growth of Calgary. The CSC's membership mushroomed after the war and the club was involved in every facet of the sport. It promoted skiing through initiatives like the *Herald* Ski School for kids, the SkiWees, a new race league for children, the Calgary Ski Patrol and a club ski hill in the Bowness district of the city. There were challenges as well. Lean snow years in the mid-fifties made skiers surly and caused membership to plummet. But this was a bump in the road. The CSC remained the only ski club in the city and was still the voice of Calgary planksters. And in the glossy Ski Annual, produced for five years near the end of the fifties, the Calgary Ski Club expressed its pride.

It was a wonderful time to be a skier. Calgary's enthusiasts were still a small community where everyone knew each other. The growth of the sport had not yet removed the feeling of adventure that was the hallmark of the days before the war. But there was also the exciting feeling that skiing was on the cusp of big things, and that the club was a part of it.

The Post-War Boom

Skiing had been a trendy, glamorous new sport in the 1930s, but its popularity exploded after the Second World War. More importantly, downhill skiing at resorts dominated the sport's development and created a major industry. Another look at the evolution of skiing sets the stage for the continuing story of the CSC.

Skiing came of age as a sport and recreational industry after the war. Over the next thirty years, a number of factors—the post-war economic boom, an increase in leisure time, the baby boom, technical advances in equipment, better roads and highways—all fuelled steady growth, especially in North America. In the United States, the industry got a major boost from returning veterans. The famous 10th Mountain Division trained thousands of men for mountain warfare, including skiing. When they returned to civilian life, many became ski entrepreneurs, especially in the west. New ski hills proliferated through the 1950s and 1960s, from small local operations with one rope tow or T-bar to massive Vail-scale resorts and established areas.

Ski hills also got better. Powerful modern bulldozers cleared larger and more challenging runs, much faster than by hand. The T-bar and the poma-lift replaced the ubiquitous rope tow and chairlifts appeared in greater numbers and improved versions. Norquay got its first chair, a single, in 1948. More and more skiers turned slopes into fields of moguls, difficult for beginners and intermediates. Slope grooming was invented, beginning with primitive devices towed behind a ski patroller, but within a few years, tractor-style groomers were in operation.[134] Grooming also helped with another great technological leap—manmade snow. The first successful use of artificial snow—where water is mixed with air and blown out over a hill in sub-freezing temperatures—was in the 1950s.[135] Artificial snow had a tendency to be very icy, however, grooming helped keep it skiable.

The local ski hill became big business, and the spiral of demand and growth made the ski industry increasingly capital intensive. To build a new ski area meant significant investment in lifts and their maintenance, as well as much better lodge facilities. To expand and improve meant the same. By the late 1960s, the profit potential attracted large corporations, which bought interests in ski areas or put up the money for new ones. Texan oil millionaires Harry and Dick Bass took control of Vail in Colorado and created Snowbird in Utah. Closer to Calgary, the Power Corporation bought a sizable interest in Sunshine and oil money started flowing into the Temple-Whitehorn area at Lake Louise. Downhill skiing became a more expensive pastime as areas charged larger sums to use their new lifts and day lodges.

New and bigger ski areas required skiers, but they were not in short supply. Through the 1950s real wages rose, unemployment was negligible and leisure time reached new highs—by the 1960s almost everyone worked a five-day week or the equivalent. Spending on vacations and recreation quickly increased. Skiing had been a trendy sport before the war, especially among the middle class, and now more and more people took it up. From a demographic perspective, the prospects were good. The generation that reached adulthood during or just after the war were enthusiastic participants in the new "leisure society" and their children would make up the "baby boom." They would keep the ski industry on a path of growth for several decades.

The growing market for equipment fuelled innovation, and better equipment in turn encouraged people to take up the sport. Until the late fifties, most people still skied on gear much like that before the war—wooden skis, lace-up leather boots and a cable binding. Change was coming. Howard Head produced the first all-metal skis in 1948, and by 1955 metal skis were the hot item. Fibreglass and composite skies followed, so by the early 1960s the wooden ski was quickly disappearing. The first release bindings appeared in the late 1940s and the familiar two-piece, spring-loaded release binding had arrived around 1960. Release bindings made the sport much safer. Norm Russell, son of Andy Russell and owner of Norm's Ski Hut, recalls that many avid skiers broke a leg or an ankle at some point before the new bindings appeared. "That made it feasible for so many people to ski who were scared to death of it before," he says.[136]

On boots, laces were augmented and then replaced by buckles. In 1957, Bob Lange created the first plastic boot.[137] Early versions butchered feet, but also provided much better support and control, and soon improved. Skiing technique evolved with the gear. The elegant, counter-rotating Arlberg, still common after the war, soon vanished, replaced with rhythmic parallel turns. The racers took the lead, developing new techniques that filtered down to the pleasure skier. Many different schools and techniques came and went—weight forward, weight back, horse kicks, wedeln, jet turns—and skiers got better and better.[138] The Graduated Length Method of instruction, another American innovation, drastically shortened the time necessary to become reasonably competent. Ski instructor Clif Taylor realized that people learned the basics faster on short skis, and invented a system that lengthened the ski used as the skier got better. This, it must be pointed out, was also a boon to skiing manufacturers and rental shops.

The spectacular growth of lift-served, downhill skiing rapidly eclipsed ski touring, ski mountaineering and cross-country skiing. Through the 1950s, skiers still went touring, often because lift-served terrain remained limited. By the end of the decade, lift skiers vastly outnumbered ski tourers. Some backcountry enthusiasts remained, many who were also mountaineers. They kept this aspect of the sport alive but on the fringes. Self-propelled skiing in the high country would stage a minor comeback starting at the end of the 1960s.

The revival of interest in high-country touring, however, was a minor phenomenon compared to the resurgence of traditional Nordic skiing. The so-called Nordic disciplines, ski jumping and cross-country racing, hung on in North America through the 1950s. The revival began in the following decade. In the early 1970s, cross-country skiing exploded into a massive fad, thanks to an increased consciousness about health and fitness (remember those "Participaction" ads comparing the 50-year-old Swede with the

20-year-old Canadian?) and a backlash against the increasing expense of downhill skiing. Using the narrow double cambered skis and light boots cross-country racers favoured, people returned to golf courses and mountain trails in droves. Nordic skiing, however, did not catch on as much as its proponents hoped. After the initial boom, the sport waned somewhat and settled into a sizable niche in North America.

THE ROCKIES

In Western Canada, the growth of the ski industry more or less mirrored what happened in the United States, but at a slower pace due to the lack of a market. Calgary and Edmonton were still relatively small cities, but provided most of the skiers in the Rockies and the British Columbia interior until well into the 1970s. Another major factor was the location of the most developed ski facilities in the national parks. Regulations hampered the ability of Lake Louise, Sunshine and Norquay to expand and attract ski tourists, especially with popular amenities, such as accommodation at the ski hill. The park administration, fairly and unfairly, came under great criticism for its policy towards skiing. It was a major issue in the 1960s, linked to efforts to bring the Winter Olympics to Banff.

Even with these impediments, the ski areas near Calgary expanded. Norquay was first. The park administration spent around $5,000 in 1946 clearing brush and widening runs, including the new downhill race course, the North American. George Encil, a Czechoslovakian émigré and entrepreneur, bought out Canadian Rockies Winter Sports Limited in 1947 and the following year installed a single chair and additional rope tows. Encil also played a role in the development of Sunshine, buying the lodge in 1952.[139] The Brewsters had by 1948 convinced the government to build a road up to the lodge, which allowed them to bus visitors right to the door. A permanent rope tow was installed on the Strawberry hill in 1945. The resort experimented with various snow machines in the 1940s and 1950s, shuttling skiers high up Lookout Mountain or onto Standish Ridge. In 1960, Cliff White Jr. bought Sunshine from Encil and soon put a T-bar on Wawa Ridge.[140] After the Power Corporation bought a controlling interest in 1965, White was able to install chairlifts and build a new day lodge and a 100-bed hotel. Sunshine had the only large scale accommodation at a ski hill in the parks.

Skoki Lodge continued to operate quite successfully as a backcountry retreat, but Temple and Whitehorn Mountain were the focus of ski development at Lake Louise. Temple had a fire road usable in winter by the early 1950s (making it easier to bring skiers to the lodge) and installed a portable rope tow in 1952 and a Poma lift two years later. A sightseeing gondola was built to above timber line on Whitehorn Mountain in 1959, which also served as a ski lift. Although slow and poorly designed, the gondola opened up a whole new area. A Poma-lift was built in 1960 to access the upper slopes of Whitehorn and made it possible to ski down to Temple via lifts. More were built in the early 1960s to link Temple back to the front side and service new runs created for the Olympic Games. A day lodge was built at the base of Whitehorn in 1966. Lake Louise, as the area became known, had a most contentious relationship with the Parks Department, mostly over the issue of accommodation for skiers.

Skiing was not just restricted to Banff. New ski areas proliferated. Many were the work of local ski clubs—hills popped up in the 1950s in Turner Valley, Nanton, Maycroft, Red Deer, Lacombe and others. Marmot in Jasper became a destination for Calgary skiers. At the end of the 1950s and early 1960s, new commercial resorts opened in British Columbia, including Kimberley, Silver Star at Vernon, Big White by Kelowna, Fernie and Panorama. They quickly became popular. Nearer to Calgary, the short-lived Pigeon Mountain was opened in 1962, and Snowridge, later known as Fortress Mountain, in 1967. Thanks to better roads and the explosion of air travel, Calgarians also began looking south across the border—Whitefish, Montana became a destination in the early 1950s. By the seventies, Calgarians might spend a week skiing in Colorado or Wyoming, or even go to Europe.

While most Calgarians wanted to downhill ski, the re-emergence of self-propelled skiing was as evident in the Rockies as elsewhere. Ski touring and mountaineering never entirely vanished, and as early as 1963 a new club appeared in Calgary to promote cross-country racing as well as Nordic-style touring in the mountains. Cross-country remained a minor part of the ski scene until the 1970s. One unexpected development from ski touring in Western Canada was the birth of helicopter skiing. Hans Gmoser built up a thriving business guiding conventional ski tours. Then he discovered that many of his American clients would happily pay handsomely to have the same quality powder skiing with the convenience of mechanical transportation.

The growth of the ski industry had a profound effect on the Calgary Ski Club. The CSC's role changed greatly through the three decades after the war. From the natural home of the Calgary skier, the CSC became one ski club among several. The club would transform from an organization with a mission to promote skiing to one that concentrated primarily on serving its members. The sport developed a life of its own, on a scale undreamed of before the Second World War. But this was a process that took several decades to complete, and it is time to return to the story of the Calgary Ski Club.

THE CLUB AT WAR

Even a world war could not keep people from the slopes, but the pace of development slowed down. Southam, Carscallen, the Armstrongs, Reg Hayden and many others went into the military. Membership dropped precipitously to a rearguard of mostly juniors and women. The ski trains were cancelled because of wartime economy as well as lack of clientele. Gas rationing made travel by private car difficult. Norquay, Sunshine, Temple and Skoki remained open for business. There were thousands of servicemen training at Currie Barracks, Sarcee Camp or the airbases of Commonwealth Air Training Scheme near the city. Some were already skiers, who must have thought they were blessed, stationed near the mountains. Others, visiting Banff on leave, took up the sport for the first time.

The ski club encouraged the soldiers and airmen to get out skiing. The CSC was very proud that, "Three of Canada's leading skiers will wear Calgary Ski Club colours this winter." The club later organized an "Air Force, Navy and Calgary Ski Club field day," featuring the inevitable slalom races.[141] Navy won, thanks to their secret weapon, ace skiers Bud Gourlay and Dick Pike, formerly of Banff.

The antics of visiting Australian airmen quickly won the hearts of local skiers. Ozzie LaRue remembered his first encounter. "I was standing at the bottom of the hill one time when one of these fellows came down, ran right over the tips of my skis and he immediately fell in a great heap and said to me, 'How do you get these blooming things to go straight?'"[142] The Australians were easily spotted on the slopes—they usually skied in their flying suits. The suits were brown and fuzzy on the outside, picked up a lot of snow and left a big brown mark on the slope when the Australians fell. And they fell a great deal. "The way the Aussies schuss, somersault and then go right back for more is a source of wonderment and amusement for the spectators at the lodge," the *Calgary Herald* reported. "The boys from down under sure can take it and still like it."[143]

It was not all fun and games: there was a war on. Like other clubs, the

CSC was keenly interested in the military applications of skiing. The success of the ski troops of the Finnish Army against the Russians in 1940 had amazed the world and energized skiers. CASA approached the federal government to advocate forming a unit of ski troops, and the CSC was one of the clubs that offered its services to military authorities.[144] The authorities did not, however, take up this patriotic overture. Some mountain troops, such as the Lovat Scouts of Scotland, trained in the Canadian Rockies but under the auspices of the Alpine Club. Major Rex Gibson of Edmonton recruited ski instructors for the Alpine Club effort in 1943. Calgary and Banff were represented through the participation of Lieutenant Bob Freeze and Sergeant Stan Peyto. Canada never formed a unit specializing in winter and mountain warfare like the Americans did with the 10th Mountain Division.

ROSIE THE RIVETER GOES SKIING

The war brought a first for the CSC: its first female president, Shirley Hill. Like the Alpine Club of Canada and other outdoor clubs, the CSC was a mix of egalitarianism and conventional chauvinism.[145] Women were welcome and encouraged, and the club tended to be balanced between male and female members. Club members of both sexes willingly took instruction from Eleanor Boyle of Lake Louise, the 1940 Dominion junior downhill champion and recognized as one of the best skiers, male or female, in the west. The club organized races for ladies and girls and they had their own cups in the club championships, and there were almost always women on the council. But at the same time, the club bylaws allowed only two members of the council to be female, and the women on the executive tended to look after social activities or act as club secretary.

The manpower shortage during the war saw a great many women move into occupations formerly the preserve of men. The ski club was no different. The vivacious and attractive Hill, a very competent skier who was also a CSC candidate for Queen of the Banff Winter Carnival, was elected president of the club for the 1942/43 season. The club also rescinded the restrictions on women council members. Betty McAlpine, Marg O'Brien and Kay Neilson joined Hill, as well as Bob Parkes (who would marry Hill), Fens Sterne, Ken Sparks and Hap Trevelyan.

After the war, gender roles were reasserted. The female members of the club formed the Skiettes, which emulated the women's auxiliaries attached to churches and most volunteer organizations. The Skiettes put on baked bean dinners, bake sales, and organized blanket drives, gathering old wool clothing to be made into blankets for the club's new ski patrol. Their activities were all quite domestic in a cliché fifties' sort of way. But women members remained well represented on the executive. Nigel Dunn, the 1948 club president and the *Herald*'s new ski reporter, would frequently take women to task in his column for not racing enough. It wasn't until 1992, however, that the club elected another woman as president.

Under Hill's energetic leadership, the club made a stab at creating its own hill in Calgary. It was a necessity, as rationing and travel restrictions made it difficult to get out to Banff.[146] The club virtually abandoned Norquay for a couple of years, and even stopped paying its club dues for the lodge.[147] The Bowness Golf Club approached the CSC about using their clubhouse over the winter, likely to get a little additional revenue out of the building.[148] The CSC had held many dances at the clubhouse, so there was much to recommend the idea. There were some reasonable sized hills available nearby and streetcar service from the city. Fens Sterne had thoroughly explored the area and ferreted out slopes that held snow. Touted as a "winter sports centre," the new CSC headquarters included a pro shop, lockers for members, a skating rink, badminton and other games indoors, and a lunch counter. The club planned regular Sunday afternoon sing-a-longs and movies in the evening, along with regular dances.

The Bowness centre, however, did not last more than a season. The perfect snow conditions of the official opening turned into sheets of ice after a couple of days of chinook winds, but poor conditions were nothing new for skiing in the city.[149] The CSC took up quarters at the less-suitable Regal Golf Course the next season. The Regal clubhouse became a ski cabin for the winter, and the nearby slopes overlooking Nose Creek were used whenever enough snow came. The club was now conscious of the idea of having its own hill in the city. Ironically, Bowness would be the site of the CSC's most sustained effort to establish a viable ski hill in Calgary.

Many of the founding members of the CSC dropped out after the war. Some found that they had drifted away from the sport after years in the service; others married and started raising families. Alan Carscallen, so keen and so involved, spent six years in the military and afterwards left his skis in the closet, resuming teaching but not schussing. Others did not return from the conflict. One indirect casualty of the war was John Southam. He served in anti-aircraft and anti-tank units with distinction, achieving the rank of

Lt. Colonel. Southam returned to Calgary and took over as publisher of the *Herald* in 1946. At least one club friend thought Southam's wartime experiences contributed to his suicide in 1954; he was only 45 years old.

THE CLUB FOR EVERYONE

As if to celebrate the end of the war, the snow came early in the autumn of 1945 and continued copiously for the rest of the winter. Everyone agreed that it was one of the best seasons in many years. Aside from the sad absence of some familiar faces, it was as if the war hadn't happened, as skiers swarmed back to Norquay, Sunshine and increasingly to Temple. The hills around Calgary were busy too, especially at the Regal Golf Course above the clubhouse. Travel difficulties took a while to sort out, and it wasn't until the following year that the club could reliably charter buses and get the ski trains going again, but it didn't stop eager skiers from cobbling together car pools and returning to the mountains.

The CSC offered the same services for members it had developed before the war: instruction, transportation, reduced rates at the ski lodges and the Norquay tow, club sponsored races, organized trips for ski touring and ski mountaineering, and lots of social activities. In the post-war period all these benefits were improved and new services created—like bus tours to exotic new hills. In many ways, the next 15 years were the golden era for the CSC. It was the club for everyone who wanted to ski.

One sure sign that skiing had bounced back was the club's rapidly increasing membership. For the 1944/45 season, membership had dropped off to around 130, hardly a third of the pre-war peak.[150] Within two years after the war, it was at over 800. By 1948 it was approaching 1,000 and the club claimed this milestone in the spring of 1950.[151] The CSC was happy for more and carried out membership drives to keep the numbers up. There is no way of knowing for certain what proportion of the city's skiing enthusiasts belonged to the club, but it was probably a majority. The skiing community was still small. Jean MacNaughton joined around 1957, and she remembers, "You knew just about every other skier in town." The club saw itself as the natural home of the Calgary skier.

The club's growth reflected Calgary's. A city of 100,000 in 1946 became one of 250,000 in 1961, fuelled primarily by the oil and gas sector. Most of the new residents were recent arrivals from the rest of Canada, the United States and some from Europe. For those who already knew how to ski, joining the CSC was a natural thing to do, especially as many came from club backgrounds elsewhere. The club was a place to meet like-minded people and get to know a large part of the skiing community. Bill Milne, an architect[152] and a mainstay of the CSC council in the 1950s, came from Winnipeg where he taught skiing and patrolled with the Kilcoran Club. Others came west and discovered the sport. Cam Mitchell, a contemporary of Milne, arrived in Calgary in 1949. During his first winter some friends took him to the top of Brewster at Sunshine. He had never been on skis before. Mitchell joined the CSC to learn how to ski. Three years later he was president, a certified ski instructor, a qualified ski guide, a ski patroller and a ski racer—all thanks to the club. Jean Robb was a young, athletic nurse bitten by the ski bug soon after becoming a Calgarian. These three were representative of the newcomers attracted to the club—young, usually single, and often middle class professionals.

Another group that stood out was the Europeans. There was a great deal of immigration to Canada from Europe right after the war. Often very proficient skiers, they had a strong influence on racing in the club. "It brought our level of racing up tremendously," says Norm Russell, a CSC diehard.[153] The Europeans often went on to establish ski businesses. Austrian Willi Leitner was the club slalom, downhill and combined champion in 1954. He later became a ski pro. Mike Wiegele, of heli-skiing fame, was the club champion in 1960. The Europeans weren't just racers, however. Hans Gmoser and Leo Grillmair, mountaineers and founders of Canadian Mountain Holidays, were members in 1952, not long after arriving from their native Austria. Even if people didn't necessarily stay with the CSC once they found their ski legs, the club was their contact with the local scene. Many remained members. Norm Russell recalls that most new arrivals gravitated to the club: "I would say, if you were going to be a skier you had to join the club to be a part of it. It just seemed to be that way."

The CSC remained the backbone of Calgary planksters, but as the skiing population burgeoned there were attempts to start new clubs. Fens Sterne had been a mainstay of the CSC during the war. A Scandinavian, he and some fellow countrymen had built two small ski jumps in Elbow Park on the Christ Church hill.[154] Deciding that not enough was being done for city youngsters, he and several others formed the Sitzmark Ski Club in 1946.[155] The new club focused on teaching children and beginners how to ski and to reintroducing Nordic skiing to the city. The Sitzmarkers held their

Nothing else to win: Mike Wiegele, club champion, 1960.
(CSC Collection, Peter Cooper.)

outings around the Bowness Golf Course and also on the Municipal Golf Course.[156] After a good start—up to 40 kids were coming out for club outings—the Sitzmark Club faded away within a season.

The Chinook Ski Club was slightly more long-lived. The club was founded sometime in the early 1950s, taking up quarters down by the Glenbow Reservoir. The Chinooks got permission from the city to use the steep hill above Sandy Beach on the Elbow River, at the end of 50th Avenue SW, and built a small shack as a clubhouse at the top. They planned floodlights for night skiing and intended to offer free lessons for their membership. The Chinooks ran bus trips out to the mountains and down to Blairmore and even Whitefish, Montana. Vandals, with a stolen bulldozer, pushed their clubhouse down the hill during the summer of 1953, but the club quickly rebuilt it. Like the Sitzmarkers before, however, the Chinook Club seemed to quickly lose steam. After 1955, there is no mention again of the club and its fate is a mystery. The poor snow years of the middle fifties may have been responsible. The drought also affected the CSC. Clearly, the ski scene in the city had not grown enough to support more than one club.

The club's central role in the ski community was also clear from its strong links to nearly all the ski retailers of Calgary. Andy Russell was not an avid skier, but Russell's Sporting Goods was a good friend to the club. Russell sold memberships, helped organize charter buses—which often met outside his store—and Russell's was a general meeting place for skiers. His son Norm was heavily involved in the club, starting as a junior racer and would be a mainstay of the racing program, serving as technical director for many years. After working in the family business, he opened Norm's Ski Hut. The other ski shop owners were also part of the club. The Compton brothers, Al, Ethan and Bruce, started the Sportsman on 17th Avenue and Premier Cycle and Sports. Premier was also the city's only purveyor of climbing equipment. All the brothers were on the executive at one time or another. Bruce Compton was the CSC president in 1957/58, and along with his brother Ethan, was a club instructor, especially involved in the *Herald* Ski School.

The ski club essentially had a column for its doings in both major Calgary dailies. Reg Hayden returned to the sports pages with "Ski Chatter" after

Club spirit: the CSC Stampede Parade Float, 1950. (CSC COLLECTION, CAM MITCHELL.)

getting out of the military. Nigel Dunn, who would serve as CSC president, replaced Hayden in 1947. Dunn's successor in 1955, Joy Van Wagner, also belonged to the club. Over at the *Albertan*, Peter Cooper took over the ski column in 1954. Cooper was heavily involved in CSC, and, in fact, edited the magnificent CSC Annual for several years at the end of the 1950s. The press coverage was great and the club also worked on raising its profile. The Calgary Ski Club's float in the 1950 Stampede Parade was an expression of pride as well as another good promotion.

A Noble Effort

Some of the club's post-war energy went into an attempt to establish a permanent ski hill in the city. Calgary's climate had convinced the club's founders to concentrate on the mountains, but not everyone could easily afford travelling to Banff, especially children without skiing parents. A hill in Calgary would provide an alternative and also allow for skiing during the week in the evening.[157] Many ski clubs had their own hill—Edmonton was a prominent example—which became increasingly sophisticated, with rope tows and floodlights. The CSC decided that it too should have a hill. It was easier said than done. The success of Paskapoo and Happy Valley, both opened shortly after the club abandoned its Bowness hill, showed the CSC was on the right track. As the *Herald* would say, "The CSC put a great deal of effort into establishing a decent ski hill within the precincts of Calgary. The club was not in the end successful in its endeavour, but it was a noble effort none the same."

When wartime travel restrictions ended, the club eagerly returned to Norquay and planned to make it a permanent home. The 1946 president, Bob Kolb, told Don Young of the Canmore Ski Club, "We have decided to direct all our activities to the mountains in the future and as a result will have monies to spend or invest there instead of in the Calgary vicinity as in the past."[158] The club announced that it was going to buy shares in Canadian Rockies Winter Sports, the owners of Norquay, and build its own clubhouse. The January 1947 edition of the club's post war newsletter, *Ski Tips*, showed the club with a good surplus and a bank balance of nearly $3,000, stated:

> Looks like we're doing O.K.! A big chunk of that bank balance will go into shares of the Canadian Rockies Winter Sports Limited to give us a say in the future development of Norquay—and we're going to

need plenty of reserve when we get around to building a club house at Norquay—that is not just wishful thinking either.

Ski filmmaker and entrepreneur George Encil's purchase of Norquay in 1948 ended the CSC's investment plans. New ownership meant wonderful innovations like a chairlift, but it meant the CSC lost most of its privileges, most importantly the exclusive quarters in the lodge. To protect the business of the holder of the ski school concession, the club was also asked to stop holding free lessons there unless it paid for an instructor of the hill's school. In the later fifties, another owner would welcome the club back, but it was the end of the CSC's special relationship with Norquay.[159] The pendulum swung the other way and the club considered a hill in Calgary.

THE SHAGANAPPI SKI HILL

The Regal slopes the club had been using locally were not really suitable for a permanent home. Enter Bob Freeze, the son of long-serving Calgary alderman and businessman Frank Freeze. Newly returned from the University of Alberta, he had helped organize the U of A ski team and Intercollegiate Ski Meet. Freeze was an avid racer and had been using the hillside above Riley Park for slalom practice. He was keenly interested in seeing a club hill, such as he had skied at in Edmonton, available for training. With several other club members he looked for a better location. They settled on the prominent gully on the north side of the Municipal Golf Course, now better known as Shaganappi.

The run was reasonably long, the north exposure would theoretically hold snow and there was a convenient bus route.[160] At the beginning of November in 1948, the CSC officially requested permission to use the Municipal Golf Course for skiing.[161] The club wanted to clear brush on one slope and transfer snow from behind snow fences on the course to the hill to build up the base. The plan included floodlights for evening skiing. The golf clubhouse would serve as change rooms, bathroom facilities and a concession with food and drinks.

In December, Freeze appeared before the Parks and Playground Committee of city council as head of the club's local ski development committee.[162] The alderman on the committee granted the club permission pursuant to approval from the parks department. Freeze remembers that the parks department was not keen to have a bunch of skiers messing about on the golf course, but he had an ace up his sleeve. "My father was an alderman so I got him to talk to the park superintendent and I'm sure they weren't happy to do it—they were happy to later kick us out."[163]

On December 11 and 12, club volunteers started clearing brush on the hill.[164] City crews installed floodlights the first week of January 1949. On the following weekend, after a "tramping bee" to pack down the available snow, the first ski runs were made.[165] Toward the end of January, the club's ski school began operating, and on the twenty-eighth the hill was officially opened with Deputy Mayor Dr. A.E. Aikenhead on hand representing the city.[166] Ceremonies included a torch-bearing escort of the CSC ski patrol for dignitaries and a demonstration by a ski school class and refreshments in the golf course clubhouse. The hill was immediately put to use for race training. The club had a slalom race a week before the official opening to look for potential talent for future development.[167] There was even a cross-country race for high-school teams on the golf course.[168]

The opening ceremonies included a demonstration of the club's snowblower.[169] The club knew all too well that adequate snow was going to be a

Opening the Shaganappi Hill, 1948. (CSC COLLECTION.)

problem, so they looked for ways to improve conditions. Bob Freeze, Ozzie LaRue and some other club members experimented with farm machinery, such as alfalfa choppers and grain blowers, to come up with a way to deposit snow quickly on the ski runs.[170] They settled on a grain blower. It was not a snowmaking machine; snow was gathered and then shovelled into the hopper of the machine and blown out over the hill. Norm Russell remembers going out with Bob Freeze and Herb Spears with a big truck Herb borrowed from his dad's trucking firm. They filled it with snow, which was carted back to the golf course and blown onto the hill.[171] The procedure worked well, but it was a labour-intensive exercise.

The city renewed its permission to use the hill the following year and also allowed the club to install a rope tow.[172] The CSC could charge a small admission fee to non-club members to protect their investment and offset the costs of running the hill.[173] The club had spent $750 the previous season starting the hill and the power bill for lights was $250—the equivalent of more than $10,000 now.[174] The parks department seemed pleased with the development. In the department's 1950 annual report, the recreation section reported:

> Calgary Chinook winds cause local skiers much concern.
> A goodly number of the hills suitable for skiing in Calgary have a westerly or southerly exposure, thus, with the friendly chinooks [sic] making life pleasant for the greater number of the population, the skiers find the snow running off and making it necessary to go farther afield for ski runs. The one exception is the gully at the Municipal Golf Course, at which the Ski Club has installed a tow and flood lighting, to enable the younger and inexperienced members to participate in the sport and receive instruction from some of the more capable members. The Golf Club-house makes a very convenient gathering place for this activity.[175]

The hill was undeniably popular with local skiers as well. Over 200 were out on the hill one Sunday in January, 1950. Without a doubt, there was demand in Calgary for just such a place.

The Shaganappi ski hill was short-lived. Despite the glowing report its own employees gave on the hill in early December, 1951, the parks department informed the club that it was no longer welcome.[176] The reason the department gave was fear that the packed snow was affecting the grass on the course. As Bob Freeze remembers, the snowblowing might have been the club's downfall—one night they accidentally drove the truck over a green, a major no-no. He suspects, however, that the real reason was that the course manager found the skiers irritating, especially because he had to open up the clubhouse for them. Nigel Dunn was infuriated, noting in his column that the areas used for skiing were almost entirely in the rough, not fairways, and any greens in the vicinity had been fenced off.[177] As far as he and the club were concerned, the city had broken faith. Some 20 years later the parks department invited a private operator to develop the Shaganappi Ski Centre exactly where the club had first cleared runs.

Back to Bowness

After getting booted from the Municipal Golf Course, the club moved fast to set up another hill. Bill Milne, who would be president of the club from 1953 through 1954, found an ideal site up on the side of Coach Hill above Bowness.[178] He arranged a lease with the owner, Alf Zimmer, who farmed nearby, and the club started working on the new hill by the end of December.[179] Milne and Wally Humphries put together a new rope tow—Milne, an architect, designed it and Humphries, an engineer, made it work. It used an old tractor and a gear reducer, and had a speed "midway between that of the Norquay tows and the speed of the Turner Valley tow last year," the *Herald* reported.[180] One of Milnes's industry contacts, Bird Construction, donated a construction shack as a clubhouse.[181]

The opening of the new hill, however, was not auspicious. The mayor, Don Mackay, and other local luminaries were invited to the ceremonies, which were to include races, ski patrol demonstrations and lessons for the public.[182] Bruce Compton remembers that the skier's nemesis, the chinook, made a travesty of the opening. "For a day or two before the opening we had one of the best Chinooks you've ever seen. I can remember standing at the bottom of the hill in the mud, with water running over my nice leather ski boots, talking to some of these celebrities and watching people golf at the Bowness Golf and Country Club."[183] But with some new snow there was skiing the following weekend, including a cross-country race for the club's Gervig Trophy, and the tow was put in operation. Another chinook ended most skiing for the year, and to add insult to injury, at the end of March the hut at the hill burnt down. It was not the best start.

Proponents of the hill, however, called the fire "a blessing in disguise."

The club had to decide whether to replace the clubhouse and it was a chance to push for development of a proper hill, with a substantial building the club could use for all its needs. After some debate, the club decided to pursue development of the site as a year-round sports centre. It was an ambitious plan and the first challenge was finding the money to do it. The CSC subsisted on membership fees and had an annual revenue of around $3,000. The club generally had no trouble spending it all—the outlay of $750 to get the Bowness hill running cut substantially into the club's surplus from the year before.[184] The proposed development was going to be a lot more expensive.

Bill Milne talked to Zimmer about purchasing the land, preparing a report on the options along with the costs of building a respectable lodge. In Milne's professional opinion, the latter was a $20,000 proposition for a 1,500 square foot building. Daunting numbers, but a finance committee was formed with Al Compton as chair, and the club set out to raise the funds for a down payment.[185] One option for financing was to issue debentures, another was a mortgage. Neither worked out. Milne tried to negotiate a better price with Zimmer, but to no avail. The club remained on good terms with their landlord and retained an option on the property.[186] Some work continued on the hill. Another donated hut replaced the one lost to fire, but it took a couple of years of negotiation with the city to get a power line installed for floodlights.[187] The tow was rebuilt and made longer. The club, however, was still a long way from realizing its ambitions for Bowness.

Not everyone in the club was in favour of the hill project. There had been little enthusiasm among the membership for clearing runs on the first hill at the Municipal Golf Course. Nigel Dunn was moved to take the members to task for their apathy in his weekly column.[188] The decision to purchase the Bowness site was controversial. The membership approved the plan at a general meeting, but the debate had been heated.[189] The Bowness hill needed a lot of work, especially removing brush for runs, yet people were reluctant to help. The work fell to a small band of volunteers and progress was slow. In his *Albertan* column, Peter Cooper lashed out at the membership. When only five people showed up for a work party, he wrote:

> Five out of an estimated 500 club members in the city. And don't think that this is something new! For the past two or three years things have been the same ... if five members are all that are interested in this hill then the time has come to act—lets drop it now.

Keeping the hill running was an uphill battle. The delay in rigging floodlights meant the area couldn't be used at night for several years. The rebuilt tow was supposed to use electricity and the club had to rebuild it again with a gas engine.[190] The tow turned out to be none too reliable, and, in fact, was finally dismantled.[191] There were problems with vandals. But the viability of the Bowness property came down to the usual two factors: snow and the proximity of the mountains. The hill was unusable more often than not, due to Chinook winds and Calgary's poor snowfall. Lack of snow interfered not just with pleasure skiing, but the club's instructional programs. The *Herald* ski reporter, Joy Van Wagner, put it aptly. "If I had $5 for every time I've written 'the ski lesson scheduled this Saturday has been cancelled owing to insufficient snow' I could go to Florida for a holiday."[192]

Snowmaking was one option the club considered. The technology had just appeared on the market and the club seriously considered buying equipment, especially when the Edmonton Ski Club installed it at their club hill in the capital. The ESC, however, had an advantage over the CSC—Edmonton was a long way from the mountains and a local ski hill was an important asset for skiers. Wagner framed the problem bluntly: "The opinion I share with quite a few others is that nothing could induce skiers to Bowness Hill instead of Banff on weekends, no matter how fancy the layout."

The club seriously reviewed the whole project again in 1957. A search committee was formed to look for a different site, but concluded that nothing in the city was better. Matters finally came to a head the following year. With its sizable investment in the hill—estimated at over $4,000—the club had to decide whether to develop it properly or cut its losses. Surprisingly, at a general meeting on the question, the vote was 80 to 7 to buy the site once and for all. But the writing was on the wall. The club just could not seem to make the hill viable. After leasing the Bowness hill for a season to Ron Smylie, the club wound up the endeavour in 1960. At almost the same time, just across the road allowance from the CSC hill, four local entrepreneurs were busy cutting runs for the Paskapoo ski area, which officially opened in February, 1961, equipped with primitive snowmaking guns.

The CSC did not give up on the idea of a local club hill. Bob Freeze, Bill Milne and C.M. Haakenstad thoroughly examined the Bow River escarpment west of the Municipal Golf Course around 1960 for possible spots,[193] and the following year council again discussed establishing a ski hill. Then, most ironically, the operators of Paskapoo, suffering financial difficulties, offered to sell their facility to the club for $45,000.[194] A committee examined the proposal, with Bob Freeze approaching oilman George McMahon about help with financing. Again, the financial outlay was just too daunting—the committee thought that the club would be looking at a $100,000 investment to make the hill viable. The club finally gave up and pursued the more modest goal of a permanent clubhouse for meetings and socials. A noble effort had come to naught.

BACK TO SCHOOL

A justification for a club ski hill was to have a place for lessons. Providing instruction in the sport continued to be one of the club's major contributions. The CSC took it to a new level of sophistication. However, by the end of the 1950s, the continued growth of the ski industry made professional instruction cheap and easy, and the club began to wind down what had been an important service for the membership.

After the war, the club once again initiated a program of professional and volunteer instruction. In 1947, pro Bill Wellman of Banff put a group of CSCers, including Stu Rosamond, Harry Armstrong, Bob Kolb, Doug Shipley, Ozzie LaRue, Stewart McPhee and Russ Bradley through a month of training sessions. This group formed the core of the club's volunteer instructors. Within a couple of years, the club took their program to a new level, thanks to the Canadian Ski Instructors Alliance. The CSIA had been founded in 1938 to train instructors and create some standards for the growing ski industry. When the CSIA started offering courses in the west, the club subsidized the cost for interested members, who then agreed to act as the club instructors. Cam Mitchell took the first subsidized CSIA training in 1951. At the end of the week, he had a badge as a junior instructor.

Ironically, the success of the CSIA in raising the quality of ski instruction undermined the CSC's efforts. The club's program had some problems. For a good part of the 1950s, thanks to George Encil, the club couldn't teach at Norquay or Sunshine and the Bowness hill was not often usable. Although some club teachers had CSIA certified training, most were only really qualified to teach beginners and there were complaints about inconsistent instruction.[195] Professional schools, meanwhile, were well-established in Banff. In 1959, the club decided to change tack. It arranged discount lessons for interested members with professional instructors and picked up most of the cost. It was the end of one of the club's traditions, but also a recognition that times had changed. The club members who had taken teacher training came in handy as the CSC turned its efforts towards children.

HERALD SKI SCHOOL

CSC had always been keen to introduce children to skiing. In 1954, the club started a regular ski school in conjunction with the *Calgary Herald*. It was the CSC's biggest effort yet in ski education. It was not an original idea; newspapers had sponsored ski lessons in Vancouver and Winnipeg. John Southam likely played a role in the *Herald*'s support, but Bill Milne, who had been involved in the Winnipeg version, was the driving force behind the school for its first couple of years.[196] The aim was simple: to teach kids the basics of skiing. It was a perfect way to promote the sport and the club, and with the baby boom in full bloom, filled a need.

The program consisted of six free lessons, subsidized by the *Herald* and the club. The newspaper printed a coupon that interested children, 12 years and over, clipped and mailed in. They then received a membership card the instructors signed after each session. The CSC provided the instructors and the venue. The teachers were all volunteers, some who had taken the CSIA course through the club. The first year the CSC could call on over 15 instructors. The goal of the ski school was for pupils to perform a stem turn at the end of the lessons, at which point they received a badge from the *Herald*. The club used their Bowness Hill for the school, which was cancelled if the temperature fell below zero degrees Fahrenheit. This left a narrow window of opportunity.

The first year over 250 kids signed up and at the first lesson the seven volunteer instructors were kept busy.[197] The ski school continued to draw sizable numbers. On one chilly January day in 1956, classes were cancelled. One of the CSC instructors, Ethan Compton, went to Bowness on a premonition. He found about 80 kids there, hoping for a lesson.[198] Fortunately for him, another instructor, Malcolm Cullen, arrived shortly afterward. Despite the frosty temperatures, the day was a success. In 1957, nearly 200 kids sent in their coupons for the program.

As long as the program used the Bowness hill, however, lack of snow lessened its effectiveness. The original six lessons were cut down to five and then four, not for shortage of pupils or instructors, but the difficulty of finding six weekends with enough snow and suitable temperatures. For a while, the uncertain fate of the Bowness hill threatened the whole endeavour. When

Paskapoo opened, the *Herald* Ski School moved there, and under Ethan Compton's capable direction, continued until the mid-1960s, when it finally ran out of steam. It was not the last CSC program that aimed to help children to ski.

BASHING THE SCHUSS-BOOMERS

With more people taking up skiing, the slopes were getting crowded. Accidents were frequent and sometimes people were seriously hurt. A major goal of the CSC, frequently stated over in the club's literature, was promoting safe skiing. Teaching people to ski better was one way to achieve this. Even before the war, however, it was obvious that someone needed to police the slopes, looking for reckless skiers and helping the injured. Another Calgary Ski Club contribution to the ski community was the creation of the first ski patrol in the Rockies.

The ski patrol was an American invention. The death of a close friend inspired Minot Dole to organize a national body, backed by the American Red Cross and the National Ski Association, to train skiers in first aid and rescue techniques. The patrol idea expanded quickly to provide policing on the slopes, especially controlling reckless skiers. In Canada, some clubs had started providing some first aid training and services in the early thirties—CASA sponsored first aid posts in the Laurentians in 1935.[199] Finally, in 1940, CASA asked Dr. Doug Firth of Toronto to organize a national patrol for Canada. Some Canadian clubs were already supplying their own patrols. The Calgary Ski Patrol was one of them.

Traffic control was the impetus for the club's patrol. By the late 1930s, Norquay was busy on weekends. Skiers climbed up some of the same slopes they came down. Many of the people at Norquay were relative beginners while some simply pointed their skis downhill until they crashed, unable to check their speed for obstacles, especially other skiers. Some speedsters were capable enough skiers, but just wanted to go fast. Nigel Dunn nicknamed them "bashers" and "schuss-boomers." For several years, he vehemently called for their expulsion from the slopes if they refused to ski safely. Help for the injured was a haphazard affair, depending almost entirely on the presence of a doctor or nurse on the hill that day, or a park warden. Injuries were on the rise and not just for beginners. On the unforgiving gear of the day, even experts frequently suffered from broken legs and sprained ankles.

At the beginning of 1942, the CSC and the Ski Runners set up their first patrol at Norquay.[200] The Canadian Ski Patrol System had been encouraging the different CASA zones and local clubs to set up patrols, with one obviously needed in Banff. Bill Ross was the organizer for the CSC.[201] He ordered crests, armbands and pins for contributors to the patrol from the CSPS, which also advised on the training patrollers should have. Ross also acquired literature on avalanches from the U.S. The CSC soon had four skiers ready to act as patrollers and planned to train 20 members in first aid with the St. John Ambulance organization.[202] One of the first matters the patrol tackled was traffic. Ozzie LaRue, later the proprietor of Ozzie's Sports, remembered making some signs to segregate the hill into a climbing area and then a descending area. The new volunteer patrollers stuck the signs in the snow.[203] It was a good start, but the war intervened and the patrol was dropped.[204]

When the crowds returned to Norquay after the war, the CSC quickly revived the patrol. "That was my baby," LaRue would later say. He was the chairman of the club patrol committee set up for the 1946/47 season and responsible for getting the patrol going again. Two club members, wearing the armbands to denote their status, first patrolled Norquay in February, 1947, helping any injured and trying to get people to ski safely. Initially the Banff Ski Runners participated as well, with the CSC looking after the main slopes and the Runners the newly created Memorial Slope.[205] Dave Spence remembers that the CSC, as the representative of the Calgary skiers and much bigger than the Banff club, soon took over sole responsibility for the patrol.[206]

In 1948, the club patrol and the CSPS re-established communication. LaRue needed advice to improve the training for his patrollers.[207] LaRue privately confessed to Dr. Firth that while he was confident about his people's skiing skills, he was less sanguine about their first aid ability. The patrollers took first aid training with St. John Ambulance—superior Red Cross instruction was unavailable, thanks to the local director.[208] The local patrol had to come up with its own procedures to supplement the St. John training. The patrol was also short on equipment. LaRue remembers that the patrol had to build its own toboggans. The patrollers bought regular toboggans from Ashdown's Hardware and then added a frame and runners to stiffen it. One patroller would ski in front yoked to the contraption, while two skied behind, each with a rope attached to help control it. The toboggan was ungainly, but it worked. In 1950, the patrol added "snowcraft"—the euphemism for avalanche safety—to its training.

The Calgary Ski Patrol did their job at Norquay, Turner Valley and the

Ski patrollers work out bugs, Ozzie LaRue at front. (CSC Collection, Ozzie LaRue.)

CSC's hill at Bowness.[209] The patrollers even accompanied CSC and Chinook Ski Club bus tours down to Whitefish in the United States! At its peak, the patrol had about 40 trained people. It was most active at Norquay. LaRue revived the traffic control tried earlier, designating uphill lanes, beginner's areas and faster areas where necessary.[210] Patrollers also asked people to fill in their "bathtubs," holes made when they crashed, and did it themselves when necessary. Another patroller duty was keeping skiers out of the Gully when it was unsafe and the time-honoured sweep at the end of the day to make sure the hill was clear. The patrollers were given the authority to deal with reckless skiers, and able, in theory at least, to kick them off the hill. They did not have the authority to take names and ban troublemakers from Norquay permanently, which limited their effectiveness.[211]

Although the patrol was quite successful, it was not trouble-free. The park administration's assessment of the patrol was critical of the level of expertise of the volunteers.[212] Another difficulty was keeping patrollers long enough for them to acquire experience. Initially there was little reward for patrolling, so the turnover was high. The patrol eventually was able to get free lunches and free passes for the Norquay lifts for use off-duty, but only grudgingly.

In 1952, the ski patrol separated from the club. This was part of a reorganization of the national patrol, which became an independent organization no longer under the umbrella of the CASA. Local patrols that the ski clubs operated were asked to join the newly independent Canadian Ski Patrol System to create one unified organization. With the blessing of the CSC executive, the members for the Calgary Ski Patrol took a vote and decided to join the CSPS.[213] There were many advantages to joining, such as access to surplus military rescue gear, including better toboggans and inexpensive first aid supplies. The links remained strong between the patrol and the CSC. Most of the patrollers were active club members and the CSC contributed to its operation. Cam Mitchell, club president for 1952, was also the patrol leader that year and several after.

Ironically, not long after the patrol became part of the CSPS, the park administration took over responsibility for patrolling the ski areas in the park.[214] The authorities had always regarded qualifications of the volunteer patrol a bit suspiciously. Initially, the Calgary Ski Patrol provided volunteer patrollers to aid the wardens. Further conflicts arose at Norquay, Sunshine and Temple over patroller privileges and their competence. The volunteers were replaced with paid patrollers. Left with little to do, the Calgary Ski Patrol nearly disappeared.[215] It wasn't until the late 1950s that the volunteer patrol was welcomed back to the mountains. It seems hard to believe now, with the yellow and blue patroller's jacket so ubiquitous.

THE CALGARY SKI CLUB GUIDES

The ski patrol was followed with another innovation, the Calgary Ski Club Guides. Many people were still ski touring after the war. Skiing at Sunshine and Temple was still largely self-propelled until the mid 1950s, and Skoki and Assinboine remained popular trips in the springtime. The CSC regularly booked an Easter outing to Skoki, often running day or weekend trips to Sunshine and Temple. Touring around Lake Louise was popular among club members, especially trips onto the Victoria Glacier and up Mt. Fairview. Ski touring had many hazards—avalanches, unpredictable weather and lack of help in case of accidents—and was not suited for the novice. Thus the CSC Guides were born.

The club had taken an early interest in avalanche safety. Before the war,

Alan Carscallen and Don Young of the Canmore Ski Club had set up a snow craft committee for the Rocky Mountain Zone of CASA. CSC president Connie Mackey claimed it was "unique in North America." By the beginning of the war, there had been a number of deaths and lots of close calls, so there was a clear need to better understand avalanche conditions in the Rockies.[216] Under Young and later Mackey's direction, the committee collected weather and snow pack data from the Banff area to allow analysis of avalanche conditions for the region. The committee also sought to educate the skiing public about avalanche hazards through talks. It lobbied the park administration to post warnings and created a sign listing the factors indicating unsafe conditions, intended for trailheads and the backcountry ski lodges. The committee even issued public avalanche warnings.[217]

Russ Bradley was an experienced skier and mountaineer. Not much is known about his background, but in 1947 he wrote a handbook on avalanche safety for the recreational skier in the Rockies. Bradley, a member of the CSC and the ski patrol, taught avalanche safety to the patrollers. He was the driving force for the club's ski guide training. The motivation was twofold. There was a lack of trained mountain ski guides in the Rockies after the war. Veterans like Vic Kutschera and the CPR's Swiss Guides had retired or moved on to other things. They were not immediately replaced. There was a dearth of local skiers with any qualifications to guide and no professional organization training or overseeing climbing and skiing guides in Canada. The park administration was concerned with the situation and came up with criteria for licensing commercial skiing and climbing guides, but was not in the business of providing instruction.

The CSC stepped into the vacuum because the club ran ski touring trips into the backcountry. Some members, including Bradley, LaRue and Cam Mitchell, felt that better leadership was necessary to prevent accidents. Bradley took charge of the program. Superintendent Coleman of Banff National Park approved the course Bradley designed as equivalent to the training of commercial guides. It was rigorous—of the 25 skiers who took it in 1952 only two passed.[218] After the ski patrol became a separate entity, the guides unit followed it. Bradley switched to providing avalanche training for the patrollers. The guides petered out soon afterward, probably because fewer people were ski touring. Bradley would drift from the CSC to the Alpine Club. His legacy with the club, however, was a guide's training program that preceded the Association of Canadian Mountain Guides by over a decade.

Ski touring at its best: Russ Bradley leading group, circa 1950s. (CSC COLLECTION.)

The need for avalanche safety was brought home to the club a few years later. Even with the training that Bradley tried to provide for the club, there were accidents and tragedies. Along with near misses on Mt. Fairview, in 1955 the club had its first skiing related death. Peggy Hind, an active member of the ski club and an ardent mountaineer with the Alpine Club, was killed in an avalanche near Temple Lodge. Hind, who as Peggy Trotter had been the club's ladies slalom and downhill champion, was caught in a slab avalanche that she triggered. Her husband Bob had returned earlier to the lodge and came back with a rescue party that included Russ Bradley, who was patrolling at Temple. Lacking proper rescue equipment, it took them five hours to find the victim. Although she was not on a club sponsored trip, the incident was a sobering reminder of the dangers inherent in mountain skiing.

BACK TO THE RACES

In 1946, the Edmonton-Calgary slalom race resumed. The CSC handily defeated their northern brethren, establishing ski superiority that lasted for the next 10 years. The Edmontonians eventually gave up in disgust, bowing to the strength of the CSC racers. Club championships, pin races, the 1948 Dominions, the Sir Norman Watson downhill, summer racing on the Victoria Glacier, the SkiWees junior league—it's no wonder that later generations would look back on the CSC as a racing club.

Competition remained a fundamental part of the identity of the post-war CSC. The club supported racing for two reasons: to create better skiers and to promote the sport and the club. "Through the medium of racing much advantageous publicity can be obtained," wrote Nigel Dunn in his column. "Competition is the backbone of skiing, as it is with any sport." Skiing, however, can be enjoyed as a purely recreational activity, and that is how most CSC skiers enjoyed it. The racers got the glory and the club took pride in them, but they were an increasingly small proportion of the club's members. Most members never raced, and as time went on, more of them started to question the club's involvement in competition. A split started to form between recreational and competitive skiers that would have consequences in the future.

THE CSC RACE TEAM

Pre-war CSC speedsters like Bill Ross and the Armstrongs were initially the scourge of Edmonton, but a new generation of racers soon joined them. Many were up-and-coming juniors who would form the core of the club's racing talent over the next decade. The CSC soon had an actual team. The main instigators were Arnold Choquette and Bob Freeze, two keen senior racers. Choquette tried to make the 1948 Canadian Olympic team, going down to Colorado to train with coach Friedl Pfeifer. He would later start the Snowridge ski area.

Bob Freeze took up skiing at 17, before the war, and had participated in high-school races. At the University of Alberta, he became a friend with Stan Ward, a talented Banff skier, and the two practiced endlessly at the club hill in Edmonton. Back in university after the war, Freeze and Norm Rault, with the support of the Alberta provincial government, started the Intercollegiate at Norquay. Teams from universities and colleges through the Pacific Northwest, British Columbia and Saskatchewan came to compete. Back in Calgary, Freeze raced for the CSC. He remembers talking the ski club council into hiring French ski racer Gerry Monod, recently arrived in Banff, for $35 a month to coach him in preparation for the 1948 Dominions.

The first CSC team was mostly juniors with a few younger senior racers. Choquette was the first coach, but when his own racing took up more time, Freeze took over.[219] To augment his own coaching, Freeze hired Gerry Monod's brother Johnny from Banff to work with the club racers. The Monods had raced successfully in Europe and at a much higher level than just about anyone in Calgary and Banff. Freeze put Johnny up at his house. He also pushed for a club hill in town to give the racers some place to train during the week. The club set up a technical committee to look after racing. The committee instituted selection races to choose members of the team to send for competitions, especially the inter-city with Edmonton and the Crowsnest Pass championships in Blairmore.

Some of the racers on the CSC team came out of the Inter-Scholastic League. The CSC had helped Calgary's high-school skiers set up a race league before the war. A slalom race for the high-school kids had even been held

CSC Racers: top, l-r, unknown, Bob Freeze, Dave Freeze, Harry Lovett, bottom, l-r, Bob Rohloff, Joe Irwin. (CSC COLLECTION.)

CSC talent: Joe Irwin slalom racing. (CSC COLLECTION, JOE IRWIN.)

at Norquay in 1940. After the war, the league started anew and expanded. Clubs from Crescent High School and St. Mary's joined Central and Western Canada High. All were affiliated with the CSC and sent a representative to the ski club council.[220] Wilson Southam, son of John Southam, took matters further by establishing the Inter-School Ski Club, which represented the school groups.

The CSC helped with the high school clubs with their races, sponsoring a giant slalom at Norquay in 1947 and again in 1948.[221] They also established the position of junior member representative on the council. Norm Russell, who was the chief talent at Western Canada High and who won the high school championship in 1948, and Joe Irwin, a powerhouse at Central who went on to collegiate racing in the U.S., both served as representatives on the CSC council. Many of the young racers participating in the high school competitions were also junior members of the ski club and competed in club races for the junior Cote trophy local realtor Clare Cote donated in 1945.

Along with Russell and Irwin, some of the other junior talents who emerged from the club were Jack Bruce and Harry Lovett. Freeze dropped out of skiing after only a couple of years to coach the Calgary Broncs football team full-time. Norm Russell would take over direction of the club's racers and would also serve as the chair of the technical committee for years. Aside from whupping Edmonton regularly, some of the CSC skiers did well at Blairmore. No one went on to bigger things. Ski racing was still a pretty small-time sport in North America. It was difficult to entertain any long-term ambitions.

The CSC Team appealed to the more serious racer, but the club encouraged everyone to participate in competition. The annual club championships were open to all members. The CSC also began standard races, which would evolve into the "pin" races. Originally, the standard was intended to divide the club's racers into different classes for competition. Predetermined times for a set course determined what class racers were put in. The club hoped more people would be encouraged to race if they only competed against skiers of similar ability. This didn't quite work, but the pin races were more successful. They were based on the Star races out at Sunshine: bettering a certain time earned the competitor a gold star, or a silver star, and so on. Skiers were essentially competing against themselves and the course. The CSC standard race became the CSC pin race in 1958, with gold, silver and bronze pins. The club ran the races several times in the season.

Two other fun events the club ran were the two summer races, the Waterton-Akimina race and the Victoria Glacier Giant Slalom. The Waterton race was held on the slopes of Mt. Custer, above the waters of Cameron Lake, on the July 1st weekend. Bruno Engler of Banff had founded the race in 1952 when he was living down in Maycroft.[222] The Victoria Glacier event was the brainchild of Franz Gabl, an Austrian immigrant and keen racer living in Banff. It was first held in May but moved to August—mostly to promote the festival atmosphere. Racers and spectators would camp out over the weekend, race in the sunshine and slush, and enjoy some boisterous socializing. The meadow by the teahouse below the Victoria Glacier turned into a little tent city. In Waterton, people stayed in the park campground, taking a boat across the lake to the slopes. The races drew a large number of Calgarians and not just the racing crowd—some came for the lark of skiing in the summer. The club took over running the Waterton event around 1955 and the Victoria Glacier event in 1959, organizing the event and setting the courses.[223]

To Sponsor or Not to Sponsor

Despite appearances, all was not well in the CSC racing efforts. Even with attempts to encourage interest, like the pin races, only a small part of the club's adult membership was interested in actively racing. Norm Russell, who served as the technical director of the club for most of the fifties, remembers that the hard-core racers were a minority. "We were more verbal, more organized than the social set. We demanded more attention. But we were a comparatively small segment. If the club was, at that time, around 300 people, maybe 50 of us would be racers." The club's waning enthusiasm for racing was first seen with race sponsorship. The club's membership dipped substantially in the mid-1950s during a succession of poor winters, which affected morale and willingness to take on big commitments.[224]

The CSC and the Ski Runners sponsored the Dominions Championships at Norquay in 1948. The event went off smoothly, but it was much more expensive than the subsidized affairs in 1937 and 1940. While ski racing in Canada was still not a big-time sport, expectations, both on the part of competitors and spectators, were rising, and so were the expenses. Sponsoring major tournaments had become an expensive affair as well as racing became more professional. Dunn estimated the costs of the 1950 North American Championships at Norquay at $12,000, well beyond what the clubs could back. That particular competition—which Joe Irwin believes came to Banff

Skiers above Lake Cameron for Waterton-Akimina Race, circa 1960.
(CSC Collection.)

Why we ski in August: Plain of Six Glaciers teahouse, circa 1961.
(Whyte Museum of the Canadian Rockies, V190 I.A.1.a-4, Bruno Engler)

due to John Southam's initiative—followed the world championships in Vail. The North Americans had its own local organizing committee. The CSC took no direct role, and this signalled, for the most part, the end of the club's sponsorship of big tournaments.

The club did continue to support local races. The CSC in fact revived the Sir Norman Watson Cup. Originally run at Skoki, the war had put the race into limbo until the CSC brought it back in 1956 to help support Temple Lodge. Norm Russell remembers that Temple's manager, Jack McDowall, a dour Scotsman, had complained to him that the lodge had almost no early season business. McDowall told Russell that January was the slowest time, so he suggested putting on a downhill race on Larch. The club heavily promoted the race, named in honour of Temple's owner, and drew a good crowd. "It was the biggest weekend Jack had ever had practically," Russell recalls. Later he asked McDowall if he was happy with the race. McDowall replied, "Yeah, but

Another reason we ski in August: skiers relax after race inside Plain of Six Glaciers teahouse, circa 1961. (WHYTE MUSEUM OF THE CANADIAN ROCKIES, V190 I.A.I.A-4, BRUNO ENGLER)

why did you have to do it on such a busy weekend?" The CSC would sponsor the Watson Downhill until 1963, when the Lake Louise Ski Club took it over.

A single day local race was one thing, but the fight in the council over the 1959 Western Canadian Championships showed how much things had changed. The previous year's council had bid on the championships. The 1958/59 executive, feeling that they were already too busy, appointed Bob Reid to look after the race.[225] Reid had supported the bid and also headed the committee for the 1960 North American Championships. He met with a hostile reception when, shortly before the event, he informed the council the club would have to put up $2,000. The club was expected to recoup the expense from selling so-called "booster tickets" to spectators.[226] The CSC council was unhappy with this plan, with the meeting degenerating into catcalling.

The championships went ahead, but the incident made it clear that support for racing in the club was more limited than enthusiasts may have realized. There were other issues contributing to the growing tension over racing. Norm Russell remembers that although the club was not really spending very much money on the racers, the non-racing members increasingly challenged any expenditures. One sore point was the Canadian Amateur Ski Association fees. Racing clubs paid a fee to CASA based on the number of club members, not just the active racers. The CSC was a large club, and even if the head tax wasn't very much, it added up. Some of the members who didn't care for racing disliked paying the fees. It was another sign that support for racing in the club was not universal.

KIDS RACING

While there were serious rumblings about racing, at the same time the club still did a lot for the sport. Enthusiasm faltered a bit in the lean snow years of the middle fifties, despite the hard work of Norm Russell. The club's racing program caught new life when Malcolm Cullen joined the council as technical director for the 1958/59 season. In his "Ski Trails" column, Peter Cooper wrote, "… response to the racing program has been gratifying, organization has been excellent and the calibre at its highest standard in many a long season."

Cullen was serious about racing, most interested in working with young racers to develop new talent. During his tenure as racing director and in conjunction with the Ski Runners, the club instituted a new SkiWees program

CSC standard race course on Mt. Norquay. (CSC Collection.)

that focused on young skiers, the "midgets" and "juveniles," as opposed to junior racers. As part of the program, the CSC and the Runners started holding a regular Sunday slalom race. It mushroomed within a couple of years into a two-day, four-way competition with new trophies for the midgets and juniors that Cullen built in his spare time.[227]

Cullen's interest in young racers was not unusual. Choquette and Freeze had also mostly coached juniors; they had the most potential. In the larger perspective, however, Cullen's efforts were being directed towards the thin edge of a demographic wedge known as the baby boom. By the late 1950s, the leading segment of the boom, which started around 1946, was approaching their teens, which accounts for the popularity of the *Herald* Ski School. Kids were everywhere. The boom coincided with the development of ski racing into a major international sport. People noticed Canada's relative lack of presence on race podiums. In the late fifties, Calgarians were actively pursuing the Winter Olympics for 1964. Cullen was not alone in his desire to develop a new generation of racers. The club continued to sponsor races for adults, but by the end of fifties the focus was on the juniors.

Skiing for Fun

For the vast majority of the members, the Calgary Ski Club was about having a good time. The club's executive spent a great deal of time and energy on the serious business of promoting skiing and the members at large benefited. These same members, however, wanted to go on fun trips to the mountains, get together to watch ski films and go to club dances. The recreational skier was still the backbone of the organization and their needs were becoming increasingly sophisticated.

After the war, Calgary skiers gained two new places to ski near the city. In Nanton, the town residents and nearby ranchers formed the Penguin Ski Club in 1946. With only 75 members, the club cleared a small hill by Mosquito Creek with a bulldozer and built a rope tow and small cabin. The Penguins would move several times in search of better snow; the hill was eventually called Timber Ridge.[228] Two carloads from the Calgary Ski Club immediately paid a visit and their Nanton hosts insisted they use the tow free of charge and even put on a lunch of hotdogs and doughnuts. In return, the Calgarians offered some ski lessons.[229] A fond relationship grew between the CSC and the Penguins. Bruce Compton remembers that the club chartered a bus to go to a summer dance hosted the Nanton skiers, "a real old-fashioned barnburner." The Calgarians spent the night after they got their driver so drunk he couldn't take them home.

Turner Valley, however, eclipsed Nanton. A group of local enthusiasts got together around 1950, formed a club and cut runs and built a rope tow on a farm near the village. For a clubhouse, they obtained an old Calgary city streetcar and put it at the base of the hill. It had a lunch counter and local women provided the food, which got high marks from Calgary skiers. The Turner Valley hill was quite popular for budget-minded Calgarians, especially those with young families. It became a commercial enterprise when a few entrepreneurs established Turner Valley Ski Tow Ltd. in 1959. The company, which numbered Ozzie LaRue among its directors, took over from the club. It moved the hill to new location, installed a Poma-lift, and set up a ski school.

Unfortunately, both the Nanton and Turner Valley hills suffered from the same curse as Calgary: limited snowfall and chinook winds. Timber Ridge petered out by 1959. The Turner Valley company went under in 1964 after suffering through several nearly snow-less winters. The opening of Paskapoo and Happy Valley in Calgary, which both had snowmaking equipment and

Do it yourself ski hill: Turner Valley, circa 1950s. (GLENBOW ARCHIVES, PA 1599-539A-4.)

served a similar market, cut into business. For over a decade, however, the two areas were a popular alternative to the mountains and Calgary Ski Club members were frequent visitors.

The small hills were a nice diversion, but Norquay remained the favourite haunt of Calgary skiers. With the chairlift, new rope tows and improved runs, Norquay was the premier ski area through the 1950s in Banff. After the road access improved, Sunshine also became a regular day trip for club members—starting in 1947 the CSC organized buses up to the area. Temple was an increasingly popular destination and the club used it for Easter trips, staying down at the Post Hotel in the cabins built for summer tourists and commuting up daily to ski.[230] Sunshine and Temple provided only limited lift skiing until later in the decade, most visitors still did some touring.

The CSC's pleasure skiers did not entirely forsake the high country away from the resorts. Trips to Skoki remained popular. The club returned after the war to favourite areas like Castle Crags and the Victoria Glacier at Lake Louise. Russ Bradley popularized new trips like Mt. Fairview and Mr. Piran, and explored the area above Sherbrooke Lake in Yoho Park. He even searched out new slopes on the east side of Mt. Cascade. Without a doubt, skiing away from the lifts lost much of its attraction in the 1950s. At one time, the CSC would have used the Easter weekend for a trip to Skoki, but by the late fifties the club preferred to bunk at the Post Hotel near the highway and shuttle daily to Temple Lodge. With the exception of Bow Summit on the Jasper highway, most skiers succumbed to the siren call of the ski hill.

GETTING THERE

Since skiing for Calgarians still meant Banff, the club continued to offer ways to get there. The most romantic was the ski train, which reached a peak in the period immediately after the war. According to the *Herald*, up to 400 people might use the train on a given Sunday. Some coaches were designated as quiet areas, for those who wanted to nap or read, while others rang with songs and music if someone brought a guitar. According to one rider, the atmosphere was fun but not raucous; there wasn't much drinking even coming home, as most people were tired at the end of the day. "We were going to ski—we were serious about skiing." The trains were a wonderful social institution and encouraged club spirit. Many mourned their passing.

In 1951, the trains were abruptly discontinued. People had started to use their cars. By the beginning of the fifties, many more people had vehicles.

The decade saw governments undertake massive amounts of road building, especially paved, all-weather highways and winter road maintenance. Although the drive to Banff still left a lot to be desired, going by car was convenient. The club switched to carpooling as the preferred method of getting to the mountains. One of the shops friendly with the CSC was already running a car pool service and the club took it over.[231] Skiers with cars who intended to drive would leave their name at one of the ski stores—usually Premier or Russell's—by Thursday. Those who wanted a ride also registered and the shop quickly matched passengers to drivers. The usual charge was $2 for Banff and $3 for Norquay. The system worked well. Later, when the club hired a part-time secretary, the car pool was run out of their own office.

Part of the etiquette of car pooling was to be ready when your driver arrived. In the grip of powder fever, not everyone was patient. Bruce Compton remembers one incident with the notorious Aubrey Willis, CSC president for 1955/56.

> ... one time Aubrey Willis was to pick up two girls. They lived on the second floor of an apartment building and were waiting for him, watching anxiously out the window for his arrival. When they saw him coming down the street they gathered up their gear and went downstairs to the front door, just in time to see Aubrey and his car disappearing down the street.[232]

The provincial government had markedly improved what is now the 1A highway to Banff, but car trips to the mountains could still be a real white-knuckle experience. The transportation department's winter maintenance was irregular well into the 1950s and snow clearing equipment was somewhat more primitive than today's standard. Chains in the trunk were mandatory. Norm Russell and his wife MJ remember traffic on the hill up from Cochrane at an absolute standstill when it became too slippery for some cars to make it up. Drivers also dreaded the Gap Hill by Exshaw. Bruce Compton recalled taking a ski jumping competitor up to Banff for the 1950 North American Championships. Everybody, jumper included, had to get up and push him up the hill. Even buses had trouble. On a gentle curve by Exshaw, the Greyhound driver flagged down Cam Mitchell to get a report on the road east. The driver got back in his bus and released the airbrake. The slight vibration started the bus sliding across the road, right into the ditch. The

Trans-Canada Highway, completed to Banff at the end of the fifties, would be a tremendous boon to skiers.

FURTHER AFIELD

Improved roads helped create a new club tradition: the bus trip. The environs of Banff and Lake Louise were becoming a bit confined to many Calgarians, especially as more and more became lift-only skiers. Thus the Calgary Ski Club bus tour was born, something that would be a big part of the club for the next 30 years. The bus trip extended the club's previous range. It consisted of finding an interesting ski area, chartering a bus, arranging for accommodation, and signing up participants. The other change that made the bus tour possible was new ski hills.

Big Mountain at Whitefish, Montana, was the destination of the first CSC bus trip out of Alberta. The resort there began in 1935 much like Norquay, with a small cabin for the local ski club to take advantage of good natural skiing. In 1947, two local entrepreneurs incorporated a company and began improvements. By the early fifties, the mountain offered attractive skiing served by a long T-bar so it wasn't long before Calgarians began to show up. For the 1952/53 season, the club decided to do something big and go to Montana. Cam Mitchell looked after organization. Leaving Friday evening, the chartered bus was to arrive at 2:30 am. Accommodations, including meals, were arranged at two lodges by the hill. The entire trip, including lift tickets, was only $25 per person, which in contemporary dollars would still be a good bargain. After two days of skiing, the busload of CSCers was to leave in the afternoon, hoping to make Calgary by midnight.

Despite the gruelling schedule, the Whitefish trip quickly became an annual event and for the 1955/56 season two were scheduled. But even with better roads and a professional driver, the trip down could be quite an adventure. Cam Mitchell remembered one blizzard vividly:

> ... The snow was drifting straight down the highway right into the face of the driver and he got kind of hypnotized by this ... my wife and I were sitting in the front seat of the bus just to the right of the driver and he started to panic. He was putting on his brakes because he felt he was going too fast ... the snow sifting under the bus was going such a speed, he had no idea how fast we were travelling. I remember he finally got a feeling that he was actually stopped and he

opened the door of the bus and looked out and he could see a few tufts of grass every now and then through the swirling snow. So he closed the door and then walked up and down the aisle of the bus a few times to kind of shake off that sensation before he was ready to proceed on into Whitefish.

The March, 1956 trip turned into a 30-hour ride back to Banff. The bus made it to Shelby, Montana before a blizzard made the roads impassable. After briefly considering trying to make for Sun Valley in Idaho, the busload of Calgarians had an impromptu party in a Shelby restaurant before returning to Alberta. Determined to ski, a bunch convinced the bus driver to continue on to Banff, where they spent Sunday at Norquay.

Options for trips were still limited for the most part until near the end of the 1950s. The Whistler and Marmot ski areas at Jasper were difficult to reach until the new Banff-Jasper highway opened. North Star Mountain at Kimberley was a small club hill until the end of the fifties, when it expanded. The club first visited the hill in 1959. It would become a favourite.[233] The ski areas in the Okanagan Valley also started up operations at the end of the decade. More hills—Fernie, Panorama and West Castle—would become available in the near future and the bus tour really took off. The Whitefish trips had established a new tradition.

APRES-SKI

A trip to Whitefish was a social occasion as well as a ski trip, the bus ride down one long party. A good dance or party remained a big part of the club for many members of the CSC and part of the glue that held the club together. Calgary's nightlife hadn't improved much over what was on tap in the 1930s. The club social was a great place for young, single adults to meet, dance and have some fun with like-minded souls.

The Al Ahzar Temple on 17th Avenue and 4th Street SW was the club's meeting place for meetings for most of the 1950s. An impromptu sing-song or some dancing sometimes accompanied club business and there were showings of the ever-popular ski movies. One addition to the social calendar was the fashion show. Held near the beginning of the season for fun and a little fundraising, members of the club modelled the latest in ski and apres-ski clothing. The local shops also brought down the latest ski gear for everyone to salivate over, and there might be a talk on equipment or some technical subject like waxing. Started in the early 1950s, the fashion show became an annual affair, a precursor to the new ski season.

The club had one or two dances a month during the fall and winter, leading up to the formal banquet and ball at season's end. The Bowness Country Club remained a favourite location for the CSC's bigger parties. For a while in the late 1940s, the club even had its own orchestra, the Ski Doodlers. Ozzie LaRue remembers it consisted of piano, accordion, clarinet and banjo. The band was popular, with white music stands and the CSC symbol on the back.

The Al Azhar Temple served well enough for meetings, but the club still felt a need for something more permanent. The development of the Bowness Hill was stalled, so the club looked for a downtown meeting place, with room for an office and a lounge, where members could drop in at any time.[234] A perfect opportunity turned up when the Calgary Tennis Club ran out of money for its new headquarters at 15th Avenue and 16th Street SW. The ski club and the tennis club worked out a deal to share the building, which was perfect considering each had a seasonal focus. The tennis club got money from the CSC allowing it to finish off the building and the CSC got use of ample quarters, with space for an office. The social set demanded the purchase of a piano and a PA system while a record player was donated in short order.[235] Vic Binnie, the social director on council, even suggested installing lights over the dance floor—thus anticipating disco by more than a decade. A well-attended weekly dance social was started on Thursday nights. The tennis club would be the club's base for almost a decade, but the dream of a permanent clubhouse lived on.

GRUMBLINGS AND RUMBLINGS

It is easy, in describing the club's activities and accomplishments, to present a picture of an organization going from strength to strength. But the decades after the war were not untroubled. After reaching a high point in the first part of the 1950s, the club suffered several hard years when membership dropped off drastically. The commitment to things like racing noticeably faltered before rebounding near the end of the decade. But even in the good years, there were rumblings from inside the club about member apathy and increasing tension about what direction the CSC was taking.

Nigel Dunn, the 1948 president and *Herald* reporter, certainly worried about a decline in club spirit. He was disappointed with the turnout of volunteers to help with the Municipal Hill and didn't hesitate to say so in his column. Praising the outgoing 1951 president, football player Harry Hood, Dunn wrote, "Harry's job was a tough one, mainly because, like other CSC presidents, he had the support of only a few persons willing to work voluntarily for the benefit of skiing in this city." Tough words but Peter Cooper expressed similar sentiments in regards to the Bowness Hill. "Those that shout the loudest you will invariably find are those that have done the least towards making Bowness or any other venture of the CSC a success."[236] Joy Van Wagner also took the membership to task, saying in 1956, "Apathy has replaced enthusiasm. There just isn't any of the old community spirit left."

It wasn't just the club's journalists who were unimpressed with the membership's commitment. Malcolm Cullen put it very bluntly in his 1959/60 president's message:

> Your council has worked long and hard this past summer, and we hope you will enjoy some noticeable improvements during the coming season. We could, however, have done much more if even a small percentage of the members had given us their much needed assistance. Similarly, our work would have been better directed if more of you had taken the trouble to attend council meetings to make known your desires.[237]

Considering that Cullen and his council were acclaimed due to lack of candidates for council, one can understand his feelings.

Apathy was one concern, but some members also worried about the entire direction of the club. The ski columns reported that people thought that the CSC was turning into a purely social club, where members cared more about parties and dances than the business of promoting the sport. These accusations probably were near to the mark. Skiing for most people was recreation. Not everyone had a missionary zeal about the sport. Many members were likely interested in the benefits they received from the club over a higher purpose. The CSC also attained its large following through membership drives and many newcomers were no doubt there mainly for the perks. In the 1930s, skiers felt the need to organize in order to grow the sport. Now it was growing fine all on its own. Most skiers were probably not in the club to work for the betterment of skiing. They were there to have fun.

Ultimately, it is difficult to say to what degree the complaints reflected major problems in the club, and to what degree it merely reflected the grumbling inherent in any volunteer organization. Most recreational clubs and societies probably tend to have a core membership who dominate the executive and do most of the work, supported by a small number of keen volunteers.[238] Part of the problem for the CSC may have been the fluctuations in its membership. When the membership was large, such as in the rapid growth of the late 1940s, the club seemed impersonal to some members, but when it was too small, nothing got done. The CSC was also at the mercy of the elements: a poor snow year meant a decline in numbers and also the commitment of members. The club faltered in the poor snow years in the middle of the 1950s—membership in January 1954 stood at a paltry 209, a far cry from a claimed 1,000 four years before. This drop clearly impacted projects like the Bowness Hill. At the annual general meeting for 1958, coming off another terrible snow year, the club couldn't field a quorum. And most skiers would agree that lack of snow makes one inclined to surliness.

THE CALGARY SKI CLUB ANNUAL

Ironically, given the complaints about apathy and selfishness among the membership, the club ended the 1950s on a high. Several energetic councils worked hard to get the club on a firmer footing. Although the Bowness project never panned out, the membership increased again, the club's racing program had new energy and the CSC ran a variety of trips for the recreational skier. The 1960 club budget reached the $10,000 level, nearly four times higher than a decade earlier.[239] Nothing symbolized this success more than the Calgary Ski Club Annual.

Modelled on the old Canadian Ski Yearbook and Canadian Ski Annuals CASA put out before the war, the ski club annuals were attractive booklets complete with photographs, informative articles about the club, skiing in general and advertising. The club had produced an ambitious newsletter, Ski Tips, in the late forties. The annuals, however, were a celebration of the club that complemented a new monthly newsletter, Ski News and Dos, and set the tone for each new ski year. Jay Joffe was recruited to council because of his advertising and publicity background and would be president in 1958. He remembers the annuals were part of a comprehensive reform of how the club was reaching the public and the membership. He served as advertising editor on the first edition in 1957, with Peter Cooper, the *Albertan* ski writer, as the general editor.

More club spirit: the ski club annual. (COURTESY PETER COOPER.)

The *Herald*'s ski columnist, Joy Van Wagner, greeted the annual with mock dismay, asking rhetorically what she could possibly write about, when the annual said it all. The publication was successful in creating club spirit—almost any member of the fifties' vintage remembers the annuals with pride. Put out in the fall, the magazine chronicled the club's previous season and laid out the program for the coming winter, including the race and social schedules. It paid for itself with advertising. The annual, which entailed a tremendous amount of work, was published for five years, from 1957 to 1961, before it finally petered out. It captured a great deal of the Calgary Ski Club's spirit in the golden age.

Into the Future

With the end of the 1959/60 season, the Calgary Ski Club was 25 years old. As the fifties drew to a close, the organization was to all appearances healthier than ever. True to the intention of its founders, the CSC had promoted skiing in a splendid public spirit. The ski patrol, the guides unit, the *Herald* Ski School, and the Bowness Hill were all examples of the club's hard work on behalf of Calgary skiers. It was still the only ski club in the city. As more than one member put it, almost everyone who was serious about skiing belonged to the Calgary Ski Club.

The fun and enthusiasm that the ski trains embodied was part of a golden age coming to an end. Challenges waited in the next decade. The skiing scene was growing and fragmenting and it soon would no longer be possible for the Calgary Ski Club to be the club for all skiers. The CSC would start the 1960s with dissension and schism and end it on the verge of crisis, but in between reach new heights of size and influence. Like so many things in the 1960s, the passage of a turbulent decade would transform the Calgary Ski Club.

CHAPTER FIVE

Movers and Shakers

SCHISM—FREEZE—RACING—TRAFFORD—
OLYMPICS—LOBBYING—RECREATION—CLUB
HOUSES—POWDER—SHELTER—KID'S STUFF—
STORM CLOUDS

The Calgary Ski Club council meeting on September 21, 1961 was not pretty. John Newman, the technical director, introduced a motion censuring club president Peter O'Neill for his actions arising from a dispute with Canadian Amateur Ski Association officials. At the Sunwapta Slalom race in May, a CASA official had disqualified two competitors skiing for the CSC on the grounds that as instructors, they were professionals.[240] The two were given a one-year ban in August. O'Neill remonstrated with CASA and later sent a letter demanding reinstatement for the CSC competitors and an apology. O'Neill was not popular among the racers in the club. "He was a funny guy," remembers one club member. "He could barely ski." The president did not consult with Newman or anyone else in the racing crowd. They felt the president had been abusive, out of line and had exceeded his power. It was time for a showdown.

Newman's resolution was voted down. He and four other directors promptly resigned. Shortly afterward, Newman, Gordon Littke, John Robertson and a few others formed a new club, Skimeisters. The Calgary Ski Club had experienced its first schism. The new club focused entirely on racing, particularly juniors. There would be no parties, no club hill, no bus trips, just racing and more racing. The Skimeisters planned to find 40 or 50 promising kids between the ages of eight and 12 and produce a Calgarian ski racer for the 1968 Olympic team.[241] Other important CSC members, like Malcolm Cullen and the Russells, switched clubs. Yet in no time, the CSC had its own junior race team, taking on their rivals, the Skimeisters, at races across the province.

The 1960s had started with a bang, and it would be a dynamic decade for Calgary Ski Club. A club of mostly young, single adults at the end of the fifties became a club of families and youngsters by the end of the sixties. Demographics and the club's efforts to promote education played a role in the change, but so did racing. The growing popularity of alpine ski racing attracted a group of keen supporters to the club, many well heeled, who wanted their kids involved in a glamorous sport. They were movers and shakers who were involved in initiatives like Olympic bids. They created a business-like atmosphere in the club and promoted the sport with vigour. And the CSC remained an important part of the local scene. When Cliff White, the new owner of Sunshine, realized that he had enough snow in early November to open, he immediately went to Calgary to make the announcement—and the first people he told were the Calgary Ski Club.[242]

THE SCHISM

The new decade did not start on a good note. There was a growing restlessness among Calgary skiers. Not everyone was happy with the CSC. Another tiff with the Calgary Mountain Club, not quite as serious, preceded the Skimeisters crisis. Ron Smylie was a CSC member and an avid mountaineer—he climbed Mt. Logan with Hans Gmoser—and later owner of the Alpine Hut ski store. He wanted an alternative to the stuffy Alpine Club for hiking, backpacking and mountaineering in the summer and founded the Calgary Mountain Club in 1960. A number of people in the new club, like Graham and Peter Cooper, Max Wolfe and Mike Voelcker were also members of the CSC. Thanks to Voelcker, editor of ski club Annual, there was a short article on the new club in the 1960 edition.

The Calgary Mountain Club was also keen on skiing. The new club's emphasis was ski mountaineering and Nordic-style ski touring, which few people in the Calgary Ski Club were still doing. The CMC emphasized that it wanted to complement the ski club, not compete with it. The article in the annual did not amuse the executive of the CSC, however. The council asked Voelcker to either quit as club publicity chairman or drop his membership in the Calgary Mountain Club.[243] The demand caused some hard feelings, and was much ado about nothing. The CMC affiliated with CASA and organized its own race, the famous Sunwapta Slalom. It was held on the May long weekend, but was more of a party than a serious event. The CMC was also much more a mountaineering club than a skiing club and hard-core climbers soon dominated.[244]

The schism that produced the Skimeisters was much more serious. The actual event that set things in motion, the dispute at the Sunwapta Slalom race, was trivial but it tapped into a well of discontent over the racing program. The non-racing members, often called the "social set," were not interested in spending money or time on racing. The keen racers didn't think the club was doing enough. Skimeisters was an expression of their ambitions. The new club was intended to stay small, essentially a group of adults keen to support and help coach the youngsters, though they inevitably became involved in some adult races. To find their promising group of juniors, the club made arrangements to start a ski school at Happy Valley, along the lines of the *Herald* Ski School program, aimed at a younger age group. The schism produced some hard feelings on both sides. When the Calgary Ski Club started its own new junior racing program, there was quite a rivalry between the two clubs.

The Skimeisters was the first time that a splinter group had broken away from the Calgary Ski Club to form another club.[245] But new organizations started appearing. By the end of the decade, there were four other active skiing clubs in Calgary, and the CSC would never again be the sole voice of the city's skiers. The two largest were the Foothills Nordic Ski Club, devoted to Nordic ski racing, and the Petroleum Ski Club, dedicated to recreational skiing. The new clubs were focused on one facet of skiing, unlike the CSC. The Calgary ski scene expanded and also fragmented. And increasingly, skiers didn't join any club. Rather, they skied on their own.

THE FREEZE YEARS

The Skimeisters affair was hard on the CSC's morale and membership took a pummeling. The club needed to reverse the tide. Enter Bob Freeze. The reappearance of Bob Freeze in the Calgary Ski Club marked the beginning of the 1960s. He had dropped out of skiing to coach the Calgary Broncs junior football team, but wanted to return to the sport and rejoined the club. Now a mature businessman, Freeze was heavily involved in community causes, especially the Calgary Booster Club. He knew how to make things happen.

Ironically, given the whole Skimeisters debacle, his strategy to turn the club around was to focus on junior racing.

Freeze became president of the club mostly by default. Peter O'Neill had recruited him in 1961 to fill the position of vice president, which was vacant. As Freeze recalls, "It was not very legitimate. I wasn't nominated, and I didn't stand for the position with the membership." O'Neill was transferred to New York for business. Freeze, as his vice president, took over the executive and then served again as president the next year. The club soon showed renewed energy. The enthusiasm was not just due to Freeze, but he helped inspire it. One way he did this was by recruiting talented people from both within and without the CSC to take over programs.

True to his booster club ethos, Freeze's goal right from the outset was to revitalize the racing program. It was focused almost entirely on juniors with the ultimate aim of producing Olympic-calibre Calgary ski racers.[246] (Which, of course, was exactly what the Skimeisters had formed to do!) As Freeze says now, "I've always been involved in competition. I believe in it." Ski racing, especially junior level, was clearly the flavour of the time. The Banff Ski Runners (as the Ski Runners of the Canadian Rockies came to be called) jumped on the bandwagon in the 1960s. The Edmonton Ski Club had a big junior program—it's CASA race fees were larger than those of the rest of the province's clubs combined.[247] Freeze thought that the three local clubs would provide a competitive environment to encourage excellence. Just a year after the hard-core racing enthusiasts split away from the CSC, the club was back in the business of promoting competition. The motto: "A Calgarian in the 1968 Olympics."

Unlike the Skimeisters, however, Freeze and his supporters did not want to reduce the CSC to a specialist club. For one thing, the membership at large would never stand for it. As Freeze recalls, support for racing was limited, not just in the CSC but the other general purpose clubs: "I don't think the club members generally wanted to spend anything on racing."[248] He realized, however, that a large and powerful club could support racing while still appealing to pleasure skiers. And Freeze, along with many other members, still believed in the need of a club to promote the general interests of local skiers, and efforts to revamp the club were not just restricted to competition. The goal was 2,000 members.[249] The emphasis on racing proved a very effective way to rally the club.

Freeze also made a few suggestions for changes to the club constitution to strengthen the council. The most important extended the term for the officers of the club (president, vice-president, treasurer and secretary) to two years from one.[250] This was intended to create more continuity. He also wanted to do away with nominations to council from the floor at the annual general meeting; instead, a nominating committee would pick candidates. A smaller quorum made it easier to get meetings together and the limit for council's discretionary expenditures was raised to $1,000. These suggestions gave the council more power and stability and made its work easier. The changes also recognized that the members were generally leaving it up to council to run the show.

The club pulled out all the stops to increase the membership. Ideas ranged from stuffing club flyers in shopping bags at Safeway to putting them on windshields in parking lots around town and in the mountains. One councillor suggested that council members recruit as many people as possible within their respective professions. The goal was ambitious. One other lasting contribution Freeze made to the club was a new crest. Designer Brian Maison created the signature symbol of the CSC for the sixties, the triangle with the buffalo head. Loved as well as hated, the crest was certainly distinctive and worn with pride.

THE CSC JUNIOR RACING TEAM

To get the club racing again, Freeze turned to Joe Irwin. A Calgary geologist, Irwin had been a junior racer for the club in the 1940s and competed at the collegiate level in the United States. Irwin remembers that, "It was all Bob Freeze's idea, he wanted there to still be racing in the club." When Freeze approached him, Irwin agreed to set up a new program. The original aim was to have as many members of the club involved in racing as possible—"We believe that participation in racing benefits skiers of all ages and abilities"—but the program quickly became dedicated to junior development. The emphasis was 10- to 14-year-olds, prime candidates for future Olympic glory. Irwin, with John Holland, Bill Ling, Isabel Elliot and other dedicated members, revitalized racing in the CSC.

The *Herald* Ski School was the recruitment ground for the racing program. In the first year, 1961/62, the club aimed to start training a group of 75 youngsters, covering midget to Junior A. A junior race team of 10 to 12 would be chosen from the group. Initially, Irwin, Holland, another talented former racer, Bill Ling and other volunteers did the coaching. They soon decided to

The Juniors, 1964. Top, l-r: Annette Barrington, Reto Barrington, Billy Trafford, Bill Strain, Mike Muir, Joe Irwin, Harry Lovett. Bottom, l-r: Allen Straum, Rick Cooper, Geoff Trafford, Stephanie Sloan. (CSC COLLECTION.)

hire a professional coach to augment their efforts. Their choice was Doug Robinson of Banff. Robinson had coached Scott and Wayne Henderson, who were two of Canada's early stars in international racing. The move served notice that the club meant business.

Paying for these ambitions was a challenge. The club finances were not particularly strong, and racing was not cheap. Robinson alone was $1,600 for four months of work. The racing budget for the second year, 1963/64, was a whopping $2,800, which represented 72 per cent of the club's expenditures. Travel expenses, lift tickets and CASA fees all took a sizable chunk. To pay for the coach, Freeze approached the Calgary Booster Club for a donation, using the Olympics angle. Club events also became direct fundraisers for the team—the 1963 fashion show was billed as support to get a Calgarian to the Games.

Another difficulty was keeping a coach. A professional in Banff was a crucial part of the program. The CSC coaches, however, tended to be young and often moved onto other things. They also had a way of getting hurt. Robinson had a crash the first season and was out of commission. George Paris, of the Banff family, replaced him the next year, but George also crashed partway through the season and broke his leg, so his assistance was limited. Ted Clark of Banff took over from Paris and lasted a couple of years. Later in the sixties, the club had some success with Wolfgang Ehnman, a young German immigrant, but lost him to the ski school at the new Snowridge Resort in Kananaskis. He died tragically in an airplane crash not long after. It was enough to think the program had a curse hanging over it.

One part of the racing program was early season conditioning, dry-land training in a gym. The club had done conditioning with racers in the fifties. In the intervening years, it had become a standard part of training for competition. Although run initially for the junior racers, the training stirred a great deal of interest in the adult skiers in the club. For the 1963/64 season, conditioning was offered to all club members. It was established as a regular CSC offering, a positive spin-off for the non-competitors in the club. School gyms were rented to hold the classes. The Sunalta School was a popular location for several years. The club's program was so successful that the Calgary

Ski conditioning for CSC kids, circa 1960s. (CSC COLLECTION.)

Continuing Education Department (known then as Adult Education) asked the CSC if it could run their ski-conditioning course in 1968. The club provided instructors and films for the city classes, reaping the benefits of good publicity and a chance to recruit for the club.[251] It was one of the first, but not the last, partnerships between the CSC and the City of Calgary. The Dry Ski School would be a part of the CSC's fall schedule from that point onward.

To create interest and support in the race program, the CSC also continued fun adult competition. The pin races were revived, in the charge of Miles Heseldin. The club moved the races out to Lake Louise, where they were held on the newly cut Olympic Ladies Downhill course. The races were a mixed success. Heseldin, however, caused quite a stir among race organizers in the province with an electronic timer he built for the races.[252] There were still the club championships, now run with the Mask-Ski-Raid costume event in March. The club also sponsored the Sir Norman Watson Downhill as well as two junior races.

Adult competition was not very robust within the club and quickly faded. The pin races were discontinued again after 1967 due to lack of interest. The Sir Norman Watson was passed on to the Lake Louise Ski Club. The club also stopped holding the summer races. The council told Ian Neilson that he could organize the Victoria Glacier race for 1964 "if he wanted to." John Holland recommended that the club drop the event in 1966, and the race was abandoned the next year. The Waterton race had already been discontinued. The Calgary Mountain Club persuaded the CSC to take over the Sunwapta Slalom in 1968, but the race only lasted for another year.

The Calgary Ski Club's junior racing program had better legs, continuing until the seventies. It was a serious affair and produced some success. One of its first stars was Randy McRoberts, who was Calgary's only Junior A racer in 1963 and touted as potential national team material.[253] In 1965, Harry Irving won the Junior C giant slalom at the prestigious Taschereau at Mt. Tremblant, the first time any westerner had won an event there. The club had drummed up enough money from local businesses to send seven skiers and the coach to Quebec for the races.[254] Bill Strain and Karen Taylor made the Alberta Junior Team. Taylor and McRoberts trained with the National Team at Kokanee Glacier in 1965.[255] Reto Barrington also aspired to the National Team and his sister Annette was one of the top junior girls in the country. The CSC can even claim Ken Read as an alumnus. When the Read family first moved to Calgary in the late 1960s, they joined the club. Ken and Gerry Read

Aggressive start: CSC racer Randy McRoberts. (CSC COLLECTION, PETER COOPER.)

were junior members and their parents Dee and Dr. John Read were racing volunteers. Dee Read also helped at the New and Used Ski Sale, and would play a role in its expansion.

The Calgary Ski Club never did place a Calgarian in the Olympics. Neither did the Skimeisters. Both clubs did play a role in establishing serious grassroots ski racing in Alberta.

The Ski Sale

One of the CSC's signature events is the New and Used Ski Sale. It is a lasting legacy of the junior racing program. The sale started as an equipment swap for parents of racing kids to get suitable gear without having to buy new stuff every year. It was not an entirely new idea. In 1948, the club had tried an equipment swap. Members were encouraged to bring their old gear to a meeting. "Following the regular program they'll be able to haggle and strike up bargains to their heart's content," the *Herald* reported. [256] "No deals have to be closed, but 'Joe Basher' might find that 'Stem Christie' has a pair of six-threes that will just suit his kid brother for Christmas." [257]

Parents quickly discovered a truth about ski racing: it is an expensive sport. Isabel Elliot, one of the members on the racing committee, heard their complaints and came up with a solution. In the fall of 1963, with the help of Jean Irwin and Betty Cooper, she set up a gear swap at the Calgary Tennis Club. [258] People bartered exchanges for their gear. The racing parents loved the swap, and it was an instant success. The organizers also discovered that there was a market for used goods among skiers in general. People did not necessarily want to do a swap, but they wanted to buy used gear and also sell their old stuff.

The club held the swap again, but made a crucial change of format. The swap became a consignment sale of used equipment. The club charged a 10 per cent commission to handle the goods. Jean Robb took over the event from Elliot, who had moved to Vancouver. The used ski equipment sale was held at the Medical Dental Building on the edge of downtown Calgary. Robb asked Norm Russell and the Comptons for help. They examined the gear people brought in to make sure it was safe to sell and to help set prices. The event went off in early October and the response was gratifying. Hundreds of people lined up the block to get in. Over a thousand dollars in sales were racked up. The revenue mostly covered expenses and the club's profit was small, but clearly the CSC was on to something.

The next year the club pulled out all the stops. The sale moved to the Agricultural Building on the Exhibition and Stampede grounds, and turned into a full-blown ski fair. The club invited local retailers and ski areas to set up booths and show off their merchandise. There were ski films and the club fashion show. A small admission was charged at the entrance and added to the proceeds. The highlight of the show was the demonstration ramp borrowed from the Hudson's Bay Company department store. It was a small portable indoor ski slope, on which ski techniques could be shown. The event got longer—one day now stretched to two and a half. The following year over 3,000 people came to the renamed Calgary Ski Club Ski Fair. More importantly, the club began to make some money out of the sale. In 1967, $18,000 in equipment changed hands and the profit after expenses for the CSC was $1,000, a significant sum at that time.[259]

The sale was growing faster than the club could handle. At the 1967 edition, Jean Robb remembers that she was afraid someone was going to get hurt in the crush at the doors on opening night. There was also a surprising amount of theft. One sale worker, Art Patterson, recalls, "It never occurred to us that people would peel a price tag off, take one off a cheaper item and put it on." Prices were painted on instead. Jean Robb says with a laugh that it was a status symbol to have gear with the painted numbers. It meant you got a good deal at the sale.

An innovation then and tradition now: the ski sale, circa 1967. (CSC COLLECTION.)

It was clear that the club volunteers needed help. So, for 1968, the CSC turned to an outfit with lots of experience in crowd control: the Canadian Ski Patrol System. As a not-for-profit organization, the volunteer ski patrol was always interested in raising money and leapt at the chance to help at the sales. Patrollers assessed the consigned gear, looking for unsafe equipment, and looked after security and crowd control. In return they got a share in the profits from the fair and sale. In 1970, the club and the patrol came to a new arrangement. The patrol took over organizing the Ski Fair while still providing overall security for the event, giving the CSC a share of the gate and picking up half the costs for sale and show.[260]

In 1970 the club also added the last element: the clothing sale. Dee Read had been an enthusiastic volunteer for the CSC and the sale. After the Reads switched to the Lake Louise Ski Club, she approached Jean Robb with a suggestion. The LLSC could set up a clothing consignment sale to complement the hard goods.[261] The ski club and the ski patrol were both amenable to the idea, and the clothing sale was born as an adjunct to the ski sale. The Lake Louise club agreed to pay a percentage of their revenue to the Ski Fair.

By the end of the decade, the Ski Fair and Sale had become a sizeable enterprise. Amazingly, except for a few security people, volunteers ran and staffed the whole show. Over a hundred people participated in setting up, running and taking down the show and handling the consigned merchandise, a far cry from the "seven friends" who helped Robb with her first sale. "It was a very social thing," remembers one of those seven, Jean MacNaughton. There was, however, a bit of a learning curve. Robb recalls that in the early years, at the end of the sale, she would take the proceeds home and put them under her pillow for the night. Finally, Ethan Compton told her, "Jean, you can't do that, somebody is going to knock you off." She then took the money to the safe at Premier and finally started using night deposits.

Since its founding, the used equipment sale has continued to grow year by year with only the occasional setback, becoming an enduring part of the CSC. And while the money's always nice, the sale was founded on the principle of serving the skiing community, a principle that has kept it going for the last 40 years. The sale has its imitators—Elliot started up a version after moving to Vancouver—but the CSC-CSPS New and Used Ski Sale was the original. The club claims that it is the largest volunteer run event of its kind in North America.

Party Time

A club aiming for 2,000 members had to be a club people wanted to join. To attract young adults, who made up a large percentage of skiers, Freeze realized that good parties were a necessity. In the turmoil following the schism, attendance at social events fell off. A memo from the social director for the 1962/63 season lamented that the club's dances "are not well attended." Only a year or two before, the club had popular weekly socials at the tennis club with mostly singles and young couples. To get those people back, the club injected a real spark of life into its social side with something new and different: dances in Banff.

Through the 1950s, Banff was a real no-man's land in winter. There wasn't much to do or many places to stay. Hans Ockermuller remembers that the Brewster Block had about the only low-cost accommodations in town, old dormitories for Brewster bus drivers. A strict older woman ran the building. There were no parties and there was a strict segregation of gender. The situation was unchanged in the new decade. Peter and Betty Cooper remember walking down Banff Avenue one New Year's eve in the early sixties. The only soul in sight was a lone drunk, who called out, "Happy New Year's to the missus and the kid," before staggering off. "Banff was very subdued at that time," recalls Jean MacNaughton. "A lot of the Banff residents didn't see the potential in skiing, and we were almost a nuisance to them. We got the feeling they wanted to close down and relax. There was nothing to do in the evenings but go to the Cascade Hotel bar and drink beer." Now that people travelled to Banff by car instead of train, they didn't need to dash to the station to get back to Calgary. The time had come for some nightlife in Banff.

Bob Freeze was the instigator. He asked Jean Robb, who would later run the ski sale, to be social director and take on the job of organizing the dances. She exceeded all expectations. Her first challenge was finding a suitable location. Robb settled on Phil's Pancake House. Phil's was a new establishment and eager to build up a clientele. Liquor licenses were still hard to come by for restaurants, so that was something the club could provide. The tea dances, which started around 4:30 and ran until 8 or 9, were an immediate success. Over a hundred people would fill Phil's. The dances got quite raucous—Jean remembers partygoers literally dancing on the tables. Admission was a $1.50 for the general public and 50¢ for club members, and there was a band. The dances were so popular that even the Skimeisters came.

Eventually Phil, who wasn't selling many pancakes to the partying skiers,

Let's dance: CSC skiers party, 1963. (Whyte Museum of the Canadian Rockies, V190 I A III-2, Bruno Engler.)

turfed them out. The dances moved over to the Banff Legion Hall and ran there for several years before finally running out of steam. Jean recalls that the local RCMP would come by and check them out, and there was sometimes a scramble to usher underage juniors out the back door. The dances also had their desired effect of building up the membership. One straw poll suggested that more than half the single members of the club were joining to go to the parties in Banff.

When the Legion became old news, the club moved the dances to the new Timberline Lodge, just off the road to Mt. Norquay. They were a little more formal than the tea dances, yet still drew crowds. The Timberline dances started on a monthly basis in the 1964/65 season, but were so popular that they became a weekly event. Even with a band—the Moonglows were lasting favourites—the Timberline dances generally turned a profit. The only drawback was that dances and socials held in Calgary, outside major events like the Final Fling or the Ski Ball, suffered in competition with the Banff parties.

Not every social event was a dance. There was fun on snow as well. The Mass-Ski-Raid Giant Fun Race, despite the ponderous title, was one of the club's crazier events. Held at Norquay, it was a Mardi Gras-style costume event.[262] It included a special Sadie Hawkins race where the gals chased guys down the hill. All the local clubs were invited. Even the dour Walter Fisher, owner of Norquay, reduced rates on the lifts for those in costume. CFAC Radio provided sponsorship and members of the Calgary Stampeders football team attended. At the end of the day, everyone repaired to the Legion hall in Banff for a party.

The social skiers also enjoyed the club's regular bus tours. The trips to Whitefish had established the tradition in the fifties. There were now more destinations available. Jaunts to Marmot, Kimberley and even Kamloops and the Okanagan became very popular, and the club usually had two or three a year. The out-of-town trips also got longer. Some weeklong adventures were organized, with the club looking at possibly chartering a flight to Europe for skiing.[263] This never quite got off the ground, so to speak, but it reflected the club's ambitions. Of the out-of-town destinations, Kimberley was particularly popular. It was a community hill and had a real small-town atmosphere. Art Patterson remembers that a cantankerous old Scot, who knew all the local skiers, ran the hill. If he saw anyone skiing recklessly, he would single them out over the PA system in his thick highland brogue: "Johnny, yer skiing much too fast for your ability. Slow down or I'll have yer parents collect ye."

Ski tourists: bus tour to Vernon, B.C., circa 1960s. (CSC COLLECTION, VERNON CHAMBER OF COMMERCE.)

The Calgarians always felt particularly at home in Kimberley—the locals would invariably arrange a party for Friday night to welcome the ski club bus. The trips to Kelowna and Vernon were a bit more gruelling. Like Whitefish, the bus left after work on Friday and arrived in the early hours of Saturday morning. The bus ride, however, was usually part of the fun. The beer and wineskins emerged once the bus left Calgary and there would be singing until people began to nod off. It was a great way to meet people. Jean Robb remembers one shy New Zealander, a newcomer to the city. "By the end of the trip, he knew all 35 people. It was an introduction to Calgary."

Despite their success, the bus trips were dropped for a year in middle of the decade, and though resumed, never had quite the same vibrancy. It reflected the club's increasing shift towards children and racing, which would have some major consequences.

The Trafford Years

Bob Freeze laid the groundwork for a revitalized club. Another dynamic president, Ted Trafford, followed him. An oil company executive, Trafford brought his talents as a businessman to the club's leadership. He had a large family with several keen skiers, and was drawn to the club's racing program. Trafford and Freeze were not the only movers and shakers to join the club in the early sixties. There were a number of professionals and business people, many associated with the petroleum industry, to be found in the club. Some went on to prominent careers, like Peter Valentine, later Auditor General of Alberta. Thanks to oil and gas, Calgary had become a prosperous, white-collar city and many organizations boasted members who went on to great things. The ski club, however, certainly had its share.

Although Freeze had put things in motion, the club's future remained uncertain. His ambitious goal of 2,000 members had not been reached. The racing program was also expensive. As Freeze put it bluntly, the club was going broke.[264] There were questions within the club about where it was going. Was the CSC a social club for young adults who skied, or was it a racing club, or was it a family club? In the spring of 1963, as ski season drew to a close, the club council had a two-week debate about the CSC's direction and the options open to the club.

The executive was equally split into two camps: a small club dedicated to racing and a big club dedicated to racing.[265] Freeze had been unduly pessimistic about the level of support in the club for a racing program. A survey of the membership in 1963 showed a high level of approval of the club's efforts and willingness to spend some money on racing.[266] The question was how to pursue it. Ted Trafford had the most ambitious vision. He argued for a big club with prominent members in the community on the board. The big club would have the influence to lobby for better ski areas, push for innovations like season's tickets and support a clubhouse and a racing team competing across Canada. Joe Irwin and John Holland both agreed with the big club, believing it would be easier to support a racing program that way.

Other councillors, however, felt equally passionate about the small club. Hans Maciej argued that a small club would be much easier to run, with an "esprit de corps." A number of councillors agreed with him. Freeze initially declared for a big club, but then changed his mind. For one thing, he presciently thought that private enterprise like the ski areas and bus companies would soon provide many of the services the CSC offered. Big clubs, he argued, were needed in places like Edmonton and Ottawa to provide a local ski hill. That wasn't true of Calgary. One thing nearly everyone agreed on was that the CSC needed to have a clubhouse to call its own, to give the club a meeting place and more identity.

CSC president Ted Trafford.
(GLENBOW ARCHIVES, PA-2351-68.)

The big club proponents won the day. Freeze stepped down as president after one and a half terms — he would soon leave for a decade in Vancouver — and Ted Trafford replaced him. The Calgary Ski Club continued on the course already charted, to be a big, general-purpose ski club that supported an excellent racing program for juniors. It pursued this agenda with new energy and vigour.

With Trafford at the helm, the affairs of council took on a brisk business-like air. The new president immediately showed his executive training with curt memos delegating tasks to his councillors. One of the first things the new council did was hire a secretary for the club, to help manage the club's affairs during the winter. Lois Warren was the first to fill this position.

Along with Warren came an office, initially donated, but the club later rented quarters in the Lancaster building for a number of years. The club now at least had an administrative headquarters, which would be invaluable as it set to work.

Dreams of Olympic Glory

The dream of a Winter Olympics in Banff was one that captivated skiers, sport fans and civic booster alike. In 1955, members of the Calgary Booster Club decided, after California's Squaw Valley landed the 1960 Olympic Winter Games, that Calgary would be a shoo-in. A group that included Ernie McCullough, Ed Davis, Peter Lougheed and Hans Maciej founded the Calgary Olympic Development Association. CODA submitted three bids: an exploratory attempt in 1964, a serious bid for 1968 and a final effort for 1972. The last bid failed amid bitter rumours that Avery Brundage, the IOC president, had personally opposed it. After the final disappointment, CODA went dormant until 1979, when another group from the Booster Club revived the dream.

The Calgary Ski Club was quite interested in the Olympic bids and had strong connections to CODA. Soon after CODA was organized, the club ran a fundraising slalom race out at Norquay. The Olympic bid fit in well with the CSC's mandate to promote the sport. A successful bid would almost certainly mean bigger and better ski facilities around Banff, where most of the events would be held. The booster element of the club, people like Bob Freeze, felt the Olympics must be a fundamental part of the club's goals. Freeze put it directly in his 1962 president's report. The CSC aimed to be: "A ski club which can assist the Calgary Olympic Development Committee in its efforts to obtain the 1968 Olympic Games for Canada."[267]

Freeze was a member of CODA. The ski club's main contribution to the movement was as a recruiting and training ground for the Olympic organization. Bob Reid, formerly of the club, was the chairman of the organizing committee for the 1960 North American Nordic Championships, which CODA used as a warm-up event. Reid was the technical advisor for the first 1964 bid. Gord Patterson, CSC vice-president in 1960–61, joined Reid on the technical committee. Jay Joffe, club president for 1957–59, worked on the publicity committee. Gordon Pogue, who operated a gym and wrote articles on fitness for the ski annual, was CODA president in 1960. Ted Trafford later joined and became events director. Peter Cooper, Malcolm Cullen, Norm

The swinging sixties: an accurate representation of the CSC end of year party
(COURTESY JEAN MACNAUGHTON)

Russell—the list goes on. But no one in the CSC was more involved than Hans Maciej. A former competitive runner, Maciej was a founding member of CODA and would spend two years as director of Olympic 72.

Maciej wrote a long article for the 1961 Ski Annual that articulated his thoughts regarding the CSC's involvement in the 1968 Olympics. The club's members would be the workhorse volunteers. Women could look after the reception centre at the airport and act as hostesses at official events and as secretaries and assistants to IOC members. The men would be gatekeepers, course wardens and other minor race officials. Maciej wanted to set up a training program, with compensation, to encourage members to volunteer at local ski tournaments and gain experience. And there were, of course, the many unglamorous jobs the club could do, like providing drivers and guides. It sounds much like the volunteer work for the 1988 Winter Games.

The Calgary Ski Club was not, however, an integral part of the Olympic bids. It mostly provided moral support. The CSC wasn't in a position to provide financial assistance. It did have some fundraising events to raise money for the National Ski Team, and lent the Foothills Nordic Ski Club $500 to send two racers to international competitions. Along with the other ski clubs, the CSC providing access to its mailing list for CODA membership drives. The club scheduled a social event, a Mardi Gras party, to coincide with the visit of some international journalists. And the CSC led a protest to the local media over the poor coverage of the 1964 Olympics, both as a matter of interest to skiers and to support the Calgary bids. Maciej was made the CODA representative on council to keep the club up to date on developments.

All in all, the direct contributions of the CSC to the Olympic movement were not extensive. This is not to say that the members were not interested. Far from it: Olympic fever gripped the club. Jean MacNaughton recalls that, even though only a few people in the club were heavily involved in the bid itself, skiers in general were very excited. "There was a feeling that it would be wonderful to have the Games, and have a chance to see all the world-class skiers compete." A big party was planned in January, 1964 at the Danish-Canadian Club for the announcement of the 1968 bid winner. Ted Trafford would telephone from Rome and let the ski club know if the bid was a success. MacNaughton remembers that Jeannie Robb was designated to take the call. "We would either cry in our beer, which we did, unfortunately, or celebrate." Sadly, two years later, the club had salty beer again when the 1972 bid went down in flames.

THE BATTLE FOR BANFF

Disappointed Olympic supporters blamed conservationists for the loss of the Games in Banff. A growing environmental movement strongly opposed the bids, especially the last one. A campaign of letters and petitions, including threats to disrupt the Games with protests, influenced the IOC's decision. The controversy over the Olympics was part of a much larger fight over the future of Banff National Park, and one of the most contentious issues was the development of ski areas. The Calgary Ski Club, in the interest of its members and Calgary skiers in general, was right in the thick of the controversy.

The issue of development versus conservation in the national parks was not a small one. It directly affected skiing. The park administration, fairly and unfairly, came under great criticism for its policy towards the sport. In the early years, it was simple: under the "dual use" mandate for conservation and tourism Commissioner Harkin formulated in the 1930s, the Dominion Parks Branch encouraged skiing, like other things, meant for the amusement of tourists, such as golf. The park department aided and abetted the nascent ski industry. It cleared runs at government expense at Norquay and on Whitehorn Mountain at Lake Louise and built and rebuilt jumps on Norquay for competition. Into the 1960s, parks employees packed and groomed the snow on the slopes at Norquay and Lake Louise, for both races and pleasure skiing.

As visits to the parks mushroomed and tourist facilities multiplied in the 1950s, concern rose in the park administration and with the general public about development. After years of studying the situation, in 1964 the government formulated a new policy for the national parks. The policy complemented the Parks Act from the 1930s. It made conservation the first priority for national parks, but reaffirmed the idea that the parks existed for the public's benefit and enjoyment. The policy, however, spelled out that this meant, "the National Parks of Canada are 'sanctuaries of nature for the rest, relaxation and enjoyment of the public.'" The government wanted visitors to appreciate the parks as places of natural beauty and preserved wilderness, and not to expect them to be resorts. Hiking, bird watching, even touring in a car was acceptable; golf courses, amusement parks and bowling alleys were not.

Skiing presented a challenge and a puzzle to park authorities and their political masters. On one hand, skiing was a popular type of outdoor recreation that took place in the mountains and had a history in Banff. On the other hand, the increasingly mechanized character and scale of modern skiing struck many people as inappropriate for a place primarily preserved as wilderness. Skiing was arguably an end in itself—one came for the skiing, not for the natural beauty, and many people perceived the facilities as most unaesthetic. Pressure, however, was growing for the government to allow more skiing. Although skiers only accounted for 8 per cent of the visits to Banff National Park in the early 1960s, according to government statistics the sport was growing at a rate of up to 20 per cent a year.

The development of true ski resorts like Vail, founded in 1960, had also changed the rules of the game. A big problem for the lift operators around Banff was that their customers largely came from Calgary and Edmonton on the weekends so the hills were empty most of the week. When skiers complained about long lineups and lack of amenities like day lodges, the area owners told them that expanding lifts and clearing more runs for weekend traffic was not economical. The operators around Banff wanted to attract ski tourists who would come for a week or more, such as were going to Vail or to Europe. These skiers, however, expected certain amenities, like accommodations close to skiing and entertainment in the evenings. This positioned skiing as exactly the sort of activity the government was trying to discourage in the parks.

Area operators and local skiers chaffed under the restrictive regime in which they operated and recreated. Some people, like Jack McDowall, the manager of Lake Louise, were convinced the government was intentionally undermining ski resorts.[268] He had reason to feel that way. "In my view, the Parks should be retained as far as possible as natural areas confined to unsophisticated recreation and enjoyment that only a natural environment can provide. I do not feel that the Parks are the right place for highly sophisticated and elaborated activities and recreation, however desirable these may be in themselves," wrote Arthur Laing, minister of Northern Affairs and National Resources, in a letter to McDowall in 1963.[269] Pronouncements like this worried skiers that downhill skiing would soon have no place around Banff.

The Calgary Ski Club and Ted Trafford leapt right into the fray. Trafford

Too much? New Sunshine hotel, circa 1965. (CSC COLLECTION.)

defended the development of skiing "as a western Canadian businessman and an individual who believes in the value of outdoor sports and recreation in the general health of this country."[270] As avid skiers, the rank and file of the club was all for better hills and amenities in the mountain parks. The club soon got a chance to influence government policy. Realizing that it had touched a nerve over skiing, the government decided to review the entire winter sport situation in the parks. In 1963, it hired Richard Street and Canadian Resort Services to carry out a study of both the current state of the ski industry in Banff and its future growth, and make recommendations on how to manage it. One of Street's first stops was the Calgary Ski Club to distribute a questionnaire to the membership.[271] The club was happy to help and even offered to assist in tabulating the results. Street got back over 300 forms. He was clearly interested in what the club had to say because he then asked the CSC to prepare a brief with recommendations "regarding winter activities and facilities."[272]

Ben Barrington, Art Patterson and Terry Hawitt prepared the CSC brief presented to Street. The document made it abundantly clear that the club stood for more development. The brief stated that the park administration should, "Emphasize enjoyment and use of parks, as opposed to wilderness concept. Generally speaking, allow more development."[273] To this end, the club wanted to see a department for recreational development, to counterbalance what was seen as predominance of conservationists in the park administration.[274] The brief called for specific improvements to the different areas, such as full road access to Sunshine lodge, more intermediate terrain at Norquay, better lifts at Louise and better slope maintenance everywhere. The club also asked for new ski areas, possibly at Copper Mountain near Castle Junction on the Trans-Canada or at Bow Summit on the Banff-Jasper highway, a popular early-season destination.

The brief also addressed general concerns, such as allowing better facilities for after-ski entertainment, especially between the hours of 4 pm and 10 pm, accommodations convenient to the ski areas and more latitude for improvements. The three authors also wanted more support of the ski clubs, especially allowing construction of clubhouses and hostels in the parks. Joe Irwin added a separate brief on ski racing. It asked for more development of runs suitable for racing and some permanent infrastructure for competition like buried phone lines, good lift access, equipment storage and cheap accommodation for young racers competing and training around Banff.

Aside from the briefs, Street also held numerous discussions with Trafford and members of his council.[275] Street later wrote to thank the club, specifically for the survey where the members "helped immeasurably."[276] He also made no bones about the fact he was including many CSC suggestions in the master plan that he was preparing for the government. A *Calgary Herald* editorial would note that at a meeting of the Banff Chamber of Commerce, Street had given a speech that was strongly in favour of developing winter sports as a means to attract tourists. One of the points the columnist took exception to was that Street "stressed the need for organizing activities to keep park visitors happy between 4 pm and 10 pm"—exactly as Patterson, Hawitt and Barrington had suggested.

Trafford, a man of the world, knew that briefs and protest letters were not enough. He assiduously courted Arthur Laing, the minister of Indian and Northern Affairs, as well as Laing's assistant, Jack Austin. Calgary Ski Club letterhead frequently crossed the desk of powerful federal cabinet ministers. Trafford argued forcefully on behalf of the club's goals, but he was quick to praise some of the government's actions and to moderate his stance on some issues. Calls for Vail-style resorts were transformed into a request for "low cost accommodations suitable for families." The CSC also hastened to support the preservation of wilderness, asking only that a few areas good for skiing be zoned for development. Laing responded with assurances that his department was not hostile to improving ski facilities, but merely wished to do it in a controlled manner. Trafford made sure to invite Laing to speak to the CSC at the Timberline Lodge to explain the government's policy, and Laing appreciated the courtesy and the opportunity. The tone between the two became almost chummy. After announcing his department's new policy towards skiing in March, 1965, Laing opened the Beehive Race at Lake Louise and joked to Trafford that he should have pre-run the course.[277]

The pressure that the Calgary Ski Club, the ski hill operators, Banff and Lake Louise businessmen, CODA, the Calgary Chamber of Commerce and ski clubs in Edmonton and elsewhere exerted had an effect. In 1965, the Department of Northern Affairs released its ski policy. Noting that the U.S. National Parks Service did not allow any downhill skiing, the policy stated that the sport would be allowed in Canada's parks, but only in certain areas. New ski hills were out, yet the existing areas would be able to expand after they developed master plans the department approved. There was even provision to allow more entertainment within motels and hotels in Banff and Lake Louise. Trafford and the CSC interpreted the new policy as a victory and an open door to better skiing. In his 1964/65 president's report, Trafford stated:

> Arthur Laing's announcement on March 12, reversing the old Park's policy and giving the go-ahead to the development of first class resort areas in the Banff National Park, has been a key event and most gratifying for the skiing public. It is fair to say, I believe, that in this achievement, the Calgary Ski Club had considerable influence. Its prestige and experience is recognized and well respected by the Parks Authorities and Government alike.[278]

It would not be the end of the club's efforts to lobby for improved skiing. Under Trafford's successor Mike Brusset, the club backed another brief that a group of concerned citizens, including present and past club members like Ethan Compton, Art Patterson and Pat Duffy, prepared. The urgency of lobby efforts, however, soon faded. The expansion allowed at Sunshine and Lake Louise created enough capacity to handle growth for a while. Ironically, despite predictions that restrictions and regulations would strangle the ski industry in the parks, it continued to grow.

THE CLUBHOUSE REVISITED

One of the issues the CSC raised with the parks department was a clubhouse in Banff. The tennis club in Calgary served well for meetings and socials, but it had certain failings. The biggest, in the eyes of the racers and racing parents of the club, was the location in downtown Calgary, not at a ski hill. They wanted a facility to serve as a dormitory for the racers as well as a headquarters for the club, one that was as convenient as possible for training. With options in the city seemingly exhausted, the club again looked longingly at Banff and Lake Louise. Ted Trafford enthusiastically seized upon the idea of a mountain clubhouse, and as was his wont, did not think small.

A clubhouse in Banff, however, faced a major obstacle: the park administration. As a matter of principle, for years the parks department had frowned upon any facilities that were not open to the general public. Hans Maciej approached Gordon Dempster, the regional head of the parks, about a CSC clubhouse. Dempster told him that the only way it might happen was if the government built a facility and leased it to the club.[279] The 1964 parks policy reiterated the principle, so a new clubhouse for the exclusive use of the ski club faced major opposition. One option was for the club to locate somewhere else in the mountains beside Banff. Canmore was considered briefly, but in 1962 it was still a small mining town and a distance from the ski hills. More exciting was Pigeon Mountain, which opened in 1962. Though not the best hill for race training, the owners had ambitious plans for Pigeon, and they expressed interest in having the CSC.[280] Discussions never went beyond the preliminary and no agreement was reached.

The news that a visitors' centre was in the works for Lake Louise, with a number of new motels, gave the CSC grounds for optimism. Trafford inquired about obtaining a site. B.I.M. Strong, the western regional manager of the parks, advised him to draw up an outline proposal. Trafford went to architect Bill Milne for some preliminary ideas. Milne put together a concept of a "village within a village." A central lodge building would contain a cafeteria, games rooms, lounge, meeting room and caretakers quarters. Sleeping accommodations were small detached two-bedroom cabins, with hostel-style bunk beds, as most of the guests would be young racers.[281] Trafford told Strong the club wanted to build a headquarters that could provide cheap meals and accommodation for some 30 to 40 girls and boys and a place for dances and after-ski get-togethers.[282]

The answer of the government was an unequivocal no. Since Trafford and the club didn't seem to understand the government's position, Arthur Laing made it clear:

> Our aim is to provide services for the maximum number of visitors and yet use the minimum amount of land within the Park for the necessary basic services required to satisfy the needs of those visitors. We certainly cannot achieve that objective by allowing private clubs to flourish to satisfy a limited number of people. To allow such a development would lead to a vicious circle of supply and demand which could only result in the expansion of park townsites and visitor services centres beyond the minimum required for park purposes.[283]

The club was not easily discouraged. A new clubhouse at Lake Louise was out, but there was Banff. Laing was somewhat sympathetic to the CSC's aspirations and opened the door to potentially leasing an existing building. The main difficulty was that not much was available in Banff in the mid-

1960s. The club council assigned Rod Whitehead and Ben Barrington the job of finding something. Barrington came up with what looked like the perfect solution, the Alpine Club of Canada clubhouse.

The ACC had obtained a lease in Banff in 1910. The ACC clubhouse was a rambling complex with a main house and detached cabins and outbuildings on a six-acre site. It was built for the summer and was closed up in the winter. By happy coincidence, the Alpine Club wanted to get more use out of their clubhouse buildings. They were in need of serious renovations and were costing the ACC money. The club realized, however, that the change in government regulations made the lease irreplaceable and it needed to keep the clubhouse viable.

The CSC quickly forwarded a proposal. The club offered to help pay for winterizing the ACC's buildings and provide a caretaker for the winter. Visiting CSC skiers would provide revenue. Trafford suggested that CSC members could become associate members of the ACC for a small fee and vice versa. He finished the proposal with a fine rhetorical flourish:

> The important advantage, to my way of thinking, is that skiers will be exposed to the fine traditions of the Alpine club and some will almost certainly take up climbing and thus be led to a fuller enjoyment of the mountains. The converse is, I believe, equally significant. I think it is most desirable that we build in Canada a strong body of people dedicated to year-round outdoor activity, and this will be a step in the right direction.[284]

The CSC even went so far as to change the constitution, adding a new associate membership category to facilitate a membership swap with the Alpine Club.[285]

It certainly was a great plan for the Calgary Ski Club and had its advantages for the Alpine Club. However, the ACC realized that it could invite all ski clubs and skiers to use the clubhouse and earn even more revenue.[286] The ACC's clubhouse committee recommended simply establishing a ski membership for the Alpine Club. The head of the committee thought that admitting skiers might "bring in new blood and new vigour" to the ACC. But he was in the minority. At the next general meeting, the Alpine Club's membership made it clear that they weren't in favour of anything that might lead "to some fundamental changes in the character of the Alpine Club of Canada, namely broadening the membership in the Alpine Club of Canada to include downhill skiers."[287]

The CSC made some last desperate attempts to find something in the park. The most promising was the old lodge at Sunshine. With the completion of the new hotel and lodge, it was no longer needed for guests. Cliff White regretfully informed CSC president Mike Brusset he was using it for staff accommodation.[288] The parks department belatedly suggested that the club might be able to take over something built for the 1972 Olympics—but this idea died with the bid.

Snowridge

Few things excited skiers more in the fall of 1968 than hearing that a long-rumoured new ski hill, on provincial land in the Kananaskis Valley, was nearly a reality. Two well-known characters in the local ski scene, Al Compton and Arnold Choquette, had spent several years tramping round the valley looking for the right combination of snow, terrain and access to the forestry roads in the valley. They found what they wanted under the towering east face of Fortress Mountain, where fire had swept a series of ridges and created open terrain. The location had a settled snow-pack measuring five feet on a bad year. It took several years to get the financing in place, but in 1968 skiers finally were able to visit Snowridge's futuristic new lodge and ride three T-bars serving novice and intermediate terrain and a chairlift for experts.

Compton and Choquette were both former members of the CSC. As founders of a new resort, they were open to the idea of the club making an alliance with Snowridge. The club's latest attempt to use the Bowness Golf and Country club for a headquarters, for the 1967/68 season, had met with little success.[289] CSC President Mike Brusset had already spoken with Choquette about Snowridge. He and Compton came to a CSC council meeting to give a presentation on the hill. Negotiations began, culminating in a tentative letter of agreement in the fall of 1967. The CSC's plan was ambitious. The club would have its own exclusive practice hill and lodge, adjacent to the main ski area, and access to the rest of the resort at reduced rates. Along with the clubhouse, there would be sites for future development of small chalets.

Snowridge, however, was very much an unknown quantity. The council hired a consultant, Dave Brewer, to check out the potential. Brewer found the terrain good, if not aesthetic, and the snow excellent, if wind blown. He was concerned, nonetheless, about the access—the winding, narrow gravel road in the Kananaskis Valley was a nightmare in the winter and the road up to the ski hill was even worse. Considering the competition near at hand in Banff, Brewer had doubts about the resort's viability, which he spelled out in no uncertain terms. "In short, the success or failure of the Calgary Ski Club development at Snow Ridge will be quite dependent on the success or failure of Snow Ridge proper. Frankly, I think the future for them is a gloomy one."[290]

The new resort suffered many teething problems and the delays were fatal to the CSC master plan. As an interim measure, Snowridge reserved for the club an area off the top of its main T-bar for the 1968/69 season. The club undertook to clear the slope, with the understanding that other race clubs could use it when the club wasn't. An area of the lodge was set aside for the CSC racers. Later that season, Snowridge, desperate for financing, came up with a new scheme. If the CSC sold 250 lifetime memberships, the resort would build the club a $25,000 clubhouse. It was a last-ditch attempt to keep the sheriff from the door. The club found the memberships a tough sell. Yet another clubhouse scheme petered out.

Powder Hounds

The Calgary Ski Club was known in the sixties as a downhill skiing club. Most of the organization's energy was spent promoting alpine racing, the Olympics, better ski resorts and mobilizing bus tours to other regions. Trafford's ideas for the club, however, extended to the pristine powder slopes of the backcountry. Art Patterson was a Calgary geologist. He had been a junior member of the club back before the war and then rejoined later in the 1950s. As Patterson recalls, Trafford called him up out of the blue and asked if the club should be arranging ski mountaineering tours. When Patterson said he thought it was a good idea, Trafford asked him to look after it. Under Patterson's direction, the club's efforts went beyond simply organizing ski touring trips. The CSC was instrumental in providing facilities for skiing on the high glaciers of the Rockies and the huts of the Wapta Icefield.

Interest in self-propelled skiing had waned in the fifties, but there were still a few enthusiasts in the club. Many members had done a little touring, especially at Skoki or Bow Summit. At that time, Bow Summit became known as the "best little ski hill in the parks" and was a popular trip for both ski tourers and downhill skiers. The highway to Jasper was completed in 1940 as a gravel road. CSC enthusiasts like Cam Mitchell made a trip in

1951. Word quickly got around that there was often snow on the slopes of the summit, right beside the road, early in the season and late into the spring. It wasn't long before skiers, the Calgary Ski Club among them, organized outings when the road was passable. The road was rebuilt between 1957 and 1959 as an all-weather highway and the summit became popular. Over 140 skiers were reported on an early-December weekend in 1957, and carloads of CSC members made the trip in October to inaugurate the 1959/60 season.[291] During the awful snow year of 1957/58, the club even held its championships there in April. The park administration put in a campground, and it was not unusual to find club members camped out there in the spring and early summer to stretch the season out. At times the hill looked like a run at a ski resort!

Trafford did not pull the idea of a ski touring program out of thin air. The 1960s were the start of a general revival of interest in this old-fashioned variant of skiing. The Alpine Club had continued to hold annual ski camps and the Calgary Mountain Club encouraged ski touring and ski mountaineering. The Foothills Nordic Club, established in 1963 to promote Nordic ski racing, also organized tours into the mountain backcountry. Guide Hans Gmoser

Not quite the backcountry: moguls at Bow Summit, circa 1960s. (WHYTE MUSEUM OF THE CANADIAN ROCKIES, VI90 I A.I.B-6, BRUNO ENGLER.)

built up a sizable business in the early sixties offering backcountry skiing holidays, based at the Alpine Club huts in the Little Yoho Valley and Glacier National Park. Trafford thought the CSC should be part of the revival.

Patterson, an experienced and enthusiastic backcountry skier, was happy to organize the program. But he was adamant about one thing: club sponsored trips would always have a professional guide.[292] Patterson had skied with Gmoser and his partner Leo Grillmair, and knew the depth of experience and judgment a good guide could offer. A guide made club trips safer and also more fun. Initially he hired Gmoser himself to lead trips; unfortunately, he was frequently unavailable. Gmoser suggested Peter Fuhrman, who was well known in the Alpine Club and one of the founders of the Association of Canadian Mountain Guides. It was the start of an enduring relationship between Fuhrman and the club.

The CSC's backcountry tours began in 1964. The trips were a combination of day trips and longer overnight trips that might involve winter camping. The tours started in March to take advantage of the longer days, deeper snow and more stable avalanche conditions of the spring. The club started with easier day trips to accustom participants to the rigours of touring. As the season progressed, the club worked up to harder tours. Fuhrman sang the praises of the country along the Icefield Parkway on the way to Bow Summit. Trips to Cirque Peak, Katherine Lake, Molar Meadows and mighty Mt. Hector—names familiar to ski tourers today—were all part of the club's agenda. Fuhrman also took them to some old chestnuts, like Mt. Piran by Lake Louise. The goal of the tours was fine mountain views and great powder skiing. Participants used alpine skis with special touring bindings and climbing skins. Patterson relied on the office secretary, Lois, to make sure everyone knew what gear was required when they called to sign up for a trip. To go on the longer overnight tours, participants first had to go on an easier trip so the guide could evaluate their ability. Generally, this simple system worked well.

The touring program was an immediate success. It basically paid for itself, with the fee for each trip covering the cost of the guide and car pool transportation. It wasn't long before there was a gang of avid touring folk in the club. Jean Robb, who went on many trips, remembers there were about 20 regulars, with others coming from time to time and always a few newcomers. By the late sixties, the club was running up to 10 trips a season, including a couple of longer trips onto the Wapta Icefield. Almost no one else was offering organized ski touring on a regular basis. Patterson remembers that they never saw anyone out in the backcountry. Ironically, Ted Trafford, who had suggested the whole program, never went ski touring.

Not every trip was an unqualified success. The first season the club went into Assiniboine. Patterson, the field geologist, was enamoured of helicopters, and, in fact, played a key role in the creation of heli-skiing. The trip into Assiniboine was long and somewhat daunting. He thought that he could speed things up by using not just a helicopter but also a Nodwell, a tracked snow vehicle, to give a little assist. He planned to use the helicopter to fly supplies and a cook up to the Naiset Cabins, where the group was staying. The Nodwell, meanwhile, would tow the skiers—some 20 all together—down the length of Spray Lake. The group would then ski some 20 kilometres into Assiniboine, which was a shorter approach than the usual one via Sunshine.

Not everything worked out as planned. Thanks to an emergency call, the helicopter arrived late, keeping the group waiting until after noon. By then, the April snow had become soft in the sun and the Nodwell kept bogging down. One track seized up and the vehicle started going in circles, flinging the towed skiers helter-skelter. Finally, the group figured out that if they all skied on one side and dug in their edges, they could keep the Nodwell going in a straight line.

The party finally arrived, already exhausted, at the end of the lake in the late afternoon. They still had to face the long ski up to their camp. By nightfall they had a long way to go. Fuhrman, their guide, led the group unerringly in the dark to the Naiset Cabins and went back with a toboggan to rescue one skier who had reached the end of his strength. Mike Brusset recalls that when they got to Assiniboine at two in the morning, to add insult to injury, the group had to dig out one of the cabins. His friend Jack Gallagher was so dehydrated that he drank most of a pot of cold dishwater in the cooking cabin before he realized what it was. Yet, despite all the hardship, the group had a tremendous time, spending the next few days touring and returning with blisters and sore muscles.

The near-disasters always make the best stories. The club never had any serious incidents over the course of almost 10 years of tours. Patterson attributes the excellent safety record to the presence of a trained guide. The tragic 1964 death of former CSC member Peggy Tefler in Glacier National Park was proof of their value. The accident occurred on an informal, unguided trip. Tefler, a young ski instructor and former racer, had felt unwell on a tour up onto the Illecillewaet Glacier and elected to turn back. Since she was a strong skier, no one thought twice about it, but Tefler, possibly disoriented in poor weather, had stopped a short distance away from the ascent route and dug in. She was not missed until the group returned to the cabin at nightfall. By the time her companions found Tefler the next day, it was too late—she had died of exposure. High-mountain skiing was a great adventure, but it was not to be undertaken lightly.

GIVE ME SHELTER

The touring program created a great legacy in the form of a system of high-altitude shelters on the Wapta Icefield. In 1935, Dudley Batchelor and Gordon Moodie of the CSC had skied on the Wapta to climb Mt. Balfour. In the late 1950s and early 1960s, adventurers like Gmoser and Fuhrman rediscovered the series of large glaciers, which parallels the highway to Jasper along the Great Divide. The high-line traverse to the Trans-Canada Highway became a favourite trip for the CSC, requiring several days and snow-camping on the way. This led to the Wapta huts, one of the more unexpected accomplishments of the club.

When climbing and ski mountaineering became more popular in the sixties, enthusiasts wanted backcountry huts and shelters in the national parks, similar to those common in Europe. The idea was not new—years earlier the Alpine Club had built a number of cabins in the Rockies for mountaineering. These were almost all located below tree line and not much help to the climber or skier caught far from shelter in an emergency. Hans Gmoser was a proponent of special high-altitude shelters in the Canadian Rockies, and even used the 1961 CSC annual as a soapbox. He argued that along with enhancing safety, shelters would help popularize the Rockies as a world-class mountaineering destination. The Calgary Mountain Club, meanwhile, built a small pre-fabricated hut in 1963 above the Valley of the Ten Peaks for climbers.

Enter Peter Fuhrman, Art Patterson, Ted Trafford and the Calgary Ski Club. Fuhrman thought the Wapta was the perfect place to put a chain of small shelters. Some American clients he had taken on the traverse in 1959 had even offered to pay for one near Balfour Pass.[293] Fuhrman tried to interest the park administration with no success. After Fuhrman started guiding tours for the CSC, he asked Patterson if the club would be interested in helping to put up a chain of huts. Patterson took the idea to Trafford, who was whole-heartedly in favour. It was another way to promote skiing, in this instance the ski mountaineering potential of the Rockies. The club added ski touring facilities like high-altitude shelters to its demands of the national parks administration.

The club was willing to put its money where its mouth was. It formed a shelter committee and set up a hut fund for donations. The project soon became a joint endeavour with the Alpine Club and the Calgary Mountain Club. "We needed the Alpine Club," says Patterson. "The parks thought the Calgary Ski Club were just a bunch of downhill skiers, so we needed the name." The ACC got permission to build the huts; the CSC helped pay for them. The CMC had tapped out its resources with the Graham Cooper hut, but the club donated equipment for the proposed shelter. Philippe Delesalle, an architect with Cohos Evamy and well-known mountaineer, designed the huts. He was a friend of Gmoser and Fuhrman and had come on several of the CSC trips. He designed a simple, prefabricated, fibreglass dome that could be broken into sections and easily moved. Disassembled, the whole thing could fit in a truck and be flown in with a helicopter. Assembled, the shelter could sleep up to 12. It was so easy to set up that a version intended for the Peyto Glacier was erected at the following year's Ski Ball.[294]

Obtaining permission for the hut was another story. The superintendent of Banff was not in favour of the shelter. He told Fuhrman and Patterson that the parks wanted a standardized design for their proposed high-altitude shelters. It was clearly a stalling tactic, and Patterson, for one, fumed about this requirement. As he put it, "[The huts] are all in the experimental stage and we have had to try different plans in order to arrive at the best solution."[295] Fortuitously, Fuhrman guided the chief planner of the Ottawa Capital Commission on a hike the summer of 1965 and bent his ear about the shelters. With this ally in the government, Fuhrman and Patterson were able to get things moving again.[296]

Finally, the first hut was flown to its location at the foot of Mt. Balfour in October 1965. Art got his friend Dave Bullock of Bullock Rotor to donate the helicopter time. Fuhrman, Patterson, his son Harry, Ed Sutton, Dr. Jim Gibson and Bruno Engler were the construction crew. The shelter soon proved its worth. On one of his first trips to the new hut, Fuhrman sat out a 30-hour storm, with winds so strong a flashlight he put down outside was blown away. The Balfour igloo, however, turned out to be a learning experience. As Art remembers, "Being a geologist and being exceedingly knowledgeable, I picked a location on a moraine, never thinking most moraines are ice core. We built the igloo and it was flat, the next year it had about a 10-degree list, the next year about a 15-degree list and eventually a wolverine got in it. The wolverine ate the fibreglass insulation." The hut was located right on a favourite route for wolverines going to the Yoho Valley. Wolverines, well known for their ability to break into cabins and food caches, soon rendered the hut unusable. In 1967, Parks Canada replaced the igloo with a Pan-abode structure.

The Peyto Hut followed Balfour. A donation from Catherine Whyte of Banff, in memory of her husband Peter, mostly financed the shelter. Catherine ran Skoki Lodge with her husband for three years in the thirties and had come on some CSC tours. The hut was once again built under the aegis of the Alpine Club. Bow Hut followed Peyto. The CSC shelter fund paid most of the costs for the hut and a work crew from the CSC, the Alpine Club and Mountain Search and Rescue, and the Association of Canadian Mountain Guides built it. Bow Hut was a wood and metal "bread loaf" structure intended for up to 20 people, and skiers called it the "Ritz." The hut almost went missing in action. Fuhrman stored it disassembled at Bow Lake late in 1967 and a heavy snowfall buried the shelter. The road plows piled up even more snow, so Fuhrman had quite a time finding it. The hut was finally put up in February 1968.

Fuhrman and Patterson planned more shelters, but the endeavour ran

Any hut in a storm: erecting the Balfour shelter, 1965. (BRUNO ENGLER, COURTESY ART PATTERSON)

out of steam after Bow. A fourth hut completing the Wapta chain would come years later, yet did not involve the CSC. The original huts did not last more than a few years. Wolverines also vandalized the original Peyto Hut and Parks Canada replaced it with two unpopular fibreglass bubbles. Eventually the Alpine Club replaced all the original Wapta huts with better structures and now run them on behalf of the parks. Few people remember the role the CSC played in their construction. Hundreds of ski tourers use the Wapta hut system every year, a fine, if little known, legacy for the Calgary Ski Club.

Kids Stuff

The Calgary Ski Club got a reputation in the sixties as a family club. Ski touring was one of the few new club programs that was generally adults only. The CSC had always taken an interest in kids, especially with instruction and racing, but in the sixties the club evolved into a family club. Aside from the racing program, there were also the Saturday Specials and the Bobcats, both of which rate a mention.

The club's focus on children is not surprising. Calgary then was basically overrun with them. Fully one-third of the city's population was 14 and under in 1966. Throw in teenagers and kids made up over 40 per cent. The baby boom, as usually defined, had started in 1946 in North America and was in full swing through the fifties and the early sixties. As early as 1960, the club was thinking of setting up a baby-sitting service at Norquay to help out young parents. Parenting likely affected the club's membership cycles. The drop seen in the club's numbers in the later fifties may well have reflected members starting families—often with someone they met in the ski club! Many of the children born in the fifties, however, were getting on skis a decade later. The interest in junior racing reflected the growing popularity of alpine ski competition, but was also a function of the sheer number of kids around.

Children certainly had an impact on the club. By the second half of the 1960s, the proportion of junior members in the club increased precipitously. At the end of the 1964 season, when membership crept up over 1,000, about half were single adults. Couples and families made up the rest and included about 300 children. In 1966, the membership went over 1,300, and kids were in the majority. By 1968, over two-thirds of the club's were juniors. Single adults were down to barely 160.[297] Towards the end of the sixties, the club was emphasizing its kids programs even more, because none of the other clubs were doing anything for them. This focus on children had transformed the club substantially over the decade. It had become known as the city's family ski club.

SATURDAY SPECIALS

One of the most successful programs for children was the Saturday Specials. It was another brainchild of Ted Trafford. It was not too surprising that a man with six kids should be interested in children's programing. The *Herald* Ski School, which was still running at Happy Valley, was getting younger kids on skis. He felt there should be something for teenagers that included skiing in the mountains. The Special would turn into another ski school, running for 10 years. It was a club service to the skiing community.

Trafford came up with the idea after joining council in 1962. It was a straightforward plan with some complicated logistics. The Special took groups of children, 10 to 16, and bused them to Mt. Norquay, where they enjoyed a lesson in the morning and free skiing in the afternoon. The trips ran every weekend from the middle of December until March. It was a package plan. The club looked after everything. Club volunteers supervised on the buses and the professionals at Norquay provided instruction. The aim was to teach kids to ski but also expose them to the joy of skiing in the mountains, especially for children whose parents themselves didn't ski. The program wasn't entirely altruistic. Trafford suggested that the Special "could bring people into the club who would never have thought of joining."[298]

The first trip ran on January 5, 1963. Tickets were sold at the ski shops and the buses had designated pick-up spots in residential areas to make it easier for parents. The response was good. By February, two busloads of kids a week were heading out to Norquay.[299] Special badges were added that kids earned for attendance and skill improvement. By 1968, an average of 200 children were hopping on the buses each week. When the *Herald* Ski School finally folded in 1967, after the newspaper pulled its sponsorship, the Special became the main club program for teaching kids to ski.

A wonderful part of the Specials was the Farish Trophies. Jack Farish, one of the club founders, decided he wanted to donate trophies to the club to recognize a worthy endeavour. The Saturday Special caught his fancy, and he arranged to give a cup each year to the boy and the girl who made the most progress over the course of the season. Farish personally presented the cups for many years, usually at the end of the year banquet. His trophies were a link between the club's origins and its continued work promoting skiing.

THE BOBCATS

The club augmented the Specials later in the 1960s with the Bobcats Program, aimed at eight- to 16-year-olds. The new program emphasized enhancing skills and was designed to advance students to expert skiing. The program also aimed to teach youngsters proper deportment on the hill. As President Mike Brusset told the *Herald*, "We don't want them to ski wild on the hill once they've learned to turn." The emphasis, though, was on fun. The program was limited to just 200 kids. It used tests modelled on swimming—passing meant a ribbon and going on to the next level, flunking merely meant repeating the lessons.

The Bobcats was not a racing program. Participants could join the Nancy Greene League, or if they showed promise, aspire to join the CSC team. But they could also become junior instructors or even get into the new sport of freestyle skiing, which had particular appeal to kids. The aim of the Bobcats was to produce good skiers, not necessarily racers. It filled a niche. Peter Cooper of the *Albertan* welcomed the program effusively. "The Calgary Ski Club has come up with something that has been wanting for a long time. It's a junior program that does not revolve around racing."[300] Cooper, a qualified instructor, liked the idea that Bobcats would teach kids to ski to a high level of technical proficiency, but without the expense and commitment of time needed to race. Cooper's praise of the Bobcat idea also showed his disenchantment with the junior competitive scene that the CSC had helped foster. And he was not alone.

The club continued to offer adult instruction sporadically but with little success. Lack of interest caused the cancellation of budget lesson plans put together under Bob Freeze's council. In the Trafford era, the club started Introduction to Skiing, a coffee-and-doughnut-style talk on getting into skiing. It was aimed at parents sending their kids to the *Herald* Ski School or the Saturday Special, to get them on skis, too. Whether it worked is debatable. Trafford, for one, had a tendency to use the talks as a platform for the Olympics or lobbying for ski facilities. A more elaborate program, Ski with A Pro, was aimed at adults, especially parents with kids in the CSC junior programs. It consisted of a weekend at Sunshine with structured lessons as well as free skiing accompanied by a pro instructor. Although it took advantage of the new hotel facilities at Sunshine, Mike Brusset remembers that the program just never took off. Ski with A Pro only lasted a couple of years.

The lack of demand for adult lessons, in retrospect, was indicative of some important changes in skiing. Already in the fifties, decent professional instruction was available commercially and the industry had grown even more in the sixties. The skiing market had changed—far fewer adult skiers around Calgary seemed to be newcomers to the sport. They already knew how to ski, and if they didn't, they could learn at a ski school. Joining a club was not as necessary to get into the sport as it had been. And within the CSC, there were fewer adults, period. Many were there to support their kids. The CSC's emphasis on children and junior racing had undermined its attraction to young adults and they weren't joining. This would have consequences.

STORM CLOUDS BREWING

Cooper's remarks about junior racing were one man's opinion, but a well-informed one. And it reflected new discontent in the Calgary Ski Club over competition. The sport was becoming the territory of dedicated racing clubs, like the Skimeisters and a revitalized Lake Louise Ski Club. In the CSC, enthusiasm was waning outside of the hard core of racing families. The emphasis on supporting the racing program, however, was affecting the rest of the club. Although no one saw it at the time, it signalled a coming crisis for the CSC.

Joe Irwin became deeply involved in the Alberta Division of CASA. He left the club in 1966 to take over the Lake Louise Ski Club, which became one of the leading competitive clubs. The junior racing program continued—Miles Patterson effectively stepped into the breach—but the momentum was slowing. There were signs the club was split into those interested primarily in seeing their kids race and everyone else. By the late 1960s, there was little interest in adult racing within the club. One race parent, Norm Gustavson, proposed setting up a subsidiary club, solely focused on junior competition as few members outside the racing families were interested.

Racing also created tension among the racers. Mike Brusset, who took over as president when Ted Trafford moved to Australia in 1966, recalls:

> Racing seemed to be the biggest problem area for the president at that time, because you had some parents who really focused on the racing and their kids were involved, so just like hockey nowadays, you got some competition between different families. So that used to take up a fair amount of time, keeping everything under control.

Racing was also expensive and the club started running deficits trying to keep up. Socials, bus trips, alpine tours and the Saturday Specials were already run on a cost-recovery basis. While the newsletter and the racing program were the club's major expenditures, the newsletter brought in some revenue. The situation was severe enough that for the first time in its history, the CSC solicited donations to help cover its costs.[301] There were cutbacks but inevitably the club had to look to the members. For 1966/67, dues doubled and it had an immediate and negative impact on membership, which plummeted from a high of nearly 1,400 down to 886.[302] The higher fees and a concentrated funding drive restored the club's financial order. But the fees drove membership down and probably disenchanted many clubbers with racing.

Some members also felt that the club was growing much less cohesive. Part of the blame was the way the entire local ski scene had changed. Peter Cooper, as the *Albertan*'s ski editor, tracked the changes. The two things that most affected the CSC's fellowship, in his opinion, were private cars and more ski hills. The Trans-Canada Highway made driving to the mountains easy. The club soon stopped scheduling buses for day trips to the mountains. The club car pool kept running, but fewer people used it. They drove out in their own cars. The rise of Sunshine and Lake Louise also spread out the skiing community. As Cooper points out, through the fifties, people did most of their skiing at Norquay. It was easy to meet many people in the ski community. By the late sixties, the crowds were spread out among the three areas. The number of skiers had also risen greatly. No longer did people know most of the other skiers in Calgary, and no longer did most of the other skiers belong to the club.

It was the club's lack of ability to attract young adults that was the most worrisome for the CSC. Junior members had several drawbacks. Children paid lower dues and couldn't help run the show. The club, however, also found that its general renewal rate was dropping fast. By 1967, two-thirds of the membership were new each year. The club was clearly having difficulty hanging on to new blood. One reason was that a good chunk of the membership were children, many there for the Saturday Special. Once they learned to ski, they did not necessarily return to the club. As for adults, if they were not joining for their kids, they seemed to find the club lacking and didn't stick around. At the end of the decade, it was clear that the CSC was no longer getting the young adults that made up the majority of avid skiers. They were going elsewhere.

THE PETROLEUM SKI CLUB

The immediate success of the Petroleum Ski Club underscored the drift of the CSC. The new club was established in 1968 with one basic goal: to organize recreational downhill skiing trips for young adults. The bus trip that the CSC pioneered was the backbone of the PSC, as were regular parties. The new club was almost entirely a social organization, dedicated to a good time at the hills—no racing, no kids' programs and no ski touring. It tapped into a serious demand and the PSC's membership exploded. By the early 1970s, the club claimed nearly 2,000 members. The PSC supplemented bus trips to closer hills with weeklong charters to the United States and Europe. The name of the new club was no accident. The oil industry was attracting thousands of young professionals to the city, accentuating a demographic shift towards young adults as the baby boom came of age. These were the sort of people who had always been attracted to skiing and they wanted a club that reflected their needs.

The Calgary Ski Club, meanwhile, was if anything more involved with children. The Bobcat program was started about the same time the Petroleum Ski Club appeared. The advent of the PSC immediately cut into the Calgary Ski Club's adult membership, which was already dropping. The CSC's long-standing character as a club for all skiers was seriously undermined. By 1970, the CSC had cut back drastically on out-of-town trips. "Due to the difficulty of competing with the Petroleum Ski club in this area, only two tours are being planned this year," recorded the minutes for the October 22 council meeting.[303] It was sign of things to come.

A DECADE OF ACCOMPLISHMENT

The 1960s were a decade the Calgary Ski Club could look back upon with pride. The club had done a great deal to promote skiing, as a sport and recreation, especially among young people. It led the fight to obtain better skiing in Calgary's mountain playground. It created new programs and services, like the Saturday Specials, the New and Used Ski Sale and the après-ski parties in Banff that satisfied the needs of Calgary's ski community. The club had recorded its highest membership ever and could boast an array of members who were leaders in the community as well as leaders in the club.

The club's very success, however, in meeting the needs of families and children ultimately forced another radical transformation. In two short years, the club's membership slid to rock bottom and its survival was in doubt.

People did not stop having families. But as the next decade dawned, those same kids who had been ski racers or had first put on skis with the help of the club were becoming young adults, with entirely new needs and desires. Calgary was on the cusp of another boom, which would attract young mobile people from across the country. The baby boomers were becoming adults, but adults with money and a desire to have some fun. With the help of another dynamic president, a tide of demographics would remake the Calgary Ski Club yet again.

CHAPTER SIX

Swinging Singles

CRISIS—DEMOGRAPHICS—SWINGERS—
THE NIGHTLIFE—CROSS-COUNTRY—DOWNHILL—
SUMMERS—CLUBHOUSE—FOLKIES—TURMOIL—
DEMOCRACY—THE FUTURE—THE PAST

Folk music and espressos? Discos? Streakers? What did any of this have to do with skiing? Well, it was the seventies. As reliable reports have it, anything went.

One of the things that almost went was the Calgary Ski Club. At the beginning of the seventies, the club had a near-death experience. The whole racing enterprise ran out of steam, and the CSC discovered that its focus on families and children had robbed it of another vital constituency, young adults. Fortunately, Calgary experienced a tremendous surge of immigration in the seventies, largely made up of the people who would revitalize the CSC, the baby boomers. One of the things the newcomers wanted to do was ski. Largely because of the boomers, the ski industry underwent a massive expansion in the 1970s. A new generation brought new life to the Calgary Ski Club.

In doing so, they took the club in a different direction. For a decade, it was one big party. Molson Breweries became a club sponsor—mostly with product. The CSC always had a big social component, young adults most interested in fun skiing, dances, parties and meeting the opposite sex. They now became the essence of the Calgary Ski Club, as it re-invented itself to serve the Me Generation. The noble goal of promoting skiing in all its forms was quietly discarded. In their desire to fill their abundant leisure time, the

Let 'er rip: a typical CSC skier in the 1970s. (ALASDAIR FERGUSSON.)

new members added all sorts of diversions to the CSC's offerings. It became an all-year, all-the-time, recreational club. At times skiing seemed lost in the whirl of disco parties, folk nights, raft races and baseball tournaments. At the core, however, the CSC remained a club for skiers. It enthusiastically embraced the revival of cross-country skiing but also created a recreational downhill program that was second to none. It would finally get a clubhouse. On the eve of its 50th anniversary in 1985, the CSC remained a vital part of the local ski scene.

The Crisis

The 1970s did not get off to a good start for the Calgary Ski Club. The club had the worst crisis in its existence, and came close to disappearing. It made the Skimeisters debacle at the beginning of the sixties look like a minor inconvenience. In his 1970/71 report to the club's annual general meeting, president Glen McArter openly wondered if the time had come to wrap up the whole enterprise. Membership crashed to its lowest level since the Second World War, finishing off the season at just 278 and only 47 single adults.[304] After years of being the sole voice of Calgary skiers, the CSC was competing with other clubs, particularly the Petroleum Ski Club. The dynamic personalities and the family atmosphere, which had the club going strong through most of the 1960s, had disappeared. The club was adrift, morale was at rock bottom.

The change had come with alarming swiftness, but the club had actually been slowly losing its adult members, especially singles, for some time. A sign something was amiss was the poor renewal rate—by 1967, only a third of the membership was renewing from year to year. Either people were trying the club and finding it wanting or joining to take advantage of discounts on the lessons for kids and then leaving. By the end of the sixties, symptoms that the club was ailing multiplied. No one was signing up for the bus trips to go skiing. Lack of attendance cancelled social events. The Ski Ball, the club's year-end party, died in 1970. A year later, the club was hard pressed to have two socials—10 members showed up.

The drastic drop in members, especially adults, also meant that it was difficult to run any programs. By the end of the 1971/72 season, the club was functioning with a council of five. The CSC came close to losing the ski sale, simply through lack of members to run it. With the help of the ski patrol and the more responsible club juniors, the CSC managed to squeak through in the fall of 1972. The Bobcat program went into precipitous decline and the race team was suddenly wound up in 1970. Many people who had been keen supporters of racing and done a lot of work in the club had left. They had either gone to more specialized racing clubs or their kids were no longer kids and ski racing was no longer part of their life.

Not everything in the club was falling apart. The backcountry tours were strong, but it was a specialized activity that only attracted a small, if loyal, following. The Saturday Special had a lot of traffic, mostly from non-members. There still was some demand for kids' programs, yet the family skiing experience was clearly not what people wanted.

DEMOGRAPHIC DRAGONS

For many years, the CSC had been a melding of two somewhat incompatible kinds of members, children and young adults. These were the two groups that made up a large amount of the membership at any one time. As early as the fifties, there had been grumbling about having junior members at socials. That interfered with partying; juniors had been banned for a while to allow the adults to play. Junior members were also more likely to be a part of the racing side of the club. The CSC had in many ways become two clubs in one.

A few common beliefs held the club together. One was that the club had a responsibility to promote skiing. Even if most members never raced, enough accepted that competition was a higher good for racing to be a part of the club. And until the late 1960s, adult members were probably just more tolerant of having children about, in a time of traditional "family values." The revitalized club of the early sixties continued to successfully combine social and recreational skiing that appealed to adults with racing and a public service ideal reflected in the programs to provide instruction to children and youth. The arrival of the Petroleum Ski Club on the scene, however, was all the catalyst needed to draw off young adults, a crucial and energetic constituency of the club.

The club was also at the mercy of demographic cycles. The same generation that gave the ski club a bloom of members in the late forties and early fifties, was the generation that wanted programs for their kids in the sixties. In 1970, the tail end of the baby boom was just starting to reach the age where they could learn to ski, but the leading edge of the boom was now in their mid-twenties. The bulk of the baby boom generation was approaching adulthood. It seems an unlikely coincidence that a club oriented towards families and junior competition would falter at the same time. Those same kids who had learned to ski with the club were now adult skiers with different needs.

The demographic shift was only one factor. There was still an ample supply of kids around Calgary, enough to keep the membership up. The ski industry, however, was once again catching up to the club, this time in offering instruction to kids. Every ski hill and ski shop had its own program and often an in-house ski club to go with it. The CSC kept the Saturday Special running as a service to the ski community. Around 1974, however, the public stopped using it and the program co-coordinator of the program blamed competition from the ski shops. In any case, it was clear that even families were no longer interested in the CSC, and nothing the council did seemed to help. The executive experimented with special parties and trips to attract teenagers, but got little interest. Whatever the exact causes of the decline, the club was in trouble.

SWINGING SINGLES

Just in time, a new man on horseback rode to rescue. His name was Tom Boleantu. He represented the sort of person coming to Calgary in droves in the early seventies. He was a baby boomer, in his early thirties, an educated professional, in this case a geologist, and employed in the oilfields. Like many of his confreres, Boleantu had extensive international experience, working in Morocco for over four years. It was people like Boleantu who brought the club back to life.

Boleantu was a skier. Like many previous newcomers, he made his way to the Calgary Ski Club. He found it almost moribund, but there was a small number of new members, mostly recent arrivals in Calgary. It still had some important assets, like the Ski Sale. Instead of being discouraged and leaving, he saw an opportunity. Like other club leaders before him, Boleantu was not solely responsible for the club's renewed success. He pushed it in the right direction, and most importantly, attracted new people to the executive. They oriented the club to people like themselves and their needs. It was a simple vision: a year-round outdoors club serving young to middle-aged adults.

The revitalization began with the formal alliance of the CSC with the Foothills Table Tennis Club. Tom Boleantu was a founder of Foothills, also known as the Double T. It was a social club. Playing table tennis (or ping-pong) was a good excuse to have some parties. The Double T had been holding regular "disco-pubs" in the Sunalta community centre. Boleantu brought the two clubs together. In March 1972, the CSC and the Double T became affiliated. In one stroke, it brought another group of young, active and social people into the CSC. The Double T organized socials and provided an activity, table tennis, for ski club members outside of the ski season. The CSC arranged the ski-related activities. The clubs also shared administrative costs. Boleantu became vice-president of the ski club and lost no time in tackling the sorry state of the organization. When council met after the 1972 April general meeting, he presented a long memo outlining his thoughts for jump-starting the CSC. Before the season was out, president Gerry Umbacht, who had taken over when the previous president resigned, also stepped down. Boleantu replaced him.[305]

Without talking to Tom Boleantu (who was not available for an interview) it is difficult to know exactly how his ideas for the club evolved.[306] Alasdair Fergusson joined the CSC shortly after Boleantu took over as president. He believes that Tom, in the course of his time overseas, had experienced the nightlife available in Europe, from quiet pubs to small discos and nightclubs. That sort of social outing was mostly lacking in Calgary. Boleantu had also visited a new innovation called Club Med. It was a resort where for one inclusive price people enjoyed a wide range of activities and entertainment for their holiday and could meet other single adults. "I remember at one Friday night social hearing Tom say that he thought the Calgary Ski Club could be a 'poor man's Glencoe Club,'" Fergusson recalls, "A club with lots of different activities to satisfy a member's social and recreational needs."[307]

Part of Tom's vision was not to be the Petroleum Ski Club. It had become the party club. Gord Cuming worked on the *Albertan*'s ski supplement. People in the ski community told him that the PSC "skied when they weren't drinking." The club was using two floors of Penley's dance hall for twice-monthly socials. "It was amazing. There were two different bands and there must have been 2,000 people there. You didn't know a single soul." The PSC also had an excellent bus tour program and started offering charter trips to the U.S. and Europe. Even on their bus trips, the PSC was acquiring a reputation for being a bit out of control. It was also an enormous club and somewhat impersonal.

Boleantu wanted a smaller, intimate club where members could get to know each other. And he wanted it to be first and foremost a ski club and part of the larger ski community. Ironically, Boleantu has become identified with the reputation the CSC developed in the seventies as a singles club, but that wasn't his intention. His May 1972 memo had not proposed anything revolutionary. However, his mission was to recruit new adult skiers, even suggesting that the club offer the old standby, lessons, to get beginners started. He believed that the club should play a role in the community and serve the public as well as members. Although he had criticized the Saturday Specials when he first joined council, Boleantu later expressed disappointment when council decided to pull the plug on them. For a couple of years, he was fond of referring to the CSC as "the ski club that skis." It was a pointed reference to the competition. It also made it clear why the club was there.

At the same time, Boleantu's revival of the CSC represented a major change in its basic philosophy. The club was now recruiting young, single adults and its focus was on recreational skiing. No one suggested reviving the junior racing program. Serving the ski community took a back seat to serving the needs of the club's new members.

I Love the Nightlife

One of those needs was a place to get a drink and meet people of the opposite sex. Ask any club member of seventies vintage and they will tell you that Calgary in that decade lacked a decent nightlife. It was still a small big city, suffering from the regime of the Alberta Liquor Control Board. The ALCB was a somewhat draconian watchdog that the province established after Prohibition to let people drink, but made sure it wasn't much fun.

Alasdair Fergusson, an import from Scotland, points out that the places to get a drink in Calgary were limited. The choices were barn-like beer parlours, dedicated to the mass consumption of draft, a few hotel cocktail bars and the occasional cabaret. Even within these establishments, socializing wasn't easy. Gord Cuming remembers that if you wanted to move between tables, the regulations said the server had to move your drink for you! It was especially unappealing to single women. Many newcomers to Calgary had more sophisticated tastes. As had been the case since the thirties, one option was recreational clubs. Under ALCB rules, they could get liquor licenses for events, dances and socials. Fergusson asserts, with perhaps a little exaggeration, that aside from house parties, the alternative to the bar scene "was ski clubs, curling clubs and tennis clubs."

The CSC provided an alternative. In the seventies, the club finally obtained a clubhouse. And not just any clubhouse, but a discotheque known as

Connecting at the Connection: Halloween party, circa 1970s. (ALASDAIR FERGUSSON.)

the "1207 Connection." The idea of a downtown headquarters, which would include a dance floor and a bar, originally belonged to the Double T. The club had been running a disco-pub for its socials in the Bowness and the Sunalta community halls. It wanted a permanent and central location and Boleantu started looking around downtown in 1972.[308] The CSC had done something similar at the Calgary Tennis Club in the early sixties, which had been a great success with the club's single members. The skiers were quite interested in sharing premises. As the larger club, the CSC quickly became the senior partner. After some searching, Boleantu found what he thought was a perfect space. It was a failed nightclub called the Banana Pie, next to the Moose Factory, a popular restaurant on 1st Street SW near 12th Avenue. He obtained an option to buy the assets of the business, including the lease for the premises.

A major sticking point, however, was finances. The CSC didn't have the cash on hand to take over the property. During the summer of 1973, Boleantu and his allies tried unsuccessfully to convince the club to buy the Banana Pie. With membership sitting at around 350, the council deemed the proposal too risky. In any case, they soon discovered that the ski club, as a non-profit society, could not take on a mortgage for purchasing business assets. Convinced the club needed the space, Boleantu came up with a complicated solution. His company, Pi Consultants, bought the Banana Pie assets and then subleased it to the two clubs. With the blessing of the ski and table tennis clubs, Boleantu got a bank loan through Pi, on the basis of their guaranteed use of the premises. Under this arrangement, the ski club rented the space for up to three days a week on a sliding scale and used it for council meetings as well as social events. To make the whole deal work, revenue from the club's sublease went into a trust fund to avoid any conflict of interest. Half of the money paid the rent and the other half paid the Pi Consultants' mortgage. Thus the "Disco-Pub Clubhouse" was born.

The first socials were held at 1207 in the fall of 1973. They took a while to catch on; at first the socials actually lost money. A year later, they were breaking even. And then the 1207 Connection became the hottest place in town. Boleantu added a couple of other important elements. One was Bill the bartender, whose full name was Bill Cantrill. He was actually a lab technician at the university who kept bar as a part-time job—for 19 years in the club's case. Tom knew him from the Jaycees, and persuaded him to work for the CSC. Bill had a phenomenal memory. As one member says, "If I ordered a rye and ginger-ale from Bill, the next time I came in I would get a rye and ginger without asking." The other important element was music. Gord Cuming thinks that Boleantu was on a mailing list from the record labels because he got new releases long before the local stores. The clubhouse soon had an amazing record collection.

It also had amazing lineups. The whole point of having the clubhouse and socials was to revitalize the club and it was working. Membership in the CSC edged back up to over 1,000 in 1975, and it was largely a result of the Friday socials. Word had got out that 1207 was a fun place with good music and a great atmosphere. The clubhouse had a limited capacity. Fewer than 200 people could be legally in the premise at any one time. This encouraged a more intimate atmosphere, rather different from the Petroleum Ski Club bashes at Penley's. It also created the block-long lineups. The core of club members meant that the social wasn't like a bar. Hans Ockermuller remembers that single women really liked it: there wasn't the stigma that was attached to the bar scene. The CSC socials had a somewhat older crowd, generally people in their late twenties and early thirties. Many were active, outdoorsy types looking to make friends. As Cuming recalls, the people flocking to join the club were almost entirely newcomers to the city. "You never met native Calgarians there," he asserts, "They already knew how to ski and had friends."

The new socials were almost too popular for the club's good. Within a couple of years, there was concern within the CSC that people were joining the club simply to have access to the Connection, and that actual skiers were falling into the minority. The downtown premises, however, had done a great deal to bring the club back from the brink. The parties attracted the young, energetic adults the club needed. They would put new life into its skiing programs.

The Cross-Country Revolution

That new life included the club founding its Nordic ski program. Cross-country suddenly became the hottest trend in skiing. Around Calgary, clubs like the Foothills Nordic Ski Club, formed in 1963, had tried to revive the sport with limited success. But in the seventies, everyone jumped on the bandwagon: the Hostelling Association, the Alpine Club, even the Petroleum Ski Club showed some interest.

The rebirth of Nordic skiing in North America was a surprise for the skiing public. Cross-country had remained a fundamental part of life and leisure in Scandinavia and most Nordic and Alpine nations had cross-country racing enthusiasts. Largely due to racing, the long, narrow, double-cambered ski had evolved out of the multipurpose wooden ski. It wasn't until the 1960s, however, that people in North America rediscovered the simple pleasures of cross-country skiing. The sport exploded in the seventies for two reasons. There was a backlash against the ever-growing expense of downhill skiing. And society as a whole developed more awareness of the importance of health and fitness, especially young baby boomers.

Cross-country skiing also became a fad that took on a life of its own, but like all fads it only lasted so long. Norm Russell, of Norm's Ski Hut, remembers his suppliers telling him he absolutely had to stock Nordic gear and he did reluctantly. It sold well at first, quickly dropping off again. He recalls that many of the people who came to buy cross-country gear had never skied before and sometimes looked like they never would. "A lot of those skis ended up gathering dust in someone's garage," he says now, shaking his head. This was probably true, but the boom left behind a well-entrenched sport.

The CSC had not entirely forsaken the traditional Nordic disciplines. It established the Gervig Cup in 1956 for cross-country racing and managed to get nearly a dozen competitors for the 1959 edition. The club considered building a ski jump to give members a chance to practice this esoteric art for four-way competitions. The CSC also raised money in the 1950s to help send Nordic racer Clarence Servold, then of Camrose, to attend the Winter Olympics. When the Foothills club was formed, the CSC immediately planned its own Nordic section for racing. Ironically, the idea was dropped when Foothills wanted to merge with the CSC, providing a ready-made Nordic ski program. The merger never happened and the club got into alpine ski touring. A couple of members saw the new trend coming. Ron Smylie started a program for the CSC in 1970, but dropped it due to work pressures.[309] The 1971 President's report noted that, according to Smylie, "this will be quite the coming thing in future years."[310]

The future, however, was now. The new council Boleantu established seized upon Nordic skiing with enthusiasm. The club took its first steps in the 1972/73 season. Barb Bell and Bernard Muller were put in charge of cross-country skiing and some lessons were held.[311] The program really got striding and gliding the next year. The club set up a cross-country committee with Len Gottselig as the chair. There was a special social with equipment and Nordic ski fashions from the Norseman Ski Shop, a new store dedicated to cross-country skiing.[312] The club also teamed up with the Norseman to offer lessons. And with little delay, people took to the trails.

The trips the club offered in that first year were, in a word, ambitious. They consisted of mountain tours on trails used for hiking in the summer. The club went to the mountains for several reasons. Gottselig, Hubert Rielinger, Hans Ockermuller and others involved in organizing cross-country skiing were also all keen hikers who wanted to get out to the mountains in the winter, away from the ski hills. The sport was also in its infancy in North America. Around Calgary and Banff, there were no purpose-designed cross-country trails. The Hostel Association cut some trails around Ribbon Creek, but the well-designed, marked and groomed trails enjoyed today in Kananaskis Country and Banff National Park were over 10 years in the future. Hiking trails were one of few options available. And there was the issue of snow. As always, Calgary's climate generally didn't allow regular skiing. So it was off the mountains.

The first season there were 10 tours despite poor weather and snow conditions. Skiers visited Paradise Valley, Healy Pass, Forty-Mile Creek and the still-thriving Skoki Lodge. The tours included an overnight venture to the Egypt Lake shelter and a tough trip over Gibbon Pass that ended long after nightfall. The trips had an average of 10 participants and up to 15 or so, which Gottselig reported was about the maximum that one trip leader could manage. The whole endeavour was long on enthusiasm but short on expertise. "We were mostly beginners, novices," he explains. "There was a lot of crash and burn."

Without much experience, it was tough to know what was a hard trip and what was an easy trip, especially with people new to the sport. "The average person in his/her mid-twenties and early thirties seems to be in such poor condition that even easy tours become endurance tests," Gottselig noted in his 1973/74 report.[313] He suggested people should take the club's ski conditioning program to get in shape. In retrospect, some of the club's trips seem pretty ambitious. Rating the outings for difficulty, however, was a subjective exercise. It would remain an issue for many years and was a problem for other groups as well. The CSC did address safety. The following year, the club took a stab at training trip leaders. The club subsidized the cost of taking avalanche awareness courses with the Canadian Ski Patrol System and then added first aid courses. It was a little ahead of the times, and according to

Gottselig, only lasted a couple of years. The club would simply rely on more experienced members to lead trips.

Cross-country skiing soon replaced the old Alpine-touring program. Art Patterson had eventually dropped out because of work and family pressures. Dr. Hugh Gallie kept the tours going until he left in the early seventies, but then the program quickly died. Alpine touring was a much more specialized sport than cross-country. The skis and special touring bindings were heavy and expensive, though they did provide excellent downhill skiing control. Patterson remembers one trip to Mt. Hector where a participant insisted on using the new-fangled skinny skis. "He was just a wild man coming down, totally out of control. He ended up breaking a tip." Nonetheless, the new gear was light and cheap and relatively easy to use. It attracted many hikers who wanted to get into the mountains in the winter, but were not necessarily keen skiers looking for powder. Confined largely to valley bottoms and easier terrain, cross-country skiing also seemed much safer than the ski mountaineering and high-country touring. A full-blown guide seemed unnecessary, making trips even cheaper and easier to organize.

Hiking on skis: CSC party at Assiniboine, circa 1980. (CSC COLLECTION.)

The mountains were the best place to go cross-country skiing, yet the city was not ignored. The CSC took an active role in promoting ski opportunities through the Calgary Cross-Country Council. The city's Parks and Recreation Department was keen on cross-country skiing and wanted to develop some facilities for the sport. The department approached the different ski clubs to ask for their advice and assistance. Most of the clubs, including the CSC, Foothills, and even the Petroleum Ski Club, participated and formed the council.

Just as in times past, when there were snow skiers headed to local golf courses. The council recommended that the city turn the public courses into ski venues. The department designated cross-country trails at several courses. In 1979, the city bought a snowmobile and track-setting equipment and volunteers from Foothills groomed the trails. With the help of the cross-country council, the city also cut trails in Glenmore Park and along the escarpment below Shaganappi. It even installed lights on the latter for night skiing. Lack of reliable snow, however, hampered the efforts of the council and the city. The Shaganappi trail, for instance, is better known these days to the city's mountain bikers than to its skiers!

Thanks to the snow problem, the CSC's Nordic program remained almost entirely focused on the mountains. It kept expanding through the seventies and into the eighties. The club ran day trips nearly every weekend and soon regularly included winter camping expeditions. Hubert Rielinger was one of the mainstays for the program, along with Dave Russum. They added weeklong ski camps to destinations like the Tonquin Valley in Jasper National Park. In the early eighties, the Nordic organizers took note of the success of the downhill crowd and their weekend bus trips. Winter camping was replaced with stays at lodges and hostelries, which skiers used as a base. The club offered trips, most weekenders but some longer, to Num-ti-jah Lodge, Beaverfoot Lodge, Wapta Lodge and others. The luxurious long weekend jaunt to the Emerald Lake Lodge was a particular favourite for years. When downhill and cross-country skiing were available at the same destination, sometimes both crowds would go on a combined trip. The council encouraged these trips to get the two groups to mingle.

The downhill and cross-country skiers formed two distinct groups in the club, although there was some crossover. For all the growth in cross-country, skinny skis were very much in the minority. It was some years before the Nordic program rated its own director on council. Initially, the program was the responsibility of the ski director, who primarily looked after downhill trips. Then cross-country was shifted to the portfolio of the sports director, who looked after the numerous new summertime activities. By 1982, thanks to the more elaborate lodge trips, the cross-country skiing program had become quite a bit of work, and the club appointed a director for Nordic skiing for the 1982/83 season.[314]

THE TELEMARK (NOT TELEMARKETING)

The club's strong cross-country program culminated in its takeover of the Telemark Race from the Alpine Club of Canada in 1979. Perhaps transition is a better term. Len Gottselig, one of the organizers of the 15 kilometre citizens' race, was active with the Calgary Section of the ACC and on the executive of the CSC as well as a member of the Foothills Nordic Ski Club.

The Telemark was a loppet, a citizens' race rather than a performance race. The emphasis was on participation and fun, often with a carnival atmosphere. Participants didn't have to be "carded" racers, which is to say having accreditation with the sport's governing body—anyone with skis could enter. Loppets were an old tradition in Scandinavia. In the seventies, the tradition made its way to North America. The Telemark can proudly lay claim to being the first race of its kind in Southern Alberta.[315]

Strangely enough, it was the Alpine Club that started the Telemark race. The ACC had shown an interest in skiing since the 1930s, but was generally restricted to ski mountaineering and high-country ski touring. Nordic-style cross-country, however, must have appealed to the many hikers and mountaineers among the Alpine Club. The seventies were also a time of cross-fertilization: ski clubs took up canoeing and hiking, canoe clubs took up cross-country skiing. In this context, it is not surprising that Nordic ski enthusiasts in the Alpine Club might decide to sponsor a race. Bruno Struck, chairman of the Calgary Section of the ACC in 1973, was the enthusiast. He organized the first Telemark in 1973, using a point-to-point course from the old 1A Highway at Wapta Lake to the shores of Lake Louise.

Jeanne Gonnason was involved with the Telemark for many years. In an article she wrote on the race for the CSC newsletter, she stated that about 30 people took part in the first race. It soon grew to over 500. The numbers forced the organizers to come up with a new course, a loop so that racers didn't have to be shuttled back to the start point. Using the 1A, some existing trails and as many natural glades and clearings as they could find, a route was cobbled together. "It was a hazardous course," she reported. "Anyone coming along after the racers had passed would see broken branches all over, many of them with assorted scarves and hats attached!"[316]

The ACC eventually remembered it was a mountaineering club, and in 1979, decided to stop sponsoring the Loppet. It was too difficult to get enough volunteers. As chief organizer, Len Gottselig didn't want to see the Telemark die so he approached one of his other clubs, the CSC. He found a sympathetic ear in Gerry Radke, the club's president. Along with many other members, Radke was concerned that the CSC was slowly turning into a social club and felt skiing needed more emphasis. He was quite enthusiastic about having the club involved in racing again. It wasn't too hard to convince the council that the Calgary Ski Club should take over the event. Ken Tatebe and Alasdair Fergusson, the next two presidents, were of like mind so the club became the new sponsor.

CSC volunteers first helped out on the 1979 edition of the Loppet. One of the volunteers was Fergusson. Primarily an alpine skier, he had only done a bit of cross-country, but was one of the more active members of the club and always ready to help out. After that first event, the Nordic bug bit him. Fergusson became increasingly involved in the race and eventually took over as the coordinator. Like a lot of helpers, he spent his first race frantically shovelling snow to help prepare the course. Volunteers used snowshoes to tramp down the course and skied it to set a track. They had to fill a lot of holes, bank corners, and when the park wardens weren't watching, judiciously remove a few obstacles. Preparing the course was a tremendous amount of work, which was why the Alpine Club had decided to retire.

Ironically, course preparation got easier just as the CSC took over. Parks Canada gave permission to run the Loppet, but the agency was stubborn about allowing any trail work. In the early years, the park was in the process of deciding if it should provide cross-country skiing facilities, particularly special trails. Thanks in part to the lobbying of the race organizers, Parks Canada decided to do some ski trail development around Lake Louise. The racecourse became the Telemark trail, with a park crew clearing and widening the route in the fall of 1979. That made it possible for snowmobiles to pack the course and use a track-setter. Volunteers from the Banff Ski Runners initially did the job, but Gottselig, Fergusson and a couple of other ski club members soon learned how to groom trails. It was the start of the CSC's involvement in track setting.

Around they go: Telemark Loppet competitors, circa 1980. (ALASDAIR FERGUSSON.)

Even more exciting for the race organizers was Parks Canada's creation of the Fairview Trail in 1982. This ran east from the Chateau and looped back on the Moraine Lake Road and the old Tramway track. The new trail allowed the club to have two different distances for the Loppet, one 20 kilometres, the other 12. Thanks to the race, park crews and ski club volunteers have constantly improved the trails, but not without many hassles. The park bureaucracy was slow to give approval for even straightforward and often much-needed trail modifications. On one occasion, the park wardens were not amused to find Gottselig doing a little unauthorized sapling removal. Moving the race was not an option. The club needed the deep and reliable snow pack around Lake Louise.

The trail work was vital for the race to continue. From a high of perhaps 800, the number of participants had slipped to fewer than 300 by 1979, probably because of the occasionally terrifying course. Though the race never again reached those record highs, it regained popularity once the route was improved. With the new trails, the Telemark was also able to get Canadian Ski Association sanction in 1982, becoming part of the Alberta Division's loppet series.[317] When telemark skiing underwent a revival in the mid-eighties, the club renamed the race the Lake Louise Loppet in 1987 to avoid any confusion. By then the race was well established as a club event, a service the CSC performed for the ski community at large.

Downhill Revival

Cross-country was an important addition to the club's skiing repertoire. But in the early eighties, the CSC was known primarily as a downhill skiing club. Busloads of happy, singing, occasionally drunk Calgary Ski Clubbers went north to Jasper, south to Whitefish and west to every ski resort in British Columbia. The club successfully revived the venerable tradition, the bus tour, but on a grand scale. And it was updated. As well as the weekend trips to resorts, club skiers could also hop on a plane for a weeklong jaunt to a giant American ski hill. Or to Hawaii, though not much skiing was done there!

The CSC can't take full credit for the revival. The club benefited from the rapid growth of downhill skiing in the 1970s and into the 1980s. As the Calgary market got larger, skiing in the Banff region improved and became a major attraction for the region. Many of the people coming to the city for the booming economy also wanted to go skiing. Newcomers looking for skiing partners flooded both the CSC and the PSC, resulting in a couple of new ski clubs. The local ski hills, however, still had many limitations that boosted interest in going farther afield. Skiers eventually got bored with the same hills. American resorts in the 1970s were bigger and offered amenities not seen much north of the border, like on-hill accommodation and a fun nightlife. The people who skied with the club were adventurous and also had money. It was not hard to fill the buses and the air charters.

Getting the bus tours going again was part of Boleantu's 1972 agenda. The Petroleum Ski Club had three or four buses going to destinations. Boleantu thought that with this kind of demand, the CSC should be able offer a strong program. He believed that it was a vital part of getting the club back on its feet and was quickly proved right. Once the club started to offer bus trips again, they quickly snowballed (so to speak) in popularity and attracted new members. By the 1973/74 season, the club ran trips to Panorama, Kimberley, Whitefish and Marmot, managing about a full bus for each. A year later, this had more than doubled to nine weekend trips plus a number of day trips, despite poor snow conditions. Now the CSC was also chartering more than one bus for some expeditions.

The bus trips were the mainstay of the downhill program, but the club soon tried more glamorous offerings. During the sixties, the club had tried to organize both European and American excursions, yet could never get quite enough interest. The new CSC was different. In 1974, the CSC piggybacked on a Calgary Jaycees trip to the Quebec Winter Carnival. Quebec was a party trip rather than a ski trip—three or four made it out to the hills in the Laurentians—but it demonstrated that members were interested in going further abroad. For the 1974/75 season, the club went to Salt Lake City, Utah for a full week. The CSC teamed up with the Petroleum Ski Club and the Bumbiters Ski Club to offer an all-inclusive charter, with hotels, lift tickets and dinners. Utah was a roaring success. By the late 1970s, the club was offering a major trip to the U.S. every year, sometimes with another club, sometimes alone. Salt Lake City in Utah and Steamboat in Colorado were popular destinations.

Several club members give much of the credit for the success of the downhill program to Murray Lowick. "He did a hell of a job," says Ken Tatebe. "He was a good businessman, he had a good head for putting the trips together." Lowick was also willing to do a lot of legwork. On one occasion he went to Kelowna and personally checked the proposed accommodations for the club's New Year's trip. Lowick wasn't the only ski director to do a good

Have skis, will travel: Linda Boleantu and Chris Eggert at Whitefish, Montana, circa 1970s. (GLENBOW ARCHIVES, PA2351-92.)

job, but he set the standard. The CSC trips were not necessarily cheap, yet as Tatebe points out, they gave good value for the money. A tour usually had four-star accommodations and good meals and went to great destinations. Unlike other downhill clubs like the PSC and Skirac, the CSC always budgeted for only two to a room, ensuring a higher level of comfort. "I don't think you could offer the same kind of trip now for the equivalent of what we paid," Tatebe claims.

One of the biggest Lowick coups was the "ski and sun" trips. These combined a ski week with a week at a sunny tropical resort. The first time it was Utah and Hawaii. The gimmick was done again at least once, though it was a bit of a stretch for the pocketbooks of most members. Ski and Sun was not the only high-end offering. For a few years, the club provided members a chance to sample the delights of helicopter skiing. A new operator flying out of Panorama gave the club an excellent deal. A member could go heli-skiing for $100 a day; a price that even in today's dollars would make any ski enthusiast drool. Despite several attempts, however, the CSC never organized an excursion to Europe.

The downhill trips were so popular that for many years the club would have a sign-up night in October. It was first come, first served, with skiers coming down to the clubhouse to get their name on the trip, or trips, of their choice and pay a deposit. For many trips, there was a waiting list. Sign-up night could be a zoo, but it quickly became something of a social event for the downhill crowd.

Some of the ski trips have become legends in club circles. One of the most famous was the New Year's Eve trip to Big White at Kelowna. The club filled a PWA 737, specially chartered for the event. The plane was to leave on December 31st but there was one small problem: fog completely socked in the Kelowna airport. No flights were landing that evening. Rather than wait around the airport, they went back to the clubhouse and threw an impromptu New Year's party. For some it continued through the night and all the way back to the airport early the next morning. The fog had lifted and the CSC's flight, full of bleary-eyed skiers, was soon in Kelowna and heading for Big White.

The downhill trips of the seventies and eighties were a big part of the club's culture for a decade. They recreated some of the atmosphere of camaraderie of the ski trains. Dedicated skiers went on at least one or two a year, and sometimes many more. "People liked to get on the bus, turn their brain

The disco bus: CSC skiers on another trip, circa 1980. (ALASDAIR FERGUSSON.)

off and have fun for the weekend," remembers Eileen Coffin, who was downhill director for several years in the eighties. Sing-alongs were common; the entire busload would sing itself hoarse. The club even produced a songbook. Alasdair Fergusson recalls one outing when he brought tapes of dance music and George the driver put them on the bus sound system. "George would flick the interior lights on and off in time with the music," Fergusson remembers. "We called it the disco bus." He limped into the office the next day, legs black and blue from dancing in the narrow aisle of the bus.

The club's downhill trips had no lofty goal beyond providing a good time. The one popular exception was the Lake Louise Ski Improvement Weekend. By the seventies, the club's historical role as an entry into skiing had pretty much ended. People joining the club were generally already able to ski. Several attempts to offer beginner lessons didn't last long. With different packaging, however, the club could still help people ski better. The Improvement Weekend offered an early season primer to get ready for the season and improve one's skills. Set in early December, the weekend was not just a lesson package, but also an early Christmas party. The club stayed at the Chateau Lake Louise for two nights and spent two days at the ski hill. Each day started with lessons divided by skill group and then free skiing in the afternoon, followed with dinner and drinks. The availability of cross-country trails right around the Chateau and on the Pipestone River by the hill meant that Nordic enthusiasts could come as well. It was wildly popular for a number of years, attracting up to 240 participants, which was half the winter capacity of the Chateau at the time.

The downhill trips were fun, with good skiing, good people and good times. They also reflected the growth of the ski industry and the club's place in it. The club had tapped into the baby boomers' desire for fun skiing and satisfied the demand with style.

SUMMERTIME MAKES ME FEEL FINE

Summer is a difficult time for any ski club. The long hiatus from snow doesn't do much for solidarity, as people hang up their skis and make do with other pursuits. One of the CSC's landmark changes in the seventies was that it became a year-round organization, the "Club for All Seasons." Through hiking, backpacking, canoeing and a host of other activities, the Calgary Ski Club's appeal spread beyond simply skiing and transformed it into a general-purpose recreational club.

Over the years, there had been sporadic attempts to have summer activities for the club. On the skiing side, there had been the summer races as well as trips down to Logan's Pass in Montana and Bow Summit to enjoy skiing in the sun. This tended to appeal to only a few fanatics. The May 1950 newsletter noted that the club council planned trail rides on horseback "in order to keep the gang together during the green months."[318] Summertime activities, however, never really caught on. This changed dramatically in the 1970s. Like skiing, there was an explosion in outdoor recreation over the decade, especially hiking. It appealed to young baby boomers, the same people joining the ski club in droves. It was only a matter of time before the club ventured out onto the summer trails.

Len Gottselig recalls that the club's hiking program really sprang out of cross-country skiing. At first, it was pretty much the same crowd, people who liked being out in the mountains. The Friday socials also played a role. The club at the time was still relying on the Double T to organize summer activities, most of which revolved around socials. Like-minded members bumped into each other at the socials in the summer and made dates to go hiking. Two of these members were Hans Ockermuller and Hubert Rielinger. They were keen hikers. Hans recollects that he and Hubert started organizing trips during the warm months of 1973. There was soon a core group of enthusiasts, like Dave Russum, who led many hikes and backpacking trips. Hiking soon became the club's flagship summer program.

The Boleantu council welcomed hiking and backpacking enthusiastically. It was an ideal sort of club activity for the summer, getting people out to the mountains as a group. And it was cheap, requiring almost no club resources, just volunteers to co-ordinate a car pool—the usual form of transportation—and lead the hikes. For the summer of 1974, Helen Twoyniuk, another eager cross-country skier, co ordinated a selection of trips for the club. It was a mix of day trips and car camping. Like cross-country, the hiking program grew quickly. In the first year up to 30 people showed up for a hike and the next year the club included overnight backpacks. By the end of the seventies the club even offered week long trips, usually consisting of a backpack into a base camp and then day hikes from there.

Most of the hikes were in the nearby mountain parks. "Just look in Trail Guide of the Canadian Rockies and that was where we went," says Hans Ockermuller, who led many of the early hikes. Kananaskis Country was not a popular destination until later, due to lack of a good road through most of

The mountains in summer: CSC hikers, circa 1974. (GLENBOW ARCHIVES, PA 2351-82.)

the seventies. The club was fairly adventurous, however, and would go up to Jasper and out into British Columbia. Eileen Coffin, a former president and one of the club's stalwart volunteers, remembers going out to Top of the World Provincial Park in southeastern British Columbia. Coffin was also a keen skier, but she remembers that the hiking program was a real draw for her and many others. It was one of the reasons she preferred the CSC to the Petroleum Ski Club.

One of the biggest challenges the hiking program faced was being too popular. More people were coming on outings than trip leaders could handle and non-members crashed the hikes in alarming numbers. There were other organizational problems and growing pains, not just for the club but for hiking in general. The trip co-ordinators soon found that they needed to give outings ratings to let people know how strenuous or challenging a hike would be. This was essentially subjective and in the early days there was no commonly accepted scale or commonly accepted criteria. Most trip leaders did not have any special training, usually just people with some experience hiking.

This led occasionally to some unintended epics when a hike turned out to be much harder than anticipated. Often it was the tour leader's fault. "Alasdair [the president] has to be told some stories about some of the hikes this year, one in particular that included a belay down a 25-foot cliff ... and no prior warning that the hike included this," recorded the minutes for one council meeting in 1980.[319] One headache for the hiking co-ordinators was trying to weed out poor trip leaders, especially those without patience for less fit or less experienced participants. It was a problem that also plagued the cross-country ski program, and would become a major issue for the club in the later 1980s as liability emerged as a real concern for outdoor recreation.[320]

In the early days, though, there was little concern with legalities. People just had fun and occasional misadventures were stories shared later over a beer. The usually reliable Hubert Rielinger led one backpacking trip to Assiniboine and miscounted the number of tents they needed. With great hilarity the hikers squeezed into the tents they had and ribbed Hubert about it for years. A marriage came out of that trip! Alasdair Fergusson remembers another trip to Floe Lake. During a violent thunderstorm in the night, Dave Russum leapt out of his tent to better secure it, clad only in underwear and boots. Everyone watching the storm was treated to the spectacle of Dave's

Len Gottselig and friend on the South Saskatchewan River, 1975.
(GLENBOW ARCHIVES, PA 2351-96.)

whiter than white undershorts fluorescing with each flash of lightning. It was an excellent advertisement for laundry detergent.

Canoeing and then cycling followed fast on the heels of hiking and were popular. The club took advantage of the interest in non-snow recreation with summer memberships in 1974. It was another measure to build up the membership, through attracting non-skiers. The club hoped that summer members would become full members, and to some extent this happened. The summer memberships brought active people into the club, which helped counterbalance the people joining for the socials. The club recognized the crossover between the hiking, canoeing and cycling crowd and the cross-country ski program. The Nordic director took them over in the early 1980s.

SLOW PITCH

Hiking and canoeing were just the start. The council soon had a new director for Sports and Activities and it was one of toughest jobs. The director had to look after a bewildering array of activities. Some were sports like tennis, but others, like wine tasting, weren't active recreation at all. An attitude of anything goes gripped the club, and there were few things that people didn't try in the quest to provide novel entertainment for the members.

It was the members, not the ski club council, who were the sources of the Sports and Activities program. The council mostly just rubber-stamped ideas that members proposed. The major requirement was that an activity couldn't run a deficit. But if a member or members thought something would be fun, was willing to act as the co-ordinator and recruited the volunteers to run the program, the attitude was go for it. The survival of a new activity was dependent mostly on the interest of other members. Some programs lasted for a surprisingly long time; others were short-lived. The enthusiasm was not hard to understand. Many members were new to the city and the activities were another way to meet people and have fun.

It would be difficult to enumerate and describe everything the club organized. There were annual events, like river rafting, the curling "funspiel" and the Okanagan Olympics—a grown-up version of sports week, held over a summer weekend in the Okanagan Valley and involving lots of beer. The club had a strong tennis program in the seventies. Softball, volleyball, horseback riding, sailing, windsurfing, car rallies—the list of things the club tried goes on. Not everything was sporty. A loyal bridge group met at the clubhouse nearly every Tuesday for years. The cultural activities, like wine-tasting or theatre-going groups, would come and go. "I set up a dining club," remembers Eileen Coffin. "About 30 people signed up at first, but after a few months it was just me, my sister and one other person. So it died. Then a couple of years later, we did it again, same thing."

The sports and activities program, however, strained the club's base of volunteers. Everyone with a pet activity competed for volunteers. "We always knew when we were doing too much and getting stretched too thin because the volunteers would suddenly drop off," claims Ken Tatebe. The programs were also a bookkeeping nightmare. Co-ordinators often did a poor job of keeping their records. "One problem we had was with budgets. People frequently couldn't put together a budget for an activity," recalls Alasdair Fergusson. "A standard format was created, but it remained a problem." In a heartfelt comment, one activities director stated in his annual report that most of his time was spent instructing the different co-ordinators on how to budget and prepare financial reconciliations. It was tough for the newsletter editor to get schedules from the co-ordinators in time for deadlines. There were many complaints from members about events not being listed in time for them to sign up.

Some people in the club were also concerned about the effect all the

Who needs to ski? CSC raft trip, circa 1980. (Alasdair Fergusson.)

activities had on the club's identity and cohesion. They asked whether a ski club should include theatre going, wine tasting or dinner outings. In one membership survey, a few people suggested that with everything going on, the organization shouldn't call itself a ski club. Gerry Radke, president in 1978/79, called for abolishing many of the sports and activities to get back to skiing. It was a question the club's Long-range Planning Committee thought it should address in 1979. The committee had mixed feelings. On one hand, it stated that "there should be no discouragement of eager and capable volunteer organizers." On the other hand, it also recommended that sports and activities be considered non-essential. If there was difficulty in attracting volunteers for an activity, it should die.[321] "It is the opinion of the L.R.P.C. that the Calgary Ski club should concentrate on doing a few activities well, than to organise a lot of mediocre activities."

Despite such misgivings, for more than a decade, the membership at large enjoyed and supported the expanded offerings. As several members of seventies and eighties vintage point out, there was something to do almost every night of the week down at the ski club. For the core of young singles in the club, it created a sense of fellowship and ample ways to fill their time outside of skiing. The CSC's official motto: "The Club for All Seasons."

THE NEW CLUBHOUSE

The 1207 Connection was great, but it still wasn't really an exclusive clubhouse. In 1976, the CSC finally got a place to call its own, and the acquisition immediately strengthened the club's identity. The Ski Centre on 10th Avenue was the central meeting place for everything, from downhill and cross-country skiing trips to most of the club's new activities. Almost any night of the week, you could head down to the clubhouse and something was going on. More importantly, the new premises were even better as a place for socials and for one night every week was essentially a nightclub for members and guests only.

Tom Boleantu had given the CSC a clubhouse of sorts, but in a short time many members were unhappy with the arrangement. The 1207 Connection was essentially a place to have socials. It did not have space for the club office and the lease restricted how often the club could use the premises. A vocal segment felt that the Connection had become a business enterprise built on the club, since the premises were rented out to other groups yet the club didn't get the revenue. Boleantu cited work pressure when he resigned as club president in the summer of 1975, but there had been a stormy general meeting about the clubhouse earlier. One long-time club member describes it as an "impeachment."

The exact order of events is a little unclear. The club executive had formed a committee to look at alternative clubhouse possibilities and it reported to the annual general meeting in April 1975. Ironically, the committee, headed by Gord Cuming, recommended the club stay with the current premises because the membership wasn't large enough to merit new digs. The club did renegotiate the lease with Pi Consultants to allow more use of the Connection, such as the Sunday night Ski Folk Coffee House. After Boleantu resigned, however, the relationship between the CSC and Pi deteriorated. Much of the squabbling centred on the maintenance and cleanup of the premises. A flood of the basement brought matters to a head. Pi refused to give rent relief to the club, expecting the club or its insurance to pay for repairs. The club felt their landlord should shoulder responsibility. The CSC went so far as to consult a lawyer. The time had come to move.

Finding new quarters was not exactly easy. Calgary was going through a boom, real estate was at a premium, and rents were rising. The club's needs were also quite specific. The clubhouse had to be cheap, have a convenient central location but be big enough for the socials and provide space for an office. The hunt for new premises had continued after the meeting in 1975, and in the nick of time, something suitable materialized. The building at 1024-10th Avenue SW was a lucky find. Marathon Realty, the property arm of the Canadian Pacific Railway, owned the one-storey commercial structure. It was located along the railroad's right of way in a somewhat rundown part of the downtown core. There was ample parking thanks to the right of way. The club could renovate the building and it was cheap.

The club used volunteer labour to do most of the renovations, and it turned into a bit of an epic. Len Gottselig remembers spending most of his spare time over the course of several months at the building, tearing down walls and partitions and building new ones to get the layout the club wanted. Rod MacDonald, who as the 1976/77 president oversaw the project, singled out Hubert Rielinger, Len Gottselig and Gerry Radke for their efforts on the new clubhouse. Upwards of 30 or 40 club members helped out regularly. Even with the volunteers, however, the renovation turned out to be much more expensive than expected, in the order of $30,000. The club had a new clubhouse, but it was broke.

Nonetheless, the CSC would get good value for the money. The new clubhouse was larger than the 1207 Connection and more versatile. The dance area was smaller, but the games area, with darts and the like, was larger and there was a lounge. The club now had a meeting room and space for the office, which moved over from its long-time location in the Lancaster Building. There was much more storage space for equipment and a place to work on skis. It was even possible to run ski-conditioning classes in the clubhouse.

The building soon began to pay for itself and then some. The regular Friday social became even more popular and lineups went out the door into frigid winter nights. The socials became a tidy little business and made up to a thousand dollars a night in profit. Along with Bill the bartender, the club hired professional disc jockeys while volunteers manned the door and did the grunt work. The crowds regularly flouted fire regulations, despite the best efforts of the clubhouse director. The Friday social was so popular that many people were joining the club simply to go to the parties. One member noted, with some chagrin, that people were starting to refer to the clubhouse as "the meat market." The issue of the social, or the non-skiing member, became a sore point in the club.[322]

Yahoo! Stampede dance, circa 1980. (ALASDAIR FERGUSSON.)

THE SKI FOLK COFFEE HOUSE

The Coffee House has to be one of the more interesting digressions of the CSC in the seventies. It started in 1975 at the 1207 Connection, benefiting from the new clubhouse. Gord Cuming, the Ski Folk founder, recalls that the club needed regular events when it got better access to the Connection. Randy Sherk, the clubhouse director, approached Cuming for ideas. He had a good one: the clubhouse was already equipped with a sound system, so why not have a folk music night?

Cuming was exactly the right person for the job. A recent arrival from Saskatchewan, he had been very involved in the Regina folk music festival. He was well connected to the folk music circuit, which was mostly based around small coffeehouses and bars and clubs like the Calgary Folk Music Club. Through his connections, Cuming was able to bring in well-known names in Canadian folk music, as well as many not-so-well-known ones. The Ski Folk Coffee House was an open stage, and local and visiting musicians were welcome. As Cuming recalls, a regular open stage was a unique offering in Calgary at the time. The Coffee House was literally that; it was not a licensed evening. Instead, the club got an espresso machine and offered a mysterious drink called CSC cider.

The folk night became a popular offering. It got a boost when Vic Close came to Calgary from Edmonton and approached Cuming. "He told me, 'I'm connected with everyone', and you know what, he really was." For several years, the Coffee House ran nearly every Sunday. The new clubhouse, with more space and expanded seating, was perfect. Like the socials, the Coffee House attracted a lot of non-members. "Members got a discount on the door charge," says Cuming. "I would say, that on any one night, 20 or 30 per cent of the people there were members, which was pretty good." Within the club, the Coffee House had a following among the cross-country crowd. Cuming says that it was not unusual for people to show up still in their ski gear after rushing back from the mountains.

The list of luminaries who graced the folk music stage is a long one. Thanks to the open stage, Cuming reckons that just about every local talent played there at one time, including James Keelaghan and Oscar Lopez. "We had some clangers as well, but we had ways of weeding them out and everyone got a chance." The bigger names included Murray McLaughlin, Stephen Fearing, Connie Calder, Amos Garret and even Raffi. "The amazing thing is, we never paid anyone. They just came. Sometimes they weren't booked; they were just in town and would come down." Cuming remembers that one time a member of a fairly well-known rock band [whose name escapes him] came in and played a few songs. "He said that he had nowhere else to do that kind of material, his usual fans wouldn't be interested."

Inevitably, energy flagged and the Coffee House was scaled back to twice a month. This was a comfortable groove and it continued on this basis until well into the eighties. Cuming left Calgary to start a ski store in Canmore in 1977, but Dave Thompson, Vic Close and other dedicated volunteers kept the Ski Folk evening going. Cuming returned in 1979 and immediately got involved again, but when he was transferred to Ontario around 1988, the Coffee House closed its doors. By that time, it was running once a month. Cuming revived it when he moved back to Calgary in 1991. When the club lost the lease on its clubhouse in 1993, the Ski Folk Coffee House faded into history.

The next Dylan: another night at the Ski Folk Coffee House, n.d. (CSC COLLECTION.)

Turmoil

The Coffee House was great, still some members wondered what it had to do with the CSC's mandate. The proliferation of activities unrelated to skiing was just one of a number of contentious issues the club had to deal with in the seventies. The problems the club experienced were in many respects good problems: it was too popular and growing too fast. Sort of like Calgary. Yet, the club's rebirth was not a smooth process. Constant turmoil marked the seventies. Along with the excitement of new programs and fun parties, there was also chaos and confusion. There were inevitable personality conflicts on the council as the club wrestled with expansion. And there was a sustained debate over the direction the club was taking, centred on the popularity of the socials.

The clubhouse difficulties were the first major conflict of the decade. No sooner had they been sorted out than the next crisis arrived. The great membership imbroglio of 1976 was one of the club's less stellar moments. The size and the composition of the membership was the source of real concern. In the space of a year, the numbers jumped from about 350 to over 800 and then to more than 1,000. Worried that the CSC might turn into another Petroleum Ski Club, Boleantu and the council debated putting a limit on membership. A steering committee made the recommendation in March 1974. It was put to the membership at the next AGM and passed.[323]

The limit kept the club at a manageable size, but it meant that membership renewal was suddenly important and it was an administrative nightmare. In 1976, the council decided to simplify renewals with a sign-up night at the clubhouse. It was on a first-come, first-served basis. The procedure proved a disaster. Inevitably, many members didn't understand or did not hear of the new policy and didn't or couldn't make it down for the night. It also swamped the club with people whose skiing credentials were shaky or non-existent, but wanted to be able to attend the disco-pub. The 1,000-member limit had to be specially relaxed that year to deal with the complaints and make sure deserving members got in, such as some of the people who had been working on the new clubhouse.

Compounding the membership problem was the fact that record keeping had declined into chaos. The club wasn't even sure how much money had come in from memberships. Ken Tatebe was the man who sorted out the mess. A member since the early seventies, his first job on council was membership director. It was the sort of task that would scare most people off for good, yet he rose to the challenge. His reforms aimed at keeping longtime and active members. Those with memberships had priority for renewal, within certain reasonable time limits, at which point it was open season.[324] The club also began to screen applications. Prospective members had to indicate whether they skied and whether they were interested in volunteering and for what. It was an honour system. But it was backed up by changes in the constitution made in 1977, which allowed the council to refuse membership to anyone it thought was not pulling their weight. People who volunteered, served on council or participated in ski trips or sports programs were in. Everyone else took his or her chances.

The appearance of the so-called social member made screening necessary. The "disco clubhouse" was quite a hit, and soon became known in Calgary as the place to go on a Friday night. It was so popular that people joined the club just to have access to the clubhouse. It was often difficult to get into the Connection on Fridays. This created a great deal of discontent. Active members, the skiers, hikers and volunteers, were irritated that they had to fight crowds they never saw out on the ski hill or at a club meeting to get into the clubhouse. There was a widespread feeling that the social members were not pulling their weight, not even as volunteers for social events. And some members worried that the CSC was getting a reputation as a party club, which might discourage serious members from joining. Ultimately, this might jeopardize the club's programs.

The tarnished reputation of the club was also creating problems in the ski community at large. Some retailers muttered that the CSC shouldn't be allowed to hold the New and Used Ski Sale if a share of the profits went to the club because it would support partiers instead of skiers. The situation got to the point that Gerry Radke openly advocated ending the regular socials in his president's message for the February, 1979 newsletter. Despite his personal regard for the Coffee House, he singled it out as another offering that didn't belong in the CSC. He was not against having socials and parties. But Radke suggested that parties should be for the people who joined the club as active, ski-minded members, not an end in themselves.

The social member was not a new problem. There had been complaints, even back in the thirties, that people joined the club more for socializing than the serious business of skiing. There has always been a bit of split personality in the CSC between those who wanted to promote the sport and those who just wanted to enjoy it. In the seventies, however, it came to members who skied and those who didn't. The critics had a point: the CSC was supposed to be a ski club.

The puzzle that the social member posed was never really solved. Even with membership screening, through the eighties there were rumblings that too many people in the club were there for the Friday night party. Long-time members like Eileen Coffin and Ken Tatebe estimate that out of 1,000 members, perhaps only 200 to 300 were avid skiers. In some ways, the problem actually got worse. The social director received complaints about the "stag" atmosphere on Friday nights as a more hard-edged crowd showed up. In the end, the problem would look after itself when the CSC's impromptu nightclub lost steam in the late eighties.

WE THE PEOPLE

The club didn't just sit back and ride out its troubles. Councils and members looked for ways to deal with the problems. A number of important constitutional changes took place in the seventies. The changes were not revolutionary or especially innovative, but demonstrated the high level of commitment, and sophistication, among club members of the era. "There was a lot of debate; we knew our Robert's Rules," says Gord Cuming. "It was a group of people who had a lot of opinions and ideas about how to run things." There were four key changes: a revision of the constitution, the creation of the advisory council and the position of past president, and finally, the institution of some long range planning for the future of the clubhouse and the club.

The new constitution came out of the troubled years of 1975 and 1976. The last major revision was more than 10 years old and things had changed, especially about membership. The club formed a committee in 1976 consisting of Gerry Radke, Hans Ockermuller, Rin Verstraten, Alasdair Fergusson and Paul Polson. They put a notice in the February, 1977 newsletter soliciting opinions from the membership about the direction of the club. Using the Alpine Club of Canada and the Norcen Social Club (a contribution from Fergusson) constitutions as reference, some basic changes were made. The membership categories were revamped. The 1,000 member limit was made part of the constitution, requiring a two-thirds majority of members to change. Family and junior memberships were eliminated; the club was now officially adults only. There was just one basic voting membership. Associate, honorary, complimentary and affiliated memberships, all without voting or nomination rights, were rewards for friends and helpers of the ski club.

The new constitution also enshrined screening applications for membership. Current members had priority for renewal, but the council reserved the right to refuse to renew based on "the effort and enthusiasm the applicant has indicated previously."[325] The constitution set out a procedure for expelling members. Another important change was the elimination of the two-year term for the officers of the club (president, vice-president, treasurer and secretary) to encourage more people to run for office. The longer term was a disincentive. The quorum for the club's general meetings was set at only 25. Good for efficiency, such a small quorum also meant a band of motivated members could have a disproportionate influence over policy.

Listen To Your Elders

The most important constitutional change was the creation of the Advisory Council. It had had three different but complementary functions. The first was to serve as advisors to the council. The second was to act as a financial watchdog. The third was to be liaison between council and membership and act as the club ombudsman. After some debate, the council was set at three people who had to be CSC members of at least three years standing and elected by the membership. The "greybeards" were a pool of experience and knowledge for the executive's benefit. They also watched out for the interests of the membership and the club. The first advisory council was perfect, consisting of Len Gottselig, Alasdair Fergusson and Hans Ockermuller, a member since the late 1950s.

A last and more controversial change was the creation of the position of past president, which sparked a lot of controversy. Many organizations use this position to ease transition between the old and new executive. Some members saw the position as unnecessary with the advisory council. A past president as a voting director might make it harder for a new president to assert his or her authority. Proponents, however, thought the position would provide continuity and be invaluable for new presidents who only served one-year terms. The president's position was also becoming burdensome. The past president could take over certain duties, like liaison with other clubs. The membership voted in favour of a past president as a full director in 1983. On the balance, it has been successful. The first incumbent was Alasdair Fergusson and he used the position to continue his advocacy work in the ski community. Subsequent past presidents would do much the same, working with bodies like Calgary Area Outdoor Council or acting as a media contact.

Looking Forward to the Future

The core of committed CSC members were forward thinking in the late seventies. The club was going great guns, yet they took the time to think of the future. The clubhouse, for instance, was great, but the short-term lease, with a six-month demolition clause, was a source of major insecurity. In 1978, the CSC council decided to form two committees to look to the future. The Building Committee researched the best alternative for a permanent clubhouse. The Long Range Planning Committee, meanwhile, had a broader but complementary mandate. It reviewed the constitutional goals of the club, analyzed the club's success at working towards them and recommended strategies to meet them. To determine where the club stood, the LRPC used a questionnaire to survey the membership. The committee created a profile of the average member and ascertained attitudes towards the size of the club, the level of fees, the importance of the clubhouse and the activities in the club.

The two committees didn't come up with anything hugely surprising, but their recommendations did map out the future of the club for nearly a decade. The building committee looked at alternatives such as buying a building, leasing different premises, sharing a clubhouse, even building one. The committee found that in Calgary's overheated real estate market, the present clubhouse was a good deal. To build in a similar location would cost $400,000, while the club's rent, at approximately $4 a square foot, was far less than the $14 to $25 in comparable properties.[326] Despite the lack of a long-term lease, the committee recommended sticking with the existing facility. The only viable alternative was to share a community association hall—an eerily prophetic finding.

The Long Range Planning Committee found that the club was made up of single adults with an average age of 30—some six years older than that reported for the Petroleum Ski Club. The membership was slightly skewed toward women, with an average annual earnings of $20,000. The members had a high level of satisfaction with the club. They approved the adults-only orientation, thought the 1,000 member limit was just about right and felt the mix of social activities to skiing and other outdoor recreation was good. As the report put it, "The Calgary Ski Club is seen to cater to the mature active skier who likes to socialize as he/she skis."[327] The committee also found the vast majority of the membership wanted the clubhouse, but wanted it renovated. One of the major recommendations of the committee was that the

CSC should try, through better financial controls and budgeting, to create a down payment for its own facilities.

The club was willing to put its money where its planning was with a building fund. One of the sticking points with previous attempts to set up a clubhouse was lack of ready money. Previous attempts to set up building funds had always petered out. Not this time. The council and membership decided at a special meeting in May, 1979 to set aside a $10 levy on the membership, the club's profits from the Ski Sale, which in the early eighties were around $10,000, and other windfalls in a capital fund. The goal was to have $100,000 by 1981. The fund could not be used for operating costs without approval of two-thirds of the members at a special general meeting. What made the new fund a success, however, were the socials. Yearly profits were in the tens of thousands of dollars. This was beyond what the club needed to cover administrative overhead and any deficits in the programs. Revenue from the socials pumped up the fund, but the member's levy was a symbol of the club's commitment. As many CSC councils had suspected, a clubhouse was a tremendous asset, a rallying point and even a source of identity for the club.

The LRPC had other recommendations to make about the club: better financial controls, better communication to members and an expansion of the club's educational and sponsorship activities to better fulfil the constitutional aim of promoting the sport. Another suggestion from the committee was a policy and procedures manual for the club, which was duly created. Essentially, however, the committee was mostly concerned about the clubhouse and it was an exercise that would be repeated in 1982 and again later in the 1980s.

Growing Up

The club, or more importantly, its swinging singles membership, was apparently growing up. Another sign of the CSC's new maturity was that it started looking outward again. With the renewed focus on skiing in the early eighties, the club tentatively took on the role again of advocate for skiers. Some members had always thought the club needed a higher purpose. Tom Boleantu believed it should play a role in promoting the sport, just like in the old days. Gerry Radke worried that the CSC was no longer fulfilling its original objects as a society and needed a stronger profile in the community. He urged the club to consider supporting fun competitive skiing. Radke was not alone and a few key members took up the cause. The club's voice was heard again on issues important to skiers. There was even a little racing.

Alasdair Fergusson says that his interest in the big picture for skiing drew him to advocacy work. He was one of the prime movers in the CSC's renewed involvement in lobbying and community action. He did it with the support of the club. "I had, and have, a group of senior ski club members to go to for advice, so in that sense the club is represented," he explains. Other club members have helped out with preparing and presenting briefs as well as giving advice and opinions. However, as with previous CSC lobbyists such as Ted Trafford, most of the work had fallen onto Fergusson's willing shoulders.

Ski Action Alberta was the catalyst. It started as an ad-hoc committee of seven ski clubs in the province, including the CSC, demanding better skiing facilities in the Rockies.[328] The group lobbied for much-needed improvements at the hills in the parks, including their expansion. But Ski Action's big issue was the proposed ski hill development on Mt. Sparrowhawk and Mt. Shark in Kananaskis Country. A group had tried for years to get permission to create a new resort. The provincial government was reluctant to allow the project to go ahead, for fear that there was insufficient skier traffic to make it viable. The selection of Mt. Allan as the site of the Olympic alpine events for 1988, however, fanned the flames much higher.

Nobody, it seemed, except the Calgary Olympic Development Association and the provincial government, wanted Mt. Allan to become a ski hill. Environmental groups across North America were appalled. The area was prime habitat for one of the largest bands of mountain sheep on the continent. The mountain was densely forested, meaning almost all the runs had to be cut, rather than use natural terrain. Skiers were upset because the proposed hill was in the same chinook belt as short-lived Pigeon Mountain. CODA considered Mt. Sparrowhawk, which had far better natural snow and natural terrain. Due to the ease of upgrading the roads, the nod was given to Mt. Allan. Nakiska was born. Its subsequent history shows the critics had a point!

The club submitted briefs against the selection of Mt. Allan. It hosted a forum at the clubhouse in February, 1983 with some heated debate.[329] The objections the CSC, Ski Action Alberta and their new bedfellows, the environmentalist lobby, raised did not change the mind of CODA and the government. They did, however, spark serious public debate. The club also participated in hearings on planning in the mountain parks later in the 1980s. It favoured the expansion plans for Sunshine and made its voice heard.

Fergusson impressed the ski area operators with his brief at the Sunshine hearings, and he was invited to meetings of the industry's representative, the Canadian West Ski Areas Association.

Lobbying was one thing, racing was quite another. The Canadian Ski Association, the successor to CASA, decided around 1980 to broaden its scope outside the narrow confines of ski racing. The association wanted recreational ski clubs, most of which had fallen away, to rejoin the association.[330] This coincided with the CSC's desire to get more involved in the community. The CSA approached the club about setting up a committee for recreational skiing.[331] When the CSA created a flat fee of $200 a year for recreational clubs, the CSC returned to the fold. In return, the club hoped that membership in the CSA and on the recreational skiing committee would give the club more clout in matters like the Mt. Allan controversy. Fergusson, the CSC's representative to the CSA as past president, became the first chair of the committee.

The CSA wanted to get more people involved in grassroots competition and put forward a proposal in 1983 for an adult recreational ski racing circuit, sponsored by Molson's Brewing. Much more surprising was that the club became a sponsor. It was the timing. The 50th anniversary was coming up and there was a sense of history in the air. The club was running the Telemark Loppet and also participating in the Inter-Club Challenge, a fun race day between the different Calgary recreational downhill clubs. (The CSC tended to get slaughtered.) It took a few years to get organized, but by 1985 the Canadian Masters Alpine Series was up and running. The CSC supplied volunteer gatekeepers for the races. It was a major contribution, as the CSC coordinator for the event pointed out in 1989, with the club looking after four of six Alberta races in the series.[332]

Some Calgary Ski Club members even joined the Masters as competitors. There was little interest in recreational racing. Ernie Chen had been running skill development evenings at Paskapoo that became weekly slalom races, just like the old days. A participant remembers that racing on the "Poo Glacier" quickly developed one's edge control! In the 1988/89 season, eight CSC members raced the Masters series.[333] The divide between recreational skier and competitor, however, was difficult to bridge. The Masters appealed mostly to former ski racers, who enjoyed some competition, yet little to people with no background in the sport. As one CSC member says, "The problem was the ex-racers. They couldn't just race for fun, but got all competitive about it. It wasn't any fun racing up against those guys." The club's involvement with the Molstar races, as they were known, would last a few years, then petered out.

Aside from the Loppet, the racing interlude was short but the club remained involved in the ski community. The CSC was a charter member of the Calgary Area Outdoor Council, a non-profit umbrella organization of the outdoor clubs and outfits of Calgary. The club was heavily involved in Cross-Country Alberta, dedicated to Nordic sport in the province. In the 1990s, the CSC made sure skiers were part of the consultations for the updated Mountain Parks Management Plans and the Banff-Bow Valley Study. The CSC may not have commanded the attention of cabinet ministers as it had in the sixties, but it once again had a presence.

Looking Back on the Past

History played a role in getting the club back into the skiing community. As the 50th anniversary of the club's incorporation approached, more members gained an appreciation for its storied history. And it showed. The CSC pulled out all the stops to properly celebrate the occasion, not only on behalf of the current membership, but also the many Calgarians who had belonged to the club in the past. It was a moment for the CSC to look back on its legacy in skiing.

The club got an impressively early start. It set up an archives and history committee in 1979 to start preparing for the fiftieth.[334] The committee was quite ambitious. Aside from preparing a celebration for the club's milestone anniversary, it was to research the history of skiing in Banff and area for a book on the club's history. Part of the committee's job was also to decide on what to do with the club's records. Len Gottselig was chief librarian at the Glenbow Museum in Calgary and arranged for the museum's archives to become the repository of the CSC's papers.

Bob LaRue, the son of Ozzie LaRue, was another member of the committee. Along with Ken Tatebe, he became the link to an older generation of CSC members. Tatebe tracked down past presidents for research into the club's history and met other older members. As part of celebrations for the 45th anniversary, he invited some of the old-timers to events like the New Members Barbecue. Jack Farish and Alan Turney came to a special anniversary banquet in 1980. Ken then had a great idea and suggested a CSC Alumni Association. Demonstrating the volunteer spirit of the club's golden era, Ozzie

LaRue and his wife Ronnie took charge of the association. The first meeting was held in January 1982, with 22 people attending. The Alumni Association would run for several years, holding several get-togethers and even a ski trip to Norquay.

The Alumni Association put the club in contact with the collective memories of past generations. They turned up old pins, crests, photographs and even skiing equipment. With all this material, the CSC decided to create a permanent historical display and produce a club history. Cam Mitchell, a member encountered in chapter four, volunteered to interview some of the old-timers for an oral history project. He eventually wrote part of a CSC history, covering the first 25 years. This manuscript, never published, remains an invaluable description of the club's early years. Jack Farish had kept in contact with the club over the years and previously given the club trophies for the Saturday Special Program. Now he donated plaques for the new club merit awards, another Tatebe innovation.

The 50th turned into one long party. Farish died in 1983 but Alan Carscallen, Ozzie LaRue and many others were there to celebrate alongside the current members. The club had set up a new anniversary committee in late 1983 that came up with a full slate of events. There were theme socials leading up to a grand banquet in May, 1985, with Ken Read, the Crazy Canuck and one-time ski club member, as a special guest. A planned float for the Calgary Stampede parade didn't materialize, but the club put together a special weekend at Sunshine, complete with races and a costume parade on skis and another dinner. In spite of some unseasonably cold weather, the event was a big success, bringing the milestone ski season to a satisfying close.

The club had a lot to celebrate. It was a very different organization in 1985 from what it had been in 1935, but no less vital. The ski industry had grown to a scale the club's pioneers could not have imagined. The CSC was now just one part of it, and the club could no longer claim to be the voice of Calgary skiers. Of the thousands who went out to Sunshine, Lake Louise, Norquay or cross-country ski trails in the mountain parks and Kananaskis Country, only a few hundred belonged to the CSC. But this was inevitable, and more evidence of the club's early success establishing the sport of skiing around Calgary. The CSC had shown itself to be remarkably adaptable, however, and as skiing evolved the club had evolved with it. It had reinvented itself into a form suitable for the times. The crazy party club of the seventies was just the latest incarnation of the spirit of skiing.

CHAPTER SEVEN

Hard Times

THE TIMES (AND DEMOGRAPHICS) WERE A
CHANGIN'—ON THE STREET—RETRENCHMENT—
FATIGUE—THE SKI SALE—NEW NORDIC NORM—
DOWNHILL SLIDE—VIVA LAS VEGAS—SURVIVAL

In the Dirty Thirties, a "Hard Times" dance lifted the spirits of people in the Calgary Ski Club. It was a tradition that could have been revived in the late eighties. Unemployment, bankruptcies, foreclosures, drought for the farmers, it all sounded depressingly familiar. The recession Calgary suffered was not really as bad as the Great Depression, but it was still tough. And the club really felt it. The glory days of the seventies became a memory. Instead of a thousand members and a waiting list, by the mid-nineties, the club got 300 to 400 and had to give up its cherished clubhouse. The CSC was not the only ski club crying the blues. And when the economy finally perked up, the organization didn't bounce back quite the way it had in the past. Something, it seemed, had changed. People were still skiing, yet they weren't joining the club.

The CSC's problems were not of its own making. Demographics, economics and changing cultural values all played a role. The sport and recreation club was, after all, a Victorian invention. In a century and a half, people's leisure habits have changed and there is now a massive global tourism and recreation industry. These days, the Calgary Ski Club exists in the wired, 500-channel society and faces a great deal of competition. Within the world of skiing, it is easy for people to master and enjoy the sport without ever joining a club.

This was not an easy chapter to write, because the 1990s were a hard time for the club. Many of the controversies that arose are still fresh in the participants' minds and there are some hard feelings. It is misleading, however, to think that the club had been a failure simply because it no longer commands the large membership of former days or its famous 10th Avenue clubhouse. The CSC became much leaner, more focused and more of a ski club after many years with a reputation as party types. And the CSC had successes, too, such as a revitalized Nordic program. The question the Calgary Ski Club faced as it entered a new century was what kind of club it will be in the future, as it passed through a period of transition.

THE TIMES (AND DEMOGRAPHICS) WERE A CHANGIN'

The club celebrated its 50th anniversary in fine style. But among the festivities there were warning signs that the CSC, like Calgary, was well past the crest of the boom. Membership numbers had dropped considerably and were running around 600 to 700 a year. In 1984, for the first time in nearly a decade, the club had instituted a membership drive.[335] After several bumper years, attendance and spending were dropping off at socials and revenue was suffering. Costs continued to go up because of inflation. The CSC was not the only club to suffer. Skirac, which started as a group of ex-CSCers who stayed in the 1st Street clubhouse, struggled to stay afloat. The mighty Petroleum Ski Club also saw its membership numbers plummet.

Two things were affecting the club. One was the hard economic times in Alberta. The first blow was the National Energy Program in 1981. Layoffs from the oil industry swelled the ranks of the unemployed. Inflation and high interest rates plagued the economy. The waiting lists to join the club evaporated and membership dropped to less than 700.[336] The NEP was followed by the oil price crash of 1986, more layoffs and more hardship. The local ski industry was affected as much as the club itself.

Troubles in the oil patch also meant the flow of migration to Calgary slowed drastically. Former president Al Ulmer reckons that this had a lot to do with the drop in memberships. The club's success over the years was in part because it served as an introduction to skiing for newcomers in the area. Even in the go-go seventies, the renewal rate was generally barely half the membership and new bodies kept the membership up. Gord Cuming observes that the club didn't have as much appeal to native Calgarians. They already knew how to ski and had friends to go skiing with. So when people stopped moving to Calgary, membership sagged.

Demographics were the second problem, especially the subtle consequences of aging baby boomers. The club successfully recruited a large core of dedicated members in the seventies and early eighties. By 1986, the leading edge of this group hit 40. The boomers had entered their chief childbearing years. Several club members of the era recall that more and more people married and started families. No single factor, except for lack of money, had more influence on taking people away from skiing as having children, especially for women.[337] Many ski club members were also at a point in their life when careers were making greater demands, and generally speaking, people tend to become less active with age. The entire ski industry experienced a slump in the late eighties and early nineties. Observers ascribed it in part to the fact the boomers had turned a certain corner on the highway of life.[338]

The question is why the club didn't continue to attract younger people. While Generation X and the Bust Generation that followed the Baby Boom were not as big, there were still more than enough people to fill the ranks of the club. This is a big question and can't really be answered here, but there are several possibilities. The generations after the baby boom suffered due to economic recession. Leisure time for most people also began to shrink in the nineties. There had also been an ever-increasing proliferation of entertainment, recreation and travel options. And the ski industry itself was in some ways much weaker. The downhill ski industry suffered a major recession in the late eighties and early nineties. It bounced back later in the decade, but at the start of the new millennium skier days across the industry levelled out and were dropping. Cross-country skiing also suffered a slow, steady decline in the nineties in terms of absolute numbers.

In addition, there had been changes in the way people recreated on snow. Many people were taking up snowboarding instead of skiing in the nineties, and the club was slow to welcome them—the first snowboard lessons didn't appear until 1996. And there had been more competition. The University of Calgary's Outdoor Program Centre or the City of Calgary's Continuing Education department offered many of the same services as the club, such as lessons and affordable trips for skiing or hiking. Travel businesses started selling ski trip packages that were competitive with club offerings. Why join a ski club when you can go on a Bust Loose ski trip and booze it up? But there was also a more intangible cultural shift. According to CSC veteran Alasdair Fergusson, the Calgary Area Outdoor Council reports that its member clubs had major drops in numbers over the nineties, and little or no recovery.

It may be that the club as a vehicle for recreation had simply fallen out of favour.

The CSC's membership slipped gradually. There was an immediate dip in memberships and attendance at the socials after the 1986 recession. Programs like downhill skiing stayed strong, probably because casual members were the first to drop away. The loss of revenue from memberships and socials, however, caused a financial pinch. The clubhouse was expensive and the rise of nearby Electric Avenue, a strip of trendy bars, drew off the party crowd. The building fund levy was suspended in the late eighties and eliminated in 1991. In 1988, the club voted to pass the ski sale profits and interest from the building fund to general revenue.[339] The club had started to take loans from the building fund to help finance operations.[340] Finally, in 1993, it began to forgive the loans, essentially drawing down the building fund. The situation deteriorated rapidly in the nineties. Membership numbers dropped under 600, then under 500 and then dipped to barely 400 in 1994. The financial difficulties mounted.

The club just couldn't seem to keep people. "We tried everything," bemoans Eileen Coffin, who was president in 1993 and then 1995. "Nothing seemed to work." The club even re-instituted family memberships to reverse the haemorrhage. It was not a new thought. In 1977, former president Tom Boleantu criticized the club's move to adult-only membership. Presciently, he pointed out that demographics would catch up with the CSC and suggested that family programs would be necessary to retain members as they got older.[341] In 1984, Alasdair Fergusson raised the issue again at the club's general meeting. He and a number of other members had doubts about the focus exclusively on single adults, for much the same reasons as Boleantu.[342] The matter of family programming would arise from time to time over the next few years.

Realizing that at least some of the members had left because of child rearing, the CSC decided to reinstate family memberships. The results were disappointing. While the club council blamed the lack of real offerings for families and kids, aside from a "jackrabbits" program Greg MacCulloch started for cross-country skiing, there may not have been much demand. It was telling that no new recreational ski club had formed in Calgary aimed specifically at families in the 20 years since the CSC became an adults-only club. In 1994, the Calgary Area Outdoor Council held a special open house to discuss the needs of families and the possibility of starting a club aimed at that market and no one showed up. The family club had its heyday in the 1960s, and 30 years later, its time had not come again.

ON THE STREET

Nothing symbolized the changed environment like the loss of the 10th Avenue clubhouse in 1994. It was a serious blow to the CSC and was first full-fledged crisis of the 1990s, which threatened to tear the club apart.

The CSC had never felt secure with the clubhouse. The landlord, Marathon Properties, had the club on a short lease and there was the six-month demolition clause. Marathon kept renewing the lease and the club made improvements and significant repairs—the roof in 1985 and the furnace in 1988. The CSC, however, also formed several building committees to find a permanent replacement. The committees essentially came to the same conclusion. With renovation and relocation costs factored, the present clubhouse was by far the best available deal unless the club relocated far from the city centre. The building fund had grown to over $250,000 and the CSC considered buying the clubhouse, but Marathon wasn't interested.

Then in 1990, the CSC discovered through Charles Hansen, a member who was an architect, that Marathon was listing its properties along the rail corridor, including the ski centre.[343] A new building committee was formed.[344] Hansen put a new idea on the table. Through his business contacts, he thought he could put together a development consortium, with the club as a partner, to buy the clubhouse property. A redevelopment would include a new clubhouse for the CSC on the same site. A feasibility committee reviewed Hansen's suggestion. After a special club meeting, Hansen was hired to prepare a proposal for the purchase and development of the 10th Avenue property.[345]

What followed were four stressful years of uncertainty. The new building committee, under former president Steve Horner, reported that were still no affordable alternatives. The club kept the lease with Marathon and got a little breathing room as another recession settled over the land. After much delay, Hansen finally put together a redevelopment proposal with several options. The club favoured buying and subdividing the property, and with the help of a developer, building low-rise townhouse-style commercial premises for sale to various businesses.[346] Before Hansen found the investors necessary for the scheme, purchasers materialized for the clubhouse property. The club entered into frantic negotiations with two prospective buyers, Jager Holdings and a neighbouring car wash business, to share the purchase and subdivide the property.[347] Neither deal worked out. The club then decided to buy the clubhouse property outright with the building fund and a $150,000 mortgage.[348] But it was too late—Marathon had accepted a firm offer the club couldn't match. In August 1993, the club got its notice.

The saga was not over. Now a frantic search began for new premises, to buy or rent. Eileen Coffin, who had the bad luck to be president and past president during this trying time, remembers looking at "dozens of properties." Ken Tatebe, Steve Horner and others helped in the search. One developer offered a site and even drew up a design for a prefabricated clubhouse to be built to the club's specifications. CODA invited the club to set up at Canada Olympic Park. The location was not ideal and the CSC feared losing its identity—and its building fund—in a project with the larger organization.[349]

The chief stumbling block in getting a new clubhouse, however, was money. The building fund was large, but not large enough to buy a suitable building without a substantial mortgage. The council went to the membership in late 1993 to get approval to apply for a mortgage towards the purchase of a property. Faced with the unknown expenses of trying to renovate a new space, the council decided to retrench. The building committee recommended that, with the continuing decline in membership, the club should hold off on any purchase and rent facilities until it recovered.[350] Feeling the membership would not support taking on a big mortgage, the council agreed. A temporary office was found and after more searching, the club finally moved into the Rosedale Community Centre in the northwest, where it remains.

To say the loss of the clubhouse was contentious is an understatement. It was the source of many recriminations within the club. Some of the long-time members, with so many memories and much emotion invested in the clubhouse, were stricken. They felt that not replacing it immediately was a horrible mistake. Many simply left, which didn't help. Losing the clubhouse also meant losing a convenient space for meetings and socials, a gathering point for trips and storage. Other members, less attached to the building, questioned its usefulness. They argued that the clubhouse mainly served the socials, which were lucrative but diluted the membership with non-skiers. Others felt that the clubhouse had become a luxury the club simply couldn't afford. The club had survived, even flourished, without a clubhouse in the past and could do so again.

Retrenchment

The clubhouse was not the only thing that had to go. With memberships sitting at a much lower level, the club took a hard look at its offerings and started cutting back. To some extent, a simple lack of volunteers did the job for the CSC, dooming some programs and activities. The process of retrenchment was painful and sometimes acrimonious.

Cutting back was not necessarily bad. One weakness that members frequently identified in the club was fragmentation. The all-encompassing range of activities and social programs meant there was something interesting for nearly everyone in the CSC. It also meant volunteer burnout. The diverse programming required a lot of people power to run. Some members also worried about the formation of cliques within the club, and there had been misgivings for years about the lack of focus. By 1995/96, the council decided to concentrate on core programs: downhill and cross-country skiing, hiking and cycling, and to subordinate both social events and the sports and activities programs to this core.[351] Anything that couldn't support itself, both financially and with volunteers, got chopped. The motto was "building a sustainable ski club."

The rise in the cost of liability insurance helped the reduction of the sports and activities program along. Rates for the club rose substantially by 1997.[352] One quote worked out to $30 per member. Car rallies and rafting became a thing of the past. There was even some thought about scrapping the hiking program, which didn't create enough revenue to cover its share of the insurance.[353] One aspect of the club that suffered from the cuts was the social side. The sports and activities were mostly an excuse to get together outside of skiing. The loss of the clubhouse had also doomed the weekly social. The Rosedale location was not well-liked for parties.[354] The club filled the gap with pub nights, but without a doubt the atmosphere was not the same.

Fatigue

The lack of interest in volunteering was more disturbing for the club than the drop in member numbers. Like any volunteer run organization, there was probably never a time when the club had enough warm bodies. Even in the boom times, there were complaints about insufficient volunteers because the club was even busier. In the nineties, it got much worse. Members were reluctant to serve on the executive or as coordinators for activities. After the contentious years of 1994/95 and 1995/96, the club didn't have a president for a year. But even before, the club had lacked a social director for several years and was forced to use a committee to look after downhill skiing. Needless to say, this affected both the number and quality of activities within the club. Successive advisory councils felt that the directors' duties were becoming too onerous, in part to make up for a lack of grassroots volunteers and discouraging people from coming forward. The increasing burden of time commitments outside of the club was also blamed. This is a problem that the club has not solved to this day.

Without new blood entering into executive positions, the so-called old guard found itself stepping into the breach, members who had been active participants in the club since the seventies. Ironically, this may have made the problem worse. It created the impression that the older members didn't want to let go (which may have been true in some cases). It was also a disincentive for the membership at large to participate, because the veterans stepped in at the last minute. As the 1998/99 president noted dryly, "The old guard would like to start stepping back but the young bucks are not exactly breaking down the doors to replace them." In recent years, however, many of the vets have finally dropped out. It has been a rare year that the council has been fully staffed with directors, which has created uncertainty about the future.

All the stress and indecision over the clubhouse and the difficulties the club faced in the nineties caused some acrimony. One president was almost asked to resign. Fairly or unfairly, the 1994/95 board left office under heavy criticism from some quarters that it hadn't done enough to arrest the slide in memberships and replace the clubhouse. A group of members brought a list of motions to the 1995 AGM and voted them through. They intended their platform to be the foundation for revitalizing the club. Other members saw their actions as a coup.[355] The 1995/96 council took office with a definite agenda to focus the club on four key areas.[356] It was a "no sacred cows" approach that ruffled feelings. The club's efforts to reform its Nordic program raised the ire of the club's downhill skiers, feeding animosity that had existed for some time between die-hards of the two groups.[357] Meanwhile, the Nordic program changes created hard feelings with some members involved with cross-country skiing for years. Perhaps inevitably, the tense times brought personality conflicts to the fore. It all wasn't good for attracting and keeping new members.

The club did not face its problems lying down. Like a lot of non-profit groups and organizations, the CSC realized that it needed to be more focused and effective. It turned to more sophisticated management techniques adopted from the business world. As early as 1989, then president Gary Davies and the council had a special planning day and put together a business plan, aimed at increasing membership and reducing costs. One member put together a marketing plan in 1994, both for practical reasons and to increase awareness that promotion and marketing had become a vital element in keeping the club healthy. The Calgary Parks and Recreation Department was an invaluable aid for the CSC through consulting services it offered to recreational and sport clubs, to help them analyze organizational strengths and weaknesses and become more effective. In the case of the CSC, the city consultant identified recruiting and using and retaining volunteers as major issues, followed by better communication between the executive, volunteers and the membership at large.[358] But even while the club had visioning sessions, refined mission statements and developed action plans, memberships stagnated.

The right combination of leadership, policies and actions might have made a difference to the club's fortunes. There was, however, reason to think differently. At the beginning of the nineties, after the Inter-Club races at Lake Louise, CSC president Gary Davies heard the same worries from the heads of the PSC and Skirac about declining membership, lack of volunteer interest and financial difficulties.[359] All the downhill ski clubs seemed trapped in the same downward cycle. The PSC and CSC have survived, in reduced circumstances, while Skirac didn't. It was not an easy time to be a ski club.

The Ski Sale

Even the venerable New and Used Ski Sale had problems in the nineties, creating more headaches for an overworked club executive. After the crisis of the early seventies, the sale had continued to grow. The contribution to the club's coffers increased until by the early eighties it was earning over $10,000 a year. The sale had become a sophisticated little business enterprise. In 1977, the sale first used borrowed computers for inventory control, which was improved upon in 1980 when a club member arranged sponsorship from Wang Computers.[360] In the age before personal computers, this was a coup—the club got the use of a mini-computer worth a quarter of a million dollars. Although there were many bugs to work out in the early years, computerization progressively reduced much of workload and paperwork for doing consignments and producing cheques.

Another satisfied customer: Ski Sale, 1987. (ALASDAIR FERGUSSON.)

Another big change was the 1984 partnership with a ski show. The club had run the sale as a ski fair in the late 1960s, with fashion shows, movies and equipment demonstrations, but had moved back to a simple sale in the seventies. At the same time, big commercial shows with the same format as the fair had proliferated in North America and often had some sort of consignment sale as a component. It was only a matter of time before one came to Calgary. The club declined a couple of invitations to hold the sale in conjunction with shows, generally because it didn't seem like the show would help the sale much. The Calgary Ski Travel and Recreation Show made such an overture in 1983. The club said no but found the show drew off people from the sale and decided to reconsider.³⁶¹ The Canadian National Sportsmen's Show, a non-profit group, had bought out the Travel Show and the CSC and CSPS came to arrangement with the new company to hold the show and sale together.

The deal had pluses and minuses. The sale moved in 1984 from the Agricultural Building to the new Roundup Centre, which was a much better facility. The ski sale partners, however, felt that the sale lost some profile to the show and also worried that the higher admission cost of the show might drive off customers.³⁶² Despite the misgivings, the partnership continued. In 1988, the Silver Group, the company of Toronto promoter Howard Silver, took over the ski show from the Sportsmen's Shows, which had been struggling to produce a profit.³⁶³ The club was initially pleased with the professionalism of Silver and the sale benefited from larger advertising and marketing budgets.

Silver found it difficult to make money. He squeezed the club and also the businesses that put booths in the show, including ski shops that consigned large amounts of skis to the sale. Another point of contention was an increasing retail presence in the ski show itself, which the CSC and CSPS felt was undermining their sale. The club was already worried about the state of the sale, due to the decline in the ski industry in general. There was some question in the club in 1991 whether the CSC should continue with the event.

The sale partners formed a Long Range Planning Committee in 1992 to come up with a strategy for the future. The chief question was whether to remain associated with a commercial show. The committee concluded that it was a good synergy, as long as costs didn't rise any further.³⁶⁴ This is exactly what happened the following year when Silver demanded larger fees. During negotiation for a contract in 1993, the relationship with the promoter deteriorated until that September, almost literally the last minute, the club and the ski patrol decided to go their own way. It was a mad scramble, first finding a location in the Marlborough area, and then getting advertising out, but the sale went on.

As it turned out, dropping Silver did not hurt the New and Used Ski Sale much, if at all. Most of the local retailers and ski areas supported the move.³⁶⁵ The club had also suspected that many people coming to the sale had little interest in the ski show and had resented paying the extra money for admission to both. The first couple of years after going independent were tough, as expenses were higher initially, especially for advertising. In 1996, the club and the patrol moved the sale to the Max Bell Arena in northeast Calgary, which it still uses today.[366] Initially, the club thought it would offer a community ski show, much like it had in the past, and in competition with the commercial shows. The workload for that was daunting and the partners have been content to just run a large consignment sale since 1995.

With the revival of the local downhill ski industry, the sale has continued to do very well, and, in fact, has grown in sales volume through the nineties. The 1992 planning committee resulted in a tightly run organization. The three partners, the CSC, the ski patrol and the Lake Louise Ski Club, drafted a formal agreement that clearly defined their responsibilities. Thanks to a series of good sale directors, there were improvements to everything from inventory to floor layout that made the sale much easier to run.

Moving into a new century, volunteer fatigue has become a weakness. A smaller club found it harder to get people out to help. At the organizational level, many of the same faces were seen year after year, people like Graham Smith, Larry Tibbitts, Helen Isaac and Greg MacCulloch of the CSC and Brian Pitulay and Dave Zdep of the ski patrol. These days, the main players have a lot of grey hairs. Some, like Al Ulmer, who was director of the sale many times and a major contributor to its continued success, dropped out. The ski patrol and Lake Louise Ski Club have had similar difficulties. This problem has not gone away. Another long-time sale director, Alasdair Fergusson, is presently worried about succession planning. With so many experienced people close to retirement, there is grounds for concern about the future of the sale.

New Nordic Norm

All was not doom and gloom in the 1990s. One thing the club did extremely well was renovate its cross-country offerings to reflect major changes in the sport. The effort earned high praise from the North American association of Nordic ski area operators.[367] The innovative program, along with the continued sponsorship of the Lake Louise Loppet, established the CSC as a major force in Nordic skiing in southern Alberta.

The need to reform the club's traditional cross-country offerings was clear by the early nineties. The program that had evolved in the seventies was based on mountain touring on light Nordic gear. It was often called "hiking on skis" because most tours followed summer hiking trails and emphasized the wilderness experience over developing good ski technique. However, the

Sleek starters at the Lake Louise Loppet, circa 1992. (ALASDAIR FERGUSSON.)

club trips had problems, mostly due to poorly trained trip leaders. Trips had a designation for difficulty and the club had special easy or "slowpoke" outings to accommodate beginners and less-fit skiers. There were still horror stories of gruelling tours beyond the ability of most of the participants and there had been several serious incidents and injuries.[368] Many easy hiking trails were fast, narrow slalom courses on skis. By the beginning of the nineties, the club's Nordic program had dwindled seriously.

Cross-country skiing had also been transformed with the advent of trail grooming and track-setting. At the beginning of the 1970s, the first mechanical packing and grooming of trails took place in Vermont. A track was an important part of classic Nordic skiing, allowing participants to "stride and glide" with greater ease. Before grooming, at the beginning of winter the first skiers on a popular route broke trail, establishing the track. This tended to be uneven and often awkward to ski. Packing down a trail with a snowmobile and then mechanically incising two perfect tracks made skiing on skinny skis much more pleasurable. With grooming and track-setting, for both the classic stride and glide technique and the new skating technique, more and more cross-country skiers were approaching the sport from an athletic perspective.

In the 1980s, track-set trail systems appeared at Bragg Creek, in Peter Lougheed Provincial Park, at Mt. Shark in Kananaskis Country, the Canmore

Nordic Centre and at various points in the national parks. Now cross-country skiers could choose wide trails designed for Nordic skiing, which were often much more suitable for beginners or intermediates. A long day of mostly uphill touring followed by a long downhill run back out could be replaced by a fun two- to four-hour workout on mixed terrain, on lighter competition style gear, emphasizing technique over endurance. One ski publication summed up it up as "wool" (the traditionalists) vs. "Lycra" (the performance skier). By the early 1990s, interest in cross-country skiing as a performance sport for fitness skyrocketed and club members were requesting track skiing more and more.

The CSC had outings to the trail systems, but the feeling remained that touring in the mountains was "real" skiing. Ironically, as the nineties approached, more and more people were discovering ski touring as it had been done years before, on much heavier gear that reduced mobility but increased control. These enthusiasts ventured into alpine terrain where skinny skis were not suitable, and the hazards, especially negotiating avalanche terrain or glaciers, were higher. These tours required much more skill and training. Caught between these two different developments, the club's program looked old-fashioned.

In 1993, a group of enthusiasts in the club, including Greg Grundberg, Greg MacCulloch, Tamsin Carlisle, Darrell Herrick, Dave Donald and a number of others started a multi-year program to expand and rejuvenate Nordic skiing. The traditional style of backcountry touring remained part of the program, but two new components were added: the groomed and track-set skiing and the Mountain Touring and Telemark programs. The main focus, however, was on track skiing. The new Nordic committee identified this as the greatest area of potential growth, based on industry figures and surveys of CSC members.[369]

More importantly, the revamped program emphasized a progression of skills and improvement, especially for the beginner.[370] The club established introductory seminars, followed by the "Never-Ever" trips, which were aimed at the novice and took place on groomed trails. Hearkening back to the early days of the club, the Never-Ever day started with a lesson and then free skiing in the afternoon. The club also offered inexpensive lessons with qualified instructors to encourage skill improvement. The reformers hoped that skiers more interested in backcountry touring would use lessons and trips on groomed trails to improve their skiing skills before venturing onto more difficult trails.

In 1994, the club hired former National Team skier and coach Kjerstin Baldwin to add a performance element.[371] Baldwin instituted a ski conditioning program, which was open to all club members, a master's program, and a jackrabbit program. The master's program emphasized developing the skills and fitness to allow participants to compete in citizen racing. It included a "learn to loppet" seminar. The Jackrabbit ski league was a national program, named after Quebec ski pioneer Herman "Jackrabbit" Johanssen. It introduced kids to cross-country skiing, increased their skills and allowed them to start competing as "Racing Rabbits." It was very much like the old Bobcats program that the club set up for alpine skiing back in the sixties. Both the masters and jackrabbit proved popular, and more than a few veteran CSC skiers were spotted in spiffy new Lycra outfits. As the new approach to cross-country caught on, the committee even produced a separate annual newsletter, the Nordic Ski News.

The revamped Nordic program reconnected the club to the larger skiing community. The club had always justified organizing the Lake Louise Loppet as a community service as well as a public relations event. Enthusiasm in the club for the Loppet had waned in the late eighties and for a couple of years there was some danger the CSC might pull out. The stronger Nordic contingent helped keep the race going. The City of Calgary Leisure Learning Services approached the club to form a partnership to provide ski lessons, and in 1995 an agreement was reached, with the CSC supplying the instructors for Leisure Learning's lessons. It complemented perfectly the club's own efforts, such as the successful Never-Ever program, and elevated the CSC's profile considerably.

Volunteer track-setting reinforced the club's new image as a Nordic club. When the Lake Louise Loppet course was first groomed, the Banff Ski Runners had done it. Several members of the CSC, particularly Len Gottselig, decided to learn the techniques involved. Meanwhile, in the early 1980s, the city's parks and recreation department decided that while grooming trails on Calgary's civic golf courses was desirable, it didn't want to do it. Members of the Foothills Nordic Ski Club took over the job as volunteers. By 1993, the FNSC was ready to have someone else take the burden; the CSC decided to step up. The club was already borrowing machinery from the city and Foothills for grooming the Loppet course. Once CSC volunteers began to groom and track-set, it was only a matter of time before the club got some grants and invested in its own equipment and bought two snowmobiles. The club actually made a little bit of money doing grooming for others, and because the track-set trails in the city were open to the public, the CSC could use funds raised through volunteer casinos.

The work opened the door to an exciting possibility for the club. In 1996, the City of Calgary started planning a major upgrade to the Shaganappi Golf Course. One item on the agenda was a new clubhouse. The city approached the CSC to see if the club would be interested in being a partner.[372] The Parks and Recreation Department wanted to encourage cross-country skiing, but did not want to pick up the costs of setting up any kind of permanent Nordic facility. Installing the CSC at Shaganappi was one way to accomplish the same end. The club, already grooming trails on the course, would get a permanent clubhouse and have the incentive to further develop the location's skiing potential. In 1997 and 1998, the club organized a cross-country festival at Shaganappi, Ski Fest, with sponsorship from the *Calgary Herald*. It attracted almost 900 participants the first year. People could take a lesson or try out demonstration gear from retailers.[373] It demonstrated that both the sport and the location could draw people. Ski Fest was ultimately discontinued because of that old problem, lack of snow.

Since the first proposals in the mid-nineties, however, the Shaganappi concept has expanded to include snow-making and snow farming to deal with Calgary's variable climate and create a true cross-country ski facility. One of the main proponents of the proposal, Alasdair Fergusson, points out that in British Columbia the provincial government offloaded many Nordic facilities to clubs. This move benefited both and the B.C. clubs have seen a growth of membership. Taking over Shaganappi also would be the ironic fruition of the club's efforts to create its own ski area. The CSC had not rushed to commit to the proposal. Obviously, there were financial risks involved and the club would be tied to a building again. It would identify the club even more with cross-country skiing, which not all members were happy about. At the time of this writing, the Shaganappi ski centre remains a proposal.

All the excitement and emphasis on Nordic skiing came with a price. It exacerbated tension with some members who primarily downhill skied and thought of the CSC as a downhill ski club. Describing how the revamped Nordic Committee worked, one Nordic director referred to the skinny ski program as "a club within a club"—perhaps an unfortunate choice of words! The concentration on cross-country skiing probably impacted membership. Eileen Coffin thinks that many downhill skiers who dropped out during the

The future? Ski Fest 1997 participants at Shaganappi. (ALASDAIR FERGUSSON.)

The community comes out: retailers at Ski Fest 1997. (ALASDAIR FERGUSSON.)

recession years simply didn't come back, in part because of the new focus.

Despite its popularity as a fitness activity, overall, cross-country skiing in Alberta has been shrinking, not growing, since the heyday in the late seventies. The further transformation of the CSC into a Nordic ski club, while perhaps good for the short term, might prove a limited niche.

DOWNHILL SLIDE

The decline in the club's downhill offerings balanced the success of Nordic skiing. Downhill skiing had been a part of the CSC's identity for so long that it seemed inconceivable it might vanish from the club. By 1995, the program was in serious trouble. And it wasn't because of the Nordic crowd. Some of the most enthusiastic participants in the revamped cross-country programs, like club presidents Gary Davies and Adam Noel, were also quite worried about the atrophy of downhill skiing. The success of the downhill trips had always varied from year to year, depending on the director and also the state of the economy, but generally had been strong for nearly fifteen years. The recession at the end of the eighties hit hard. Ed Kaminishi, the 1991 director, saw the trips were affected badly.[374] As the membership fell, it became harder and harder for the club to get enough people on trips to make them pay. The cancellation of the venerable Lake Louis Ski Improvement Weekend signified the program's disarray.

In 1996, the club called a special meeting to develop a strategy to revive downhill trips. It proved difficult to get the downhill program back on its feet. The CSC made it a high priority, but despite hard work, downhill skiing in the club had not rebounded the way it had in the past. Snowboarding lessons were added, somewhat belatedly in 1996, to tap this growing segment of ski resort patrons, but did not draw in significant numbers. The introductory seminar and Never-Ever approach, which the Nordic folks used to good effect, were less effective in bringing people to downhill skiing. Unlike cross-country, offering lessons did not seem to have much appeal. Even when the ski industry in Alberta recovered in the mid-nineties and showed considerable growth, the club's trips generally languished.

The shrinking membership no doubt was a big part of the problem. Fewer members made it much more difficult to get a large trip together or have many trips. Lack of volunteers to coordinate trips had been a real problem. Differing habits also played a role. Skiers usually want to go where the snow conditions are the best. Based on his research into ski industry trends,

Alasdair Fergusson believes that modern skiers are less interested in committing to trips in advance. They have the information and mobility to follow the snow. A run of bad snow years in the late nineties and the first part of the new millennium also had a dampening effect.

The difficulty in keeping the downhill program healthy was probably related to changes in the ski industry. In 1997, Ski and Sun, a travel agency specializing in ski trips, reported that it was only getting 40 per cent of the traffic it had in 1990.[375] According to statistics Fergusson gathered, downhill ski clubs in places where people had to travel great distances to ski, like Toronto or Saskatchewan, still boast strong memberships.[376] Clubs in locales close to good venues, like Denver or Calgary, have shrunk significantly. Once again, it seems fewer people see the need to ski in a club if they can easily get out on their own.

More recently, the CSC downhill program has revived and the club manages a modest offering of day and weekend trips.[377] It is too soon to see if this signals another change, but at the very least, the club has been able to keep its long legacy of downhill skiing alive.

Viva las Vegas

Another ray of sunshine in the gloomy nineties was a source of new funds for the club, the government grant. A benefit of the club's Nordic program expansion was that it finally made the CSC eligible for this exciting funding stream. Before the 1970s, government money for recreational clubs was extremely limited. The CSC investigated possible grants in the 1960s, when the Canadian Sports Council was formed, but there was nothing available. By the latter half of the seventies, governments at all levels were more involved in supporting cultural aims, including sport and outdoor recreation. Governments took on the responsibility of promoting health and wellness and grants of various kinds became increasingly available.

In Alberta, charities and non-profit organizations benefited greatly from government sanctioned casinos. The casino operators are allowed a certain return and the rest of the money is given to non-profits, which have to supply volunteers to help at the casino. Legalized gambling has become wildly popular. The funds derived from casinos have increased dramatically and are a major revenue source for many groups. As a matter of provincial policy, money from casinos and grant money generally went to organizations that provided services that benefited the larger public. The CSC, however, with its emphasis on recreation and serving its members, did not qualify for most grants and not for casinos. It had applied, starting in the eighties, but was turned down.

This changed due to the CSC's involvement with Nordic skiing and more specifically, track-setting. One of the club's first major grants obtained was from the Alberta Sport, Recreation, Parks and Wildlife Foundation in 1994 to buy grooming equipment, a utility trailer to transport it and a shed to store it.[378] The big score, so to speak, was qualifying for a casino in 1996. Along with the grooming and track-setting work, many of the costs involved in running the masters and jackrabbit programs, such as the coach's salary, were also eligible for casino funding. More importantly, the whole Nordic program, with the introductory seminar and Never-Ever lesson and the partnership with Calgary Leisure Learning, could be presented as a public service. It aimed, after all, to encourage participation in a healthy outdoor pursuit.

Casino profits have grown steadily in Alberta since the club's first event and have become a fairly important and stable source of additional funds. While the CSC can't use the money for general operating expenses, it relieves some of the financial burden indirectly. More recently, the club has determined that it can apply for provincial grants for building and maintaining facilities. This funding stream may make the Shaganappi proposal viable in the short and long term for the club. There are some interesting possibilities out there.

Survival

The story of the Calgary Ski Club through the 1990s was not an entirely happy one, but the club survived challenges that might have finished a less vital organization. In some ways CSC moved forward, such as with the reinvention of its Nordic ski program. A new member who joined to go cross-country skiing in the winter and hiking in the summer might not have thought there was anything wrong with the club. Hiking and backpacking, in fact, became even more popular over the decade to the extent the club had to split trips and start policing to make sure non-members weren't taking up space. It is tempting, especially for long-time members who remember a different era and a different atmosphere, to see the recent history of the club as somehow a failure compared to its so-called glory days. It is premature to make judgments. What might be said, with some certainty, is that the club once again is reflecting changes in the ski industry and in society.

As the CSC moves into a new century and celebrates its seventieth anniversary, the club is clearly in a period of transition. For the moment, the club could be described as staying the course set after the retrenchment of the nineties. The Nordic skiing program has a strong masters contingent and a good jackrabbit program directed by coach George Smith. The downhill skiers have day trips to the local hills and visit several more distant hills every year for a weekend. The club also offers snowshoeing, one of the fastest growing winter sports. For the summers, there is the ever-popular hiking program. The raucous Friday socials of the past have been replaced with more sedate but also more intimate pub nights. While the club may no longer be a one-stop recreation buffet, it offers a great deal for the active adult who wants to get out to the hills.

The CSC has found a new equilibrium. Membership numbers have remained steady at around 400 for a number of years and recently have climbed a little, despite several poor winters in Calgary and area. It also has major assets in the building fund, which has continued to grow and now sits at an impressive amount, and the ski sale, which generates revenue and publicity. Of greater concern is the difficulty finding individuals willing to take on executive positions, as leadership has been a crucial element in the club's success. In both relative and absolute terms, however, the club has weathered far worse crises in its past and shown an amazing resilience.

So where will the CSC go from here? Will it pursue the Shaganappi proposal and once again have its own clubhouse, at the risk of becoming essentially a Nordic ski club? Will it once again embrace families and try to recreate the successes of the sixties? Or will the CSC remain a club for single adults until the so-called Echo generation—the children of the baby boomers—comes of age and revitalizes the sport of downhill skiing, as the industry hopes? Will it embrace the snow sports that are presently growing rapidly and return to backcountry skiing or further promote snowshoeing? Or is the age of the general purpose, recreational ski club finally coming to an end? One thing is certain. No matter what might happen in the future, the Calgary Ski Club has created a tremendous legacy.

CONCLUSION

Back to the Future

Every fall, while others groan at the shortening days and dropping temperatures, avid skiers excitedly look to the skies for the first big snowfall. A few fanatics even put their skis on their shoulders and hike up to the nearest glacier in their eagerness to get back on the boards. They flock to the ski sales, not the least the New and Used Ski Sale, looking for bargains. Whatever the statistics might show about the health of the industry, the passion for skiing is alive and well, and so is the Calgary Ski Club.

In looking to its future, the Calgary Ski Club can look at its past. It is abundantly clear that the CSC has evolved constantly in response to changes in the sport of skiing and the needs of Calgary skiers. Sometimes change has been brought about through a crisis; sometimes it has been a gradual development. As is probably the case with other recreational clubs and sports organizations, demographics and economic conditions have played a powerful role. It is also clear that the leadership has mattered a great deal. A strong council, especially a strong president, could do a great deal to energize the club and especially attract committed volunteers. John Southam, Bob Freeze, Ted Trafford and Tom Boleantu stand out in this regard, but there were others. And sometimes, as was the case in the early fifties and early eighties, no one personality stands out. Instead a core of committed people, serving on the executive and acting as volunteers, moved the club along.

The Calgary Ski Club has its roots in the second great age of skiing, the 1930s, when thanks to an evolution of gear, technique and technology, the adventurous took up the sport wherever there were hills and snow. In

Calgary, the club was the pioneer, and like ski clubs around the world, it did a great deal to promote the sport. Both in its charter and its culture, the club was dedicated to promoting the sport of skiing. Even in the quiet years during the war, the Calgary Ski Club continued to display missionary zeal. After the war, the club experienced a boom that coincided with that of the sport itself and also Calgary's oil fuelled prosperity. The CSC remained the backbone of the Calgary ski scene, the best way to get introduced to and participate in the sport. Most active skiers joined the club. It was the first place newcomers to the city would go to find fellow enthusiasts.

In the fifties, the club developed a strong interest in lessons and racing for kids. It was the sign of major change and a reflection of demographics. The CSC would become known in the 1960s as a family racing club. The expansion of the sport also created more specialization, and encouraged the formation of other ski clubs. By the end of the sixties, there was a downhill racing club, a cross-country racing and touring club, a climbing club that also ski-toured and enjoyed ski-mountaineering and a club dedicated purely to recreational skiing. Ten years before, there had only been the CSC.

The seventies would start with another sea-change and possibly the most radical change in direction the club had experienced. Calgary became a city of the baby boomer, many educated, financially secure, eager participants in the leisure society and relative newcomers to the city. Under their direction, the CSC blossomed into a general-purpose social and recreational club that skied. Its character as a booster of skiing faded as it became more and more driven by the recreational needs of its membership. The downhill ski industry itself continued to expand and mature. The need for a ski club to promote the sport was much diminished, and the CSC concentrated on taking advantage of the industry's offerings. Later, as the club decided that it should be a ski club that socialized and did other things, rather than a recreational club that skied, it would find its voice once again to represent the Calgary skiing community. At its 50th birthday, the CSC was a vital organization built around a large core of dedicated members and a tried and tested formula.

A poor economy and the ageing of the boomers would soon upset the club's equilibrium, and the nineties became a period of upheaval and retrenchment. A steady decline in the membership led to a loss of revenue from the regular social events established in the seventies, and eventually, loss of the clubhouse. The club became smaller and much more focused on skiing and complementary summer recreation, like hiking. The CSC has found a new balance in terms of size and activities, but the lack of volunteers from within the membership is a continued concern for an organization that relies on them to fulfill its mandate. In this regard, the club may reflect a larger problem that plagues many organizations, especially clubs and groups dedicated to sport and recreation.

In essence, the club that formed in 1935 was part of a well-established culture of recreational and social clubs that began with the Victorians in the middle of the nineteenth century and very much a part of a dominant middle-class leisure culture in Europe and North America. The Calgary Ski Club was dedicated to establishing and promoting skiing. As the sport of skiing has evolved, the club has evolved with it, and as this book has shown, reflected larger changes in society. There is more that the history of the Calgary Ski Club could say about the development of sport, recreation and leisure. That gets into a more academic realm. Suffice to say the club has been an integral part of the history of the sport in Calgary.

In the end, it really comes down to skiing. People go skiing for the same reasons they always have: challenge, excitement, friendship, meeting the opposite sex. The sport has become a global industry worth billions, yet it is still about sticking boards on feet and sliding around for no other good reason than pure fun. The obsession people have with skiing is no different in the age of the high-speed quad chairlift and groomed cross-country trail than it was in the time of wooden skis, leather boots and climbing skins. The exhilaration, excitement and good fellowship a member of the Calgary Ski Club feels today is echoed throughout the story of the club, right back to the first pioneers.

Acknowledgements

Many people contributed to this book. First and foremost are the members of the club, past and present, who agree to be interviewed, including Mike Brusset, Eilleen Coffin, Peter and Betty Cooper, Gord Cumming, Alasdair Fergusson, Bob Freeze, Len Gottselig, Joe Irwin, Jay Joffe, Jean MacNaughton, Hans Ockermuller, Art Patterson, Jean Robb, Norm and MJ Russell, Ken Tatebe and Al Ulmer. My apologies as well to the many deserving members who could not be interviewed. Thanks are also due to Alasdair Fergusson, Jennifer Hamblin, Len Gottselig, Helen Isaac, Lindsay Moir, Ken Tatebe Al Ulmer and Bill Yeo for reviewing drafts of the manuscript and offering comments and editing. Special thanks to Chic Scott for the preview of his latest book, Powder Pioneers.

The staff of the Glenbow Library and Archives and the Whyte Museum of the Canadian Rockies were very helpful, as always. The financial support of the Calgary Ski Club and the Alberta Historical Resources Foundation, for both research and publication, made this book possible. Finally, many thanks to David Finch and Rocky Mountain Books for taking on this project.

Endnotes

[1] I. William Berry, *The Great North American Ski Book* (New York: Scribner, 1982), pg. 15

[2] ibid, pg. 16

[3] ibid, pg. 17

[4] Raymond Flowers,. *The History of Skiing and other Winter Sports* (Toronto: Methuen, 1976), pg. 24; Berry, pg. 17

[5] E. John B. Allen, *From Ski Sport to Skiing* (Amherst: University of Massachusetts Press, 1993), pg. 8

[6] Berry, *The Great North American Ski Book*, pg. 19

[7] Allen, *From Ski Sport to Skiing*, pg. 29

[8] Flowers, *The History of Skiing*, pg. 27-28

[9] Berry, *The Great North American Ski Book*, pg. 22

[10] Flowers, *The History of Skiing*, pg. 24

[11] Allen, *From Ski Sport to Skiing*, pg. 17-18, 35

[12] Flowers, *The History of Skiing*, pg. 62-63

[13] Ski pioneer Erling Strom records, in *Pioneers on Skis*, (Central Valley, N.Y.: Smith Clove Press, 1977) a long ski tour in the mountains of Colorado in 1926. Many people had not seen a skier before.

[14] Berry, *The Great North American Ski Book*, pg. 25

[15] Rolf Lund, *A History of Skiing in Canada prior to 1940* (University of Alberta, MA thesis, 1971), pg. 19

[16] Rolf Lund, "Skiing in Canada:The Early Years" *The Beaver* 308 (3), pg. 51

[17] Lund, *A History of Skiing in Canada*, pg. 34

[18] ibid, pg. 187

[19] ibid, pg. 205

[20] Flowers, *The History of Skiing*, pg. 63. See also Arnold Lunn, *The History of Skiing* (London, Oxford University Press, 1927), pgs. 15-31

[21] Flowers, *The History of Skiing*, pg. 28

[22] Dennis Brailford, *British Sport: A Social History* (Cambridge: Lutteworth Press, 1992), pg. 83; Richard D. Mandell, *Sport: A Cultural History* (New York: Columbia University Press, 1984), pg. 188; John Lowersen, *Sport and the English Middle Classes* (Manchester: Manchester University Press, 1993), pg. 12

[23] Lowersen, *Sport and the English Middle Classes*, pg. 18

[24] Berry, *The Great North American Ski Book*, pg. 21

[25] Allen, *From Ski Sport to Skiing*, pg. 11, 48-49

[26] Lunn, *History of Skiing*, pg. 72

[27] Flowers, *The History of Skiing*, pg. 87-88

[28] Allen, *From Ski Sport to Skiing*, pg. 83

[29] Henry Percy Douglas, "Canadian Skiing" In *Skiing: The International Sport*. ed. R. Palmedo (New York: The Derrydale Press, 1937), pg. 302-303

[30] Lund, *A History of Skiing in Canada*, pg. 50

[31] ibid, pg. 52

[32] ibid, pg. 90-98

[33] John Laffoon, *May I Help You: The First Fifty Years of the Canadian Ski Patrol System* (Ottawa: Canadian Ski Patrol System, 1994), pg. 7-10. Other clubs in the country established their own ski patrols independently, creating several claims about the founding of the ski patrol system.

[34] Dudley Batchelor et al, "Ski ing in Canada," *Canadian Geographical Journal*, 14 (2), 1937, details the growth of clubs in different parts of Canada.

[35] ibid, pp. 58, 64, 69

[36] Elliot Katz, "The Golden Era of Laurentian Skiing," *Canadian Geographic* 97 (3), 1978-79, pg. 13. Batchelor et al, "Ski-ing in Canada", pg. 61

[37] Berry, *The Great North American Ski Book*, pg. 23

[38] ibid, pg. 31

[39] Allen, *From Ski Sport to Skiing*, pg. 109

[40] Flowers, *The History of Skiing*, pg. 118

[41] ibid, pg. 109

[42] Benjamin G.Rader, *American Sports: From the Age of Folk Game to the Age of Televised Sports* (Upper Saddle River, N.J.:

Prentice Hall, 2004), pg. 125-126
[43] Gary H. Schwartz, *The Art of Skiing, 1856-1936*, (Tiburon, CA: Wood River Publishing, 1989), pg. 73
[44] Katz, "The Golden Era," pg. 16
[45] Lund, *A History of Skiing in Canada*, pg. 313
[46] Lund, *A History of Skiing in Canada*, pg. 118; Batchelor et al, pg. 65
[47] Rolf Lund, "The Development of Skiing in Banff," *Alberta History*, 25 (4), 1977, pg. 26
[48] ibid, pg. 26
[49] ibid, pg. 26
[50] ibid, pg. 27
[51] ibid, pg. 27
[52] Rolf Lund, "Recreational Skiing in the Canadian Rockies," *Alberta History*, 26 (2), 1978, pg. 30
[53] ibid, pg. 31
[54] Michael Boyle, *The Boyle Family of Lake Louise*, (Unpublished manuscript, Glenbow Archives) no pg.
[55] Rodney Touche, *Brown Cows, Sacred Cows: A True Story of Lake Louise* (Hanna, AB: Gorman and Gorman, 1990), pp. 47-48
[56] Robert W. Sandford, *Sunshine: Its Human and Natural Heritage*, (Banff, AB: Sunshine Village Corporation, 1984), pg. 24
[57] Lund, *A History of Skiing in Canada*, pg. 181-182
[58] B.G. Moodie, "First Ski Ascent of Mt. Balfour," *Canadian Alpine Journal*, 23, 1934-1935
[59] *Edmonton Bulletin*, February 1, 1913
[60] *Calgary Herald*, October 29, 1919
[61] ibid
[62] ibid, November 13, 1919. A later article states the club members built the scaffold themselves.
[63] ibid, February 19, 1920
[64] ibid, February 17, 1920
[65] ibid, November 19, 1920
[66] ibid, December 23, 1920
[67] ibid, December 21, 1920
[68] ibid, January 17, 1922; January 21, 1922
[69] Douglas, "Canadian Skiing", pg. 316
[70] www.nordicway.com/places_vancouver.htm
[71] Douglas, "Canadian Skiing", pg. 316
[72] Bruce Compton remembers taking his home made skis to the hill above Riley Park in Hillhurst as a kid. Running into a fence was the major hazard. "It was like riding two narrow toboggans, and you had to be pretty tricky to survive." Bruce Compton interview transcript, n.p.#, file 3, Mitchell History, CSC Fond, Glenbow Archives. See also interviews by the author with Art Patterson, who remembers his older brothers making jumping skis in the late twenties or early thirties.
[73] Mitchell History, pg. 6, file 1, CSC Fond, Glenbow Archives
[74] *Calgary Ski Club Annual, 1961*, pg. 9. Alan Carscallen, who wrote this article, notes that Moodie and Batchelor said they had the book and "chocolate cake" in hand, but suspected this was the more respectable version of actual events.
[75] Mitchell History, pg. 5, file 1, CSC Fond, Glenbow Archives
[76] ibid, pg. 6. I was unable to find the notice of this meeting. An article of skiing and the club in the December 27, 1934 edition of the *Herald*, stated the club was less than a year old, so presumably the meeting was held late in 1933 or early 1934.
[77] Carscallen interview, pg. 14, file 2, Mitchell History, CSC Fond, Glenbow Archives
[78] *Calgary Herald*, January 16, 1936
[79] H.P. Douglas, ed. *Canadian Ski Year Book, 1938*, (Montreal: Canadian Amateur Ski Association, 1935), pg. 162
[80] *Dominion Ski Championships in the Canadian Rockies,1937*, (Calgary: Calgary Ski Club, 1937), pg. 18
[81] Carscallen interview, pg. 3, file 2, CSC Fond, Mitchell History, Glenbow Archives. *Calgary Herald*, January 16, 1936
[82] "Sunshine and Powdered Snow", unpublished manuscript, pg. 2, Herb Paris Fond, Whyte Archives
[83] File 1938, box 90, subseries 7, Series 3, Facilities Administration, Parks and Recreation Department Fond, City of Calgary Archives
[84] ibid
[85] *Calgary Herald*, January 30, 1936
[86] ibid, Jan 21, 1938

[87] ibid
[88] CSC Newsletter, September 14, 1938, John Dixon Whetham Fond, Glenbow Archives
[89] *Calgary Herald*, November 29, 1938
[90] Or perhaps not. Wintergreen Resort, begun in 1971 as Lyon Mountain, closed at the end of the 2003 season.
[91] Carscallen interview, file 2, Mitchell History, CSC Fond, Glenbow Archives
[92] *Calgary Herald*, April 2, 1936
[93] ibid
[94] *Calgary Herald*, January 22, 1937. The article refers to the ski special and early start time. It is not entirely clear if this was a specially scheduled train, or just the early train to Banff with a reduced rate.
[95] *Calgary Herald*, December 7, 1937
[96] Mitchell History, pg. 11, file 1, CSC Fond, Glenbow Archives. This would mean about 800-1000 skiers, which seems rather high. However, in the post war period, when the trains were still running, club membership reached 1000, and possibly with non-club skiers on board the trains might have been this big.
[97] *Calgary Herald*, April 6, 1938
[98] National Archives, RG84, Series A-1-I, vol. 674, file B16-111, pt. 3
[99] *Calgary Herald*, December 14, 1938; December 20, 1938
[100] Registers, 1939, file 2, Ski Club of the Canadian Rockies Fond, Whyte Archives. Both the Harvies and J.B. Cross were registered as winter guests at Skoki.
[101] CSC newsletter, February 1st, 1940, John Dickson Whetham Fond, Glenbow Archives. No records were found to show how many shares club members bought.
[102] Mitchell History, pg. 14, file 1, CSC Fond, Glenbow Archives. McPhalen was Stuart McPhee at the time.
[103] National Archives, RG04, Series A 1 I, vol. 674, file B16-111, pt. 3
[104] *Calgary Herald*, January 13, 1941. Mitchell History, pg. 46, file 1, CSC Fonds, Glenbow Archives.
[105] A small, portable rope tow was used at Sunshine by 1940, but the Norquay lift was much more substantial.
[106] ibid, January 30, 1936
[107] ibid, February 20, 1936
[108] ibid, January 10, 1939
[109] "Early Skiing in Banff," unpublished manuscript, file 2, Cyril Paris Fond, Whyte Archives
[110] *Dominion Ski Championships in the Canadian Rockies, 1940*, pg. 30
[111] *Calgary Herald*, December 27, 1934
[112] ibid, January 13, 1939
[113] ibid, March 13, 1939
[114] ibid, February 4, 1937
[115] ibid, February 26, 1947
[116] *Canadian Ski Yearbook, 1937*, pg. 137
[117] *Dominion Ski Championships in the Canadian Rockies, 1937*, pg. 18
[118] Carscallen interview, pg. 4, file 2, Mitchell History, CSC Fond, Glenbow Archives
[119] *Calgary Herald*, March 30, 1938
[120] ibid, February 20, 1936
[121] Carscallen interview, pg. 4, file 2, Mitchell History, CSC Fond, Glenbow Archives
[122] ibid, pg. 8
[123] Edward John Hart, *Battle for Banff, Exploring the heritage of the Banff-Bow Valley*, (Banff: EJH Literary Enterprises, 1999), pg. 47
[124] *Calgary Herald*, December 13, 1938
[125] CSC newsletter, January 31, 1941, John Dixon Whetham Fond, Glenbow Archives
[126] Carscallen interview, pg. 12, file 2, Mitchell History, CSC Fond, Glenbow Archives
[127] CSC newsletter, November 28, 1940, John Dixon Whetham Fond, Glenbow Archives
[128] Mitchell History, pg. 53, file 1, CSC Fond, Glenbow Archives.
[129] *Calgary Herald*, March 18, 1938
[130] ibid, January 16, 1936. The gelandesprung was a leap using the two ski poles to propel oneself off the ground.
[131] Mitchell History, pg. 22, file 1, CSC Fond, Glenbow Archives
[132] CSC newsletter, January 31, 1941, John Dickson Whetham Fond, Glenbow Archives
[133] *Calgary Herald*, February 6, 1938. Jack Haylock, formerly of Calgary and the CSC, served as president of the Red Deer club in 1937-38
[134] Richard Needham, *Ski: Fifty Years in North*

America, (New York: Harry N. Abrams, 1987), pg. 51
135. "How Snow-Making Equipment Works" *Ski*, (February 1957). The process was patented in 1950 and first used commercially in 1952.
136. Norm Russell interview with author
137. Needham, *Ski*, pg. 73
138. Peter Cooper, the *Albertan* ski editor in the 1950s and 1960s, says he once made up a type of turn for his column as a joke, and couldn't believe how much serious mail it generated. Peter Cooper interview with author.
139. Sandford, *Sunshine*, pg. 25
140. ibid
141. *Calgary Herald*, December 4, 1940; March 2, 1943
142. LaRue interview, pg. 2, file 5, Mitchell History, CSC Fond, Glenbow Archives
143. *Calgary Herald*, February 5, 1941
144. ibid, January 20, 1941
145. See Siri Louie, *Gender in the Alpine Club of Canada, 1906-1940*, (University of Calgary, MA Thesis, 1996). Louie argues that the ACC was founded on a theoretical basis of gender equality, but informally discouraged women from taking a role in riskier climbing activities.
146. *Calgary Herald*, December 12, 1942
147. National Archives, RG 84, Series A-2-a, vol. 674, file B16-111, pt. 3
148. *Calgary Herald*, March 20, 1942
149. ibid, December 15, 1942
150. 1944-45 membership list, file 110, Membership, CSC Fond, Glenbow Archives
151. *Calgary Herald*, February 7, 1947
152. Milne designed the Husky Tower, now the Calgary Tower, while working for A.Dale and Associates
153. Russell interview
154. ibid
155. *Calgary Herald*, December 14, 1946
156. ibid, February 11, 1947
157. File 2591, Box 394, City Clerks Correspondence, City of Calgary Archives
158. Letter, October 27, 1946, file 111, CSC Fond, Glenbow Archives
159. *Calgary Ski Club Annual, 1959*, pg. 9, file 18, CSC Fond, Glenbow Archives
160. File 2591, Box 394, City Clerks Correspondence, City of Calgary Archives
161. ibid
162. Calgary City Council Minutes, 1948, pg. 1006, City of Calgary Archives
163. Robert Freeze interview with author
164. *Calgary Herald*, December 10, 1948
165. ibid, January 4 & January 11, 1949
166. ibid, January 28, 1949
167. ibid, January 21, 1949
168. ibid, January 14, 1949
169. ibid
170. LaRue interview, pg. 23, file 5, Mitchell History, CSC Fond, Glenbow Archives
171. Russell interview
172. File 2742, box 417, City Clerks Correspondence, City of Calgary Archives
173. File 5, box 1; Parks and Playground Committee, Council Committees; Calgary City Council Minutes, December 7, 1949, pg. 976, City of Calgary Archives
174. *Calgary Herald*, December 23, 1949. Multiplying the amounts by 20 gives a rough approximation of present day costs.
175. Annual Report, 1950, pg. 30, file 45, box 6, Series 2, Reports and Publications, Parks and Recreation Department Fonds, City of Calgary Archives
176. *Calgary Herald*, December 14, 1951
177. ibid
178. Bill Milne interview, pg. 4, file 6, Mitchell History, CSC Fond, Glenbow Archives
179. *Calgary Herald*, December 21, 1951
180. *Calgary Herald*, February 1, 1952
181. Milne interview, pg. 3, file 6, Mitchell History, CSC Fond, Glenbow Archives
182. *Calgary Herald*, January 18, 1952
183. Bruce Compton interview, no pg.#, file 3, Mitchell History, CSC Fond, Glenbow Archives
184. Statement of Receipts and Disbursements, 1952, file 101, CSC Fond, Glenbow Archives
185. Council minutes, August 5, 1952, file 8, CSC Fond, Glenbow Archives
186. Council minutes, October 7, 1952, file 8, CSC Fond, Glenbow Archives. Milne reported at that meeting that Zimmer wouldn't sell except under conditions of the

187 *Calgary Herald,* January 8, 1954
188 ibid, December 17, 1948
189 *Calgary Ski Club Annual, 1958,* pg. 4
190 November 1953 newsletter, file 188; January 1954 newsletter, file 189, CSC Fond, Glenbow Archives Although the exact circumstances are not known, it is clear from later descriptions that the club set up a permanent engine for the tow.
191 *Calgary Herald,* January 17, 1958. Wagner claimed in her "As I Ski It" column that the tow "seldom functioned anyway"
192 *Calgary Herald,* December 20, 1957
193 File SK0001a, Proposed Ski Hill – Edworthy, unprocessed records, Parks and Recreation Department Fond, Calgary City Archives
194 Council minutes, file 8, CSC Fond, Glenbow Archives
195 *Calgary Ski Club Annual, 1960,* pg. 47, file 18, CSC Fond, Glenbow Archives
196 Norm Russell thinks John Southam might have inspired the Herald Ski School, as a similar program had been done on the coast under the aegis of the *Vancouver Sun,* but Bill Milne remembers organising the school, "patterned on what we had been doing at Winnipeg." See previously cited interviews.
197 February 1954 newsletter, file 189, CSC Fond, Glenbow Archives
198 *Calgary Herald,* January 17, 1956
199 Lafoon, *May I Help You,* pgs. 7-8
200 Lafoon, *May I Help You,* pg. 31. In the *Calgary Herald,* January 23, 1942, it was noted "This weekend the Ski Clubs will endeavor to patrol the hill."
201 File 4, Calgary Ski Patrol Correspondence, Canadian Ski Patrol System Fond, Glenbow Archives
202 ibid
203 LaRue interview, pg. 2, file 5, Mitchell History, CSC Fond, Glenbow Archives. The *Calgary Herald,* January 30, 1942, states climbing lanes would be set up for the upcoming weekend. It is not entirely clear if LaRue is talking about 1942 or the renewed ski patrol in 1946, of which he was head.
204 Lafoon, *May I Help You,* pg. 31.

205 File 4, Calgary Ski Patrol Correspondence, 1941-50, Canadian Ski Patrol System Fond, Glenbow Archives
206 Dave Spence interview, pg 14, file 8, Mitchell History, CSC Fond, Glenbow Archives
207 File 4, Calgary Ski Patrol Correspondence, 1941-50, Canadian Ski Patrol System Fond, Glenbow Archives
208 ibid. In a January 18, 1949, letter, Dr. John Firth opines that "I still think the Red Cross course is vastly superiour to anything St. John can give us."
209 ibid
210 *Calgary Herald,* January 9, 1948
211 ibid, January 26, 1951
212 File 6, Calgary Ski Patrol Correspondence, 1953, Canadian Ski Patrol System Fond, Glenbow Archives
213 *Calgary Ski Club Annual, 1957,* pg. 27, file 18, CSC Fond, Glenbow Archives
214 File 6, Calgary Ski Patrol Correspondence, 1953, Canadian Ski Patrol System Fond, Glenbow Archives. The full story of relations between the patrol, the hill operators, and the park administration is quite interesting and also quite complicated. See Laffoon, *May I Help You,* pgs. 36-39
215 File 6, Calgary Ski Patrol Correspondence, 1953, Canadian Ski Patrol System Fond, Glenbow Archives.
216 At least four skiers had died in the Banff region by 1940. Ozzie LaRueLaRue recalled a near miss at Skoki, and there were doubtlessly many others, although the Rockies was often called "avalanche-free!" In one incident, fourteen skiers were caught in a slide off Quartz Ridge near Sunshine in 1938, with no fatalities. They formed the Quartz Hill Club and tried to get together in the following years to celebrate their good luck.
217 *Calgary Herald,* December 20, 1946. This may have been an isolated endeavor.
218 Council minutes, October 7, 1952, file 8, CSC Fond, Glenbow Archives
219 *Calgary Herald,* November 3, 1947
220 *Ski Tips,* CSC newsletter, January 1947, pg. 6. Copy possessed by author.

[221] *Calgary Herald*, January 17, 1947; February 1948, file 185, Newsletters 1948, CSC Fonds, Glenbow Archives.

[222] This date is not certain. The CSC annuals for 1960 and 1961 both refer to the 9th Annual Akimina race, while *A Mountain Life, The stories and photographs of Bruno Engler*, ed. Robert Stanford (Canmore: Alpine Club of Canada, c1996), states that Bruno Engler founded the race; a photo caption gives the date 1952. *Calgary Ski Club Annual, 1960*, pg. 59, file 18, CSC Fond, Glenbow Archives; Engler, *A Mountain Life*, pg. 89, 95

[223] Council minutes, April 11, 1961, file 8, CSC Fond, Glenbow Archives

[224] See below for further discussion of this.

[225] *Albertan*, January 30, 1959

[226] The Parks Branch did not allow charging admission for events in the park at the time.

[227] *Calgary Ski Club Annual, 1959*, pg. 23, file 18, CSC Fond, Glenbow Archives

[228] *Mosquito Bites Again: An Appendage to "Mosquito Creek Roundup" Parkland, 1946-2000*, (Stavely, AB: Hamlet of Parkland and District Historical Society, 2001), pg. 64-65. According to this source, there was a schism in the Penguin Club and a new group set up a longer hill called Timber Ridge, which seems to have replaced the original hill.

[229] *Calgary Herald*, March 1947.

[230] Cam Mitchell interview, pg. 7, file 7, Mitchell History, CSC Fond, Glenbow Archives

[231] *Calgary Ski Club Annual, 1957*, pg. 12, file 18, CSC Fond, Glenbow Archives

[232] Mitchell History, pg. 4, file 1, CSC Fond, Glenbow Archives

[233] *Calgary Ski Club Annual, 1959*, pg. 10, file 18, CSC Fond, Glenbow Archives

[234] *Albertan*, December 12, 1958

[235] *Calgary Ski Club Annual, 1960*, pg. 9, file 18, CSC Fond, Glenbow Archives

[236] *Calgary Ski Club Annual, 1957*, pg. 15, file 18, CSC Fond, Glenbow Archives

[237] *Calgary Ski Club Annual, 1959*, pg. 5, file 18, CSC Fond, Glenbow Archives

[238] There seems to be very little in the literature of sport sociology and sport history addressing the dynamics of recreational clubs. My search was admittedly somewhat limited, but it is difficult to say if the CSC's problems were typical.

[239] Financial statement, 1960, File 101, CSC Fond, Glenbow Archives. This would be in the neighborhood of $100,000 2004 dollars.

[240] One of the interesting elements of ski racing, both domestic and international, was the strict insistence on amateur status, even for full time athletes.

[241] *Calgary Herald*, November 3, 1961

[242] Sandford, *Sunshine*, pg. 25

[243] *Albertan*, November 18, 1960

[244] Chic Scott, *History of the Calgary Mountain Club: its members and their activities, 1960-1986*, (Calgary, 1986), pg. 2

[245] The Sitzmark club was founded by a CSC member and could be considered a splinter group. It is also possible that the Chinook Ski Club might have involved former CSC members, but there is no evidence either way.

[246] President's Report, January 2, 1962, CSC Records

[247] CASA file, CSC Records

[248] Freeze Interview

[249] Letter, Freeze to Calgary Booster Club, September 20. 1962, file 57, CSC Fond, Glenbow Archives

[250] Council minutes, Feb. 28, 1962, file 8, CSC Fond, Glenbow Archives

[251] Council minutes, June 23, 1969, file 9, CSC Fond, Glenbow Archives

[252] CASA file, CSC Records

[253] Racing Program pamphlet, 1963-64, file 112, CSC Fond, Glenbow Archives

[254] Presidents Report, April 12, 1965, file 19, CSC Fond, Glenbow Archives

[255] Council minutes, September 7, 1965, Minutes 1965-66 file, Mike Brusset Papers

[256] *Calgary Herald*, December 10, 1948

[257] ibid

[258] September 1968 newsletter, file 196, CSC Fond, Glenbow Archives. Most of the early history of the sale comes from this article and the author's interview with Jean Robb.

[259] *Calgary Herald*, October 2, 1968

[260] Letter, CSC to Dave Marchant, CSPS,

August 31, 1970, Ski Fair 1970 file, Mike Brusset Papers

[261] Letter, Read to Robb, September 7, 1970, Ski Fair 1970 file, Mike Brusset Papers

[262] Letter, Dick Berien to Doug Whan, March 1, 1964, file177, CSC Fond, Glenbow Archives

[263] Council minutes, July 5, 1963, CSC Records

[264] Council Minutes, April 17, 1963, file 8, CSC Fond, Glenbow Archives

[265] ibid

[266] Memo, E. Trafford to Committee Chairmen, July 19, 1963, CSC Records

[267] President's Report, January 2, 1962, CSC Records

[268] Letter, McDowall to Trafford, Feb. 26, 1964, file 27, CSC Fond, Glenbow Archives

[269] ibid

[270] Letter, Trafford to Laing, Feb. 21, 1964, file 27, CSC Fond, Glenbow Archives

[271] Letter, Trafford to Laing, October 5, 1964, file 27, CSC Fond, Glenbow Archives

[272] Council minutes, May 21, 1964, file 8, CSC Fond, Glenbow Archives

[273] Draft of Calgary Ski Club brief, file 27, CSC Fond, Glenbow Archives

[274] Calgary Ski Club brief, CSC Records

[275] Letter, Trafford to Laing, October 5, 1964, file 27, CSC Fond, Glenbow Archives

[276] Letter, Street to Trafford, June 26, 1964, CSC Records

[277] NA, RG-84, Series A-1-a, vol. 974, file b312-4 pt. 7

[278] President's Report, April 12, 1965, General 1965-66 file, Mike Brusset Papers

[279] Council minutes, July 5, 1963, CSC Records

[280] Kon Road would propose, years after Pigeon closed, developing a special purpose Alpine ski training facility on the mountain.

[281] Letter, Milne to Trafford, April 17, 1964, Property file, Mike Brusset Papers

[282] Letter, Trafford to Strong, April 21, 1964, Clubhouse and Office National Parks file, Mike Brusset Papers

[283] Letter, Laing to Trafford, February 8, 1966, CSC Records

[284] File 19, Alpine Club of Canada Calgary Section Fond, Glenbow Archives

[285] President's Report, 1964-65, file 19, CSC Fond, Glenbow Archives; letter, E. Trafford to membership, April 12, 1965, CSC Records

[286] File 19, Alpine Club of Canada Calgary Section Fond, Glenbow Archives

[287] ibid. It seems fair to characterise the ACC as "stuffy" on pg. 2 of this chapter

[288] Letter, White to Brusset, February 11, 1967, Clubhouse and Office National Parks file, Mike Brusset Papers

[289] President's Report, April 13, 1968, Minutes 1967-68 file, Mike Brusset Papers

[290] Brewer Report, March 26, 1968, Clubhouse Snowridge file, Mike Brusset Papers. Brewer was prescient: the original Snowridge would soon go bankrupt and was bought by Greyhound. It would later shut down for several years. The improvement of Highway 40 and growth of the ski market in the 1970s would later make it viable as Fortress, but as 2004 it has been once again mothballed.

[291] *Calgary Herald*, December 13, 1952; CSC Annual, 1960, pg. 9

[292] Art Patterson interview with author

[293] ibid

[294] *Ski News & Dos*, Spring 1966, Mike Brusset Papers

[295] File 27, CSC Fond, Glenbow Archives

[296] Herbert Kariel, *Alpine huts in the Rockies, Selkirks and Purcells*, (Banff, AB: Alpine Club of Canada, c1986), pg. 46

[297] Membership report, 1967-68, Newsletter 1968-69 file, Mike Brusset Papers

[298] Council minutes, May 16, 1962, file 8, CSC Fond, Glenbow Archives

[299] Council minutes, Feb. 6, 1963, file 8, CSC Fond, Glenbow Archives

[300] *Albertan*, December 6, 1968

[301] The club had certainly received donations before, especially of goods and services for prizes and give-aways, as well as cash gifts, or solicited money for certain programs, but this was to the best of my knowledge the first time it was suggested the club should solicit ongoing donations to clear up debt.

[302] President's Report, April 6, 1967, file 9, CSC Fond, Glenbow Archives

[303] Council minutes, October 22, 1970, file 9, CSC Fond, Glenbow Archives

304 Membership summary, May 23, 197, file 12, CSC Fond, Glenbow Archives
305 Council minutes, September 21, 197, file 9, CSC Fond, Glenbow Archives
306 Boleantu was contacted. He initially agreed to an interview, but when contacted again to set a date, did not respond. In later communication, he said this was due to work pressures.
307 The Glencoe Club in Calgary is a sport and recreation club for curling, skating, golf, tennis, badminton and swimming, which has become the preserve of upper middle class families
308 Letter, Boleantu to Mr. Rodgers, Canadian Imperial Bank of Commerce, April 18, 1973, file 46, CSC Fond, Glenbow Archives
309 Minutes, AGM, April 24, 1972, CSC Fond, Glenbow Archives
310 President's Report, April 14, 1971, file 9, CSC Fond, Glenbow Archives
311 Council minutes, November 28, 1972, January 9, 1973, file 9, CSC Fond, Glenbow Archives
312 Cross-Country Programme Report, 1973-74, file 20, CSC Fond, Glenbow Archives
313 ibid. Those who know him might also say that Len's standards are pretty high!
314 Report, Sports and Activities, 1982, Alasdair Fergusson Papers
315 March 1984 newsletter, file 210, CSC Fond, Glenbow Archives
316 ibid
317 Newsletter, February 1997, CSC Records
318 May 1950 newsletter, file 187, CSC Fond, Glenbow Archives
319 Council minutes, July 14, 1980, Alasdair Fergusson Papers
320 See, for example, council minutes, August 11, 1980, Alasdair Fergusson Papers
321 CSC Records, Report of the Long Range Planning Committee, April 25, 1979
322 March 1979 newsletter, file 207, CSC Fond, Glenbow Archives
323 Report of Steering Committee, March 20, 1974, file 13; minutes, AGM, April 24, 1974, file 12, CSC Fond, Glenbow Archives
324 August 1978 newsletter, file 206, CSC Fond, Glenbow Archives
325 Constitution, March 1977, file 7, CSC Fond, Glenbow Archives
326 Report of the Building Committee to the Calgary Ski Club, April 25, 1979, CSC Records
327 Long Range Planning Committee Report, April 25, 1979, CSC Records
328 Council minutes, August 11, 1980, newsletter, October 1980, file 208, CSC Fond, Glenbow Archives
329 April 1983 newsletter, file 210, CSC Fond, Glenbow Archives
330 Council minutes, July 28, 1980, Alasdair Fergusson Papers
331 Minutes, joint councils, May 19, 1981, Alasdair Fergusson Papers
332 April 4, 1989, "CSC's Involvement in the Canadian Masters Alpine Series", CSC Records
333 ibid
334 December 1979 newsletter, file 207, CSC Fond, Glenbow Archives
335 Membership statistics, 1984-85; minutes, General Meeting, November 21, 1984, CSC Records
336 ibid, membership statistics, 1984-85
337 Simon Hudson, *Snow Business, A Study of the International Ski Industry*, (London: Cassell, 2000), pg. 76
338 David K. Foot, *Boom, Bust, and Echo 2000* (Toronto: Macfarlane Walter & Ross, 1998), pg.
339 Minutes, AGM, April 27, 1988, CSC Records
340 Advisory Committee Report, 1986, CSC Records
341 Letter, Boleantu to council, Constitution file, CSC Records
342 Council minutes, September 24, 1984, CSC Records
343 Report of Clubhouse Feasibility Committee; Report to Ski Club Council, April 23, 1990, CSC Records
344 Building Committee, Report to November General Meeting, November 24, 1993, CSC Records
345 Notice of special general meeting, May 23, 1990, CSC Records
346 Agenda, Special General Meeting, September 30, 1994, CSC Records

[347] Council minutes, June 14, 1993, CSC Records
[348] Council minutes, March 1, 1993, CSC Records
[349] Draft Proposal to COP/CODA, January 19, 1994, CSC Records
[350] Council minutes, January 31, 1994, CSC Records
[351] Memo, May 1995, Gary Davies to council, CSC Records
[352] Minutes, AGM, April 30, 1997, CSC Records
[353] Cost-Benefit Analysis, Hiking Program, July 1997, CSC Records
[354] Survey results, socials, 1996-1997 council minutes, CSC Records
[355] Minutes, special forum, May 9, 1995, CSC Records
[356] Memo, May 1995, Gary Davies to council, CSC Records
[357] Council minutes, rough copy, October 2, 1990, CSC Records, makes reference to "the animosity between DH and XC seems to be alive and well" during a discussion about the Nordic budget
[358] Transcript, Parks and Recreation assessment session, June 28, 1994, CSC Records
[359] Council minutes, February 1990, CSC Records
[360] Report of Long Range Planning Committee, New and Used Ski Sale, history of ski sale, CSC Records
[361] 1984 Ski Sale Report, CSC Records
[362] ibid
[363] Letter, Howard Silver to Brian Nock, Canadian Ski Patrol, July 21, 1988, CSC Records
[364] Long Range Planning Committee Report, February 9, 1993, CSC Records
[365] Council minutes, October 4, 1993, CSC Records
[366] New and Used Ski Sale report, 1996, CSC Records
[367] Newsletter, August 1996, CSC Records
[368] Marketing Plan for CSC Nordic Programs 1994-95; Nordic Committee Report, 1994, CSC Records
[369] ibid
[370] Report, "Trends in Nordic Skiing with the Calgary Ski Club", September 25, 1996, CSC Records
[371] Calgary Ski Club, Nordic Ski Programs, July 12, 1994, CSC Records
[372] Council minutes, January 21, 1997, CSC Records
[373] Ski Fest 97 Report and Recommendations, January 20, 1997, CSC Records
[374] Council minutes, July 9, 1991, CSC Records
[375] Council minutes, April 1, 1997, CSC Records
[376] Newsletter, April 1997, "A Ski Club – the What, Where and Why?", CSC Records
[377] Minutes, AGM, April 24, 2003, CSC Records
[378] Letter, Terry Archer, Director, to Eileen Coffin, CSC president, September 28, 1994, CSC Records

Index

A
Advisory Council 191
advocacy
   Ski Action Alberta 194
   ski development, Banff National Park 132
Alpine Club of Canada
   clubhouse proposal 139
   relations with CSC 37
   ski camps 26
   Telemark Loppet 169
   Wapta huts 146
Alumni Association 196
Al Ahzar Temple 107
archives and history committee 196
Assiniboine 22, 144
Australians 70
avalanche accidents 91
avalanche safety 89

B
Baldwin, Kjerstin 212
Balfour Hut 146
Banana Pie 163
Banff early skiing 19
Banff-Bow Valley Study 196
Banff National Park
   ski development 132
Banff Ski Club 20
Banff Winter Carnival
   origins 20
Batchelor, Dudley 33, 58
Bobcats 150
Boleantu, Tom 159, 183
Bowness Golf Course 39, 72
Bowness ski hill 85
Bow Hut 147
Bow Summit 141
Bradley, Russ 90
Bragg Creek 40
Bragg Creek Ski Club 40
Brewer, Dave 140
Brusset, Mike 140, 151
Building Committee 192
Building Fund 193
bus tours 106, 127, 172

C
Calgary-Edmonton competition 50
Calgary Area Outdoor Council 196
Calgary Continuing Education 120
Calgary Cross-Country Council 168
Calgary Golf and Country Club 39
Calgary Leisure Learning 217
Calgary Mountain Club 114
   Wapta huts 146
Calgary Olympic Development Association 130, 194
Calgary Parks and Recreation 206, 213
Calgary Ski Club
   club championship 49
   CSC Race Team 92, 117
   instruction 46, 84
   ski mountaineering 58, 141
   ski racing 92, 116
   ski touring 55, 89, 141
   social activities 60, 107, 125, 184
   summer activities 176
Calgary Ski Club Annual 110
Calgary Ski Club Guides 89
Calgary Tennis Club 108
Calgary Winter Carnival 31
Camrose 8
Canadian Amateur Ski Association 13
   dispute with 113
Canadian Masters Alpine Series 195
Canadian National Sportsmen's Show 208
Canadian Rockies Winter Sports 45, 77
Canadian Ski Association 195
   Recreational Skiing Committee 195
Canadian Ski Instructors Alliance 84
Canadian Ski Patrol System 86, 89
ski sale 124
canoeing 180
Cantrill, Bill 163
Carscallen, Alan 33, 38, 55, 56, 58, 60
car pooling 105
casinos 216
Chinook Ski Club 75, 76
Choquette, Arnold 92, 140
Close, Vic 186
clubhouse
   10th Avenue Ski Centre 183, 202
   1207 Connection 161, 183
   Alpine Club proposal 139
   Banff National Park 137
   Braemar Lodge 60
   Calgary Tennis Club 108
   Lake Louise 138
   Rosedale Community Centre 203
   Shaganappi Proposal 213
   Snowridge 140
club championship 49
Compton, Al 140
Compton, Bruce 76
Compton, Ethan 76, 85
Compton brothers 76
constitutional changes 190
   past president 191
   Advisory Council 191
constitution committee 190
Cooper, Peter 77
Cross, Jim 45
Cross-Country Alberta 196
cross-country skiing
   CSC involvement 165, 209
   Glenmore Park 168
   jackrabbits 212
   Lake Louise Loppet 172, 212
   mountain parks 166
   "Never-Ever" 211
   revival 67, 164

Shaganappi 168
Ski-Fest 213
Telemark Loppet 169
track-setting 210, 212, 217
Cullen, Malcolm 85, 100, 109
Cuming, Gord 186
cycling 180

D
dances 61, 108, 125, 126
Dominion Ski Championships, 1948 96
Dominion Ski Championships, 1937 52
Dominion Ski Championships, 1940 54
Dry Ski School 120
Dunn, Nigel 77

E
Edmonton ski clubs 50
Edwards, Rupe 47
Ehnman, Wolfgang 119
Elliot, Isabel 122
Encil, George 68
Engler, Bruno 96

F
Farish, Jack 39, 58, 149, 197
Fergusson, Alasdair 191, 194, 195
50th anniversary 196
Foothills Table Tennis Club 159
Fram Ski Club 9
Freeze, Bob 78, 92, 115, 128
Friday social 184
Fuhrman, Peter 143, 145
Fullerton, Jake 40

G
Gabl, Franz 96
Gmoser, Hans 142
golf courses
  use for skiing 39, 72, 78, 168, 213
Gonnason, Jeanne 169
Gottaas, Christian 28
Gottselig, Len 165, 169, 196
grooming, slopes 66

H
Hansen, Charles 202
Harvie, Eric 45
Hayden, Reginald 37
Herald Ski School 85
hiking 177, 217
Hill, Shirley 71
Hind, Peggy 91
Holland, John 117
Humphries, Wally 81

I
Instruction
  Calgary Ski Club 46, 84
Inter-Club Challenge 195
Inter-Scholastic League 93
Interscholastic Ski Committee 50
Introduction to Skiing 150
Irwin, Joe 117

J
Jasper 22
Joffe, Jay 110
Johnson, Gus 20

K
Kelowna 175
Kimberley 127
Knight, Norm 47
Kutschera, Vic 47, 58

L
Laing, Arthur 136
Lake Louise 21, 57, 69
  ski area 69
Lake Louise Loppet 172, 212
Lake Louise Ski Club
  ski sale 124
LaRue, Ozzie 34, 80, 87, 103, 197
Long Range Planning Committee 182, 192
Lunn, Arnold 11

M
Maciej, Hans 129, 131
Marathon Properties 202
Mass-Ski-Raid Giant Fun Race 126
McDowall, Jack 134

McRoberts, Randy 120
membership limit 188
Milne, Bill 74, 85, 138
Mitchell, Cam 74, 84, 197
Monod, Gerry and Johnny 93
Montreal Ski Club 12
Moodie, Gordon 33, 56, 58
Moxness, Jack 28
Mt. Allan 194
Mt. Sparrowhawk 194
Municipal Golf Course 39, 78

N
Nanton 102
Newman, John 113
New and Used Ski Sale 122, 206
Norheim, Sondre 7
Norquay
  CSC investment plans 77
  CSC use of 43
  first CSC trips 38
  new lodge 45
  origins 21

O
O'Neill, Peter 113, 116
Ockermuller, Hans 177
Okanagan Olympics 181
Olympic Winter Games 130
Ottawa Ski Club 13

P
Paskapoo 83
Patterson, Art 141, 145
Penguin Ski Club 102
Petroleum Ski Club 153, 160
Peyto Hut 147
Phil's Pancake House 125
Pi Consultants 163, 183
Premier Cycle and Sports 76

R
Radke, Gerry 170, 109, 193
Read, Dee 122, 124
Read, Ken 120
Regal Golf Course 39, 72
Revelstoke 8
Richardson, E.L. 31
Robb, Jean 74, 122, 125
Robinson, Doug 118

Rosedale Community Centre 203
Ross, Bill 87
Rossland 8
Russell, Norm 67, 76, 96, 99
Russell's Sporting Goods 35

S
Saturday Specials 149
Scandinavians
  Canada 8
  North America 7
Shaganappi Golf Course 39, 78, 213
Silver, Howard 208
Sir Norman Watson Downhill 99, 120
Sitzmark Ski Club 74
Ski-Folk Coffee House 186
Ski-Wees 100
Skiettes 71
skiing
  ancient 6
  Europe, beginnings 9
skiing gear
  bindings 67
  improvements 66
  Innovations 13, 15
  Skimeisters 113
Ski Action Alberta 194
Ski Club of the Canadian Rockies 21
ski conditioning 119
Ski Doodlers 108
Ski Fair 123
ski films 61
ski jumping
  Calgary Winter Carnival 31
ski lifts
  chairlift, origins 19
  rope tow, origins 17
ski mountaineering
  Calgary Mountain Club 114
  CSC involvement 58, 141
ski patrol, Calgary 86
ski racing
  1937 Dominion Ski Championships 52
  1940 Dominion Ski Championships 54

1948 Dominions Championships 96
  Calgary-Edmonton competition 50
  Canadian Masters Alpine Series 195
  CSC 92, 116
  CSC Race Team 92, 117
  downhill, origins 11
  four-way competition 54
  Inter-Club Challenge 195
  Inter-Scholastic League 93
  Sir Norman Watson Downhill 99, 120
  Ski-Wees 100
  slalom, origins 11
  Sunwapta Slalom 115, 120
  Victoria Glacier Giant Slalom 96, 120
  Waterton-Akimina race 96, 120
Ski Runners of Canadian Rockies
  origin 26
ski sale 122
ski touring
  Calgary Mountain Club 114
  CSC involvement 55, 89, 141
ski trains
  Banff and Norquay 42, 64, 104
  Laurentians 13
ski trips 173
  helicopter skiing 174
  Lake Louise Ski Improvement Weekend 176
  Quebec Winter Carnival 173
  Ski and Sun 174
ski troops 71
Skoki Lodge 55
  origins 21
Snowridge 140
snow craft committee 90
snow making 66
Southam, John 32, 35, 48, 72
sport
  Victorian concepts 10

Sportsman 76
Sports and Activities 180
ski sale 206
Sports and Activities 204
Sterne, Fens 74
Street Study 135
summer activities 176
Sunshine 57
  origins 22
Sunwapta Slalom 113, 115, 120
Swiss Guides 21

T
Tatebe, Ken 188
tea dances 125
Tefler, Peggy 144
Telemark LoppetRace 169
Temple Lodge
  improvements 69
Timberline dances 126
Timber Ridge 102
Trafford, Ted 128, 134, 149
trophies 49
Turner Valley 103
1207 Connection 183

V
Van Wagner, Joy 77
Verne, Rudy 28, 31
Victoria Glacier Giant Slalom 96, 120
Victoria Park
  ski jump 31

W
Wapta huts 145
Wapta Icefield 145
Waterton-Akimina race 96, 120
Watson, Sir Norman 21
White, Cliff Jr 68
Whitefish, Montana
  bus trips 106

Z
Zdarsky, Mathias 10
Zimmer, Alf 81